Y0-BCM-792

DATE DUE			
Apr 24 '69			
May 13 '70			
Apr 21 '71			
May 21 '74			
Jul 2 '74			
Nov 21 '80			
GAYLORD M-2			PRINTED IN U.S.A.

WITHDRAWN
L. R. COLLEGE LIBRARY

CHRISTIAN TEACHINGS

AFFIRMATIONS OF FAITH FOR LAYPEOPLE

Martin J. Heinecken

Fortress Press
Philadelphia

CARL A. RUDISILL LIBRARY
LENOIR RHYNE COLLEGE

230.41
H36c

63492
Oct. 1968

© 1967 BY FORTRESS PRESS, PHILADELPHIA

Library of Congress Catalog Card Number 67-21529

Biblical quotations from the Revised Standard Version
of the Bible, copyrighted 1946 and 1952 by the
Division of Christian Education of the
National Council of the Churches
of Christ in the United States
of America, are used
by permission.

4062B67   *Printed in the U.S.A.*   1-1004

PREFACE

This book is written primarily for those who believe themselves to be Christians and who hold membership in a church. It is written, however, with the profound conviction that, in spite of noble efforts, neither inside nor outside the church have the great biblical-Christian words recaptured their specific Christian meanings. Christian language has, as Kierkegaard said, lost its cutting edge and been reduced to a "toothless twaddle."[1] As a result we are given no clear articulation of Christian doctrine (teaching). In fact, the word "doctrine" is a dirty word, associated with "doctrinaire," "prejudiced," "opinionated," "closed-minded." In light of the fact that Christian faith has been so narrowly interpreted as assent to Christian doctrines, some have gone to the other extreme where faith is interpreted merely as a subjective state of courage in which one believes without any regard for the content of what is believed. The disastrous result is "faith in faith," not faith in God and his sure word of promise.

Today there is a repudiation of revelation as "propositional truth." God reveals himself in acts in history and not in the form of true sentences or propositions dictated to "inspired" biblical writers. The Bible, therefore, is testimony literature, recording the witness to God's great deeds. This, however, sets up a false disjunction between God's "acting" and God's "speaking." There is no revelation of God in deeds, apart from the interpretation of those deeds in words. It was the "word" which "became flesh." Deeds without words are meaningless and words without deeds are an empty boast. It is "speech" that characterizes the human I-Thou relation and therefore also the God-man relation. The Christian faith, then, cannot dispense with "doctrines" in the form of various "propositions" which may be judged either true or false, although the method of doing this (the verification) may itself be quite different from the way in which propositions in mathematics, chemistry, or history are judged.

It is the purpose of this book to show the so-called "existential character" of the affirmations of faith. That is to say, that no "affirmations of faith" can be made in spectator fashion by one who only stands unaffectedly before the truths he affirms. They can be made only by one who is himself involved in either "faith" or "offense"; they concern the existence of the entire human being. In the face of these affirmations, no one can be neutral, because they put a claim upon a man and make him either warm around the heart (faith) or hot under the collar (offense).

The central theme with which we shall be concerned is: God's personal dealings with man in the establishment of *life together in love*. This is what binds all doctrines into one organic whole so that each doctrine presupposes the whole structure and can only be understood in a total context.

This whole concerns an intense cosmic drama of which the sovereign and hidden creator-God is the author, by whose "thoughts" and "words" the stage as well as the players and their several parts are not only conceived but brought into being. But the drama differs from an earthly drama inasmuch as the actors are not just given a role to play (the Latin word, *persona,* means the actor's mask), but are given a responsible part to work out in their own way before the unseen auditor, critic, judge. Here is not just a play; here is the one-way street of life and history on which an eternal destiny is decided. What is certain is the beginning and the end, the eternal purpose of God's love "before the foundation of the world" (Eph. 1:4), and the final fulfillment of God's purpose, when "time" itself is over.

This drama of "God's personal dealings with men" really has its origin in eternity, "beyond" this bourne of space and time. The author sets the stage, he "creates" the actors, he metes out the responsibilities, he watches with concern over what man does with his "freedom," he takes measures to restore what has gone wrong, he himself becomes involved in the play, he himself wins the decisive victory, the crisis of the drama, from which point all "hastens" to the end (*finis*) and the fulfillment (*telos*). And throughout this drama God only deals with man personally, respecting his personhood, intending to bring it to fulfillment in a life which binds God, all men, and the world inseparably together in love.

By no means is everything covered in these pages and many will marvel at the glaring omissions. But all cannot be said at once. If only the very basic doctrines can be made clear in their "existential" import and their own uniqueness, we will have succeeded. Here we have no "timeless truths" stated unchangeably for all times and all places. Our words are addressed to no vacuum but to a particular situation. This is an attempt in the advent of the space age to say to this generation of Americans that which will elucidate God's message to them and his dealings for them and with them. And at the same time we attempt in our words to maintain continuity with the church of all the ages. If these words are too stodgy for some and too far out for others, there may be some to whom, by God's grace, they will speak as a true witness.

Many will recognize in the form and content of this book material identical to much of my *Basic Christian Teachings*, first published in 1949 and revised in 1959. Alterations, deletions, and additions have been so numerous, however, as to justify the identification of this as a new work.

MARTIN J. HEINECKEN

Philadelphia, Pennsylvania
Trinity Sunday, 1967

CONTENTS

CHAPTER I

THE CHARACTER
OF FAITH

The Pattern of Life

G. K. Chesterton once said that it was more important for a landlady to know her boarder's beliefs than the size of his weekly pay check. Beliefs determine actions. What we believe about where we came from and why we are here and where we are going and how we are to act along the way is all-important. The whole pattern of a man's life and his eternal destiny are determined by his beliefs. Martin Luther said, "Where your heart is there is your god." That to which we cling and to which we give the first place in our life is our god.

Paul Tillich has called this determiner of our actions our "ultimate concern." Of course, we are justified in giving concern in our life to many things—to our own good name and fame, our children, our property, the fulfillment of our dreams, the relief of our desires' itch. But only that upon which our very being or not-being depends should be of *ultimate* concern to us; only to that should we give our hearts. Everything less than that is an idol. Only the God upon whom we depend for all we have and are is to be the object of our worship, praise, thanksgiving, trust, love, and obedience. Luther thus interprets the first com-

1

mandment, "Thou shalt have no other gods before me," as meaning, "We should fear, love, and trust in God above all things," that is, above everything else there is in the whole wide world.

The Christian's pattern of life is determined by his relation to the one sovereign God of holy love, revealed in Jesus, the Christ. This life may be best described in terms of a *community of life together in love*. Christians live in trust toward God and love to each other in a world that is a fit theater for such a life. No one can be a Christian in isolation. To be a Christian is to be in a community which is bound together in love. Such a community does not exist for its own sake; the very nature of the love knits the members together, shapes them into the form of a servant and makes them into a mission to the world. The community exists only in order that this love may flow through it out to the world's needs.

We are concerned now about what such Christians "believe"—about what determines their actions. But we must first be clear about what we mean by "believing."

Faith Over Against Belief

There are many words—and they are the crucial and decisive ones—in the Bible and in Christian vocabulary which have a meaning peculiar to the Bible and to the Christian community. Words which have one meaning in ordinary usage often have a quite different meaning in the Bible and in the Christian community. They have a meaning, in fact, which only the Christian understands. But this should not surprise us. Words are merely agreed-upon signs—certain sounds made with the vocal chords or other sound-producing device or scratches on some more or less permanent medium, in the sand or on stone or on paper—with which we call attention to something those words represent.

The same word may stand for different things. "Pig," for example, stands first of all, by agreed usage, for a certain barnyard animal. But we also use the word to designate certain kinds of people; and iron at a certain stage is called "pig" iron. We understand the word in each case because that for which the word stands has come within the range of our experience. There are no words which have a meaning or value in themselves or a magic power to do certain things like "abracadabra" or "hocus pocus."[1]

Humpty Dumpty in Lewis Carroll's *Through the Looking Glass* makes this point delightfully. You may recall that Humpty Dumpty explains that since a person has only one birthday a year while there are 365 days in the year, it is much better to get unbirthday presents on 364 days than only one on the birthday. He concludes triumphantly, "There's glory for you!" When Alice complains that she doesn't understand what he means by glory, he answers: "Of course you don't—till I tell you. I meant 'there's a nice knockdown argument for you!'" "But 'glory' doesn't mean 'a nice knockdown argument,'" objected Alice. And Humpty Dumpty answers as arrogantly and scornfully as any music critic in defense of his esoteric jargon, "When I use a word it means just what I choose it to mean—neither more nor less." "The question is," said Alice, "whether you *can* make words mean so many different things." "The question is," said Humpty Dumpty, "which is to be master—that's all." Then after defining "impenetrability" as meaning, "we've had enough of that subject, and it would be just as well if you'd mention what you mean to do next, as I suppose you don't mean to stop here all the rest of your life," he explains that when he makes a word do a lot of work like that he always pays it extra.

That we know the meaning of words only when they have come within the range of our experience is manifestly true when they refer to objects in space and time, objects which we can see and grasp with our senses. It is equally true of such words as love, trust, hate, despise, which designate inner experiences that are discovered to be common to human beings. Moreover, we should also be aware that even after we have looked up the accepted meaning of a word in our dictionary (and dictionaries are in need of constant revision as usages change), we cannot be sure of the meaning except as it is used in a sentence in a certain context. Ludwig Wittgenstein[2] has said that the meaning of a word is its use in a sentence. This involves an awareness of the purpose language is intended to serve. For example, when someone in exasperation says to another, "Aw, go to hell, will ya," he may not mean at all that he wants the other to make a certain trip to a certain torrid place. All he means is: "Keep still. Your everlasting chatter is 'bugging' me." Or he may mean, "Get out of my hair, will you; I want nothing more to do with you." The context will have to determine

4

which it is. But these same words in the mouth of the true judge of all men would mean something quite different, for "it is a fearful thing to fall into the hands of the living God" (Heb. 10:31). And then obviously the meaning of the word "hell" would need some clarification too. Does it mean a place of fiery torment located somewhere in the bowels of the earth, or what?

Much confusion has been caused in this connection by Wittgenstein's description of "language games." Some have concluded that language is a game we play and therefore not to be taken seriously. And some play around endlessly with the meaning of the simplest sentences without ever arriving at a conclusion—an endless game of chess in which the king is never checkmated. But Wittgenstein was only using an analogy and the validity of an analogy depends upon observing the point of comparison (the so-called *tertium comparationis,* the third term which is common to the two things compared when in other respects there may be great differences). Then the analogy is this: Each game we play is played according to its own rules, for its own purpose, within its own definite limitations, with specified equipment on a specified area of play. Some of these games have certain things in common and may be classified accordingly. Thus, there are games played with a ball and within that broad classification are games where the ball is kicked and those where the ball is hit with a stick. But each game has its own rules which must be carefully stated and observed even to the point where in baseball each playing field has its own specific "ground rules." Then there are the altogether different games which are played on a board with moveable pieces. There are card games and party games and solitary games, all in bewildering proliferation. Yet we manage and have loads of fun as long as we stick to the rules of each game. And no one complains because there are no strikeouts in football or no touchdowns in baseball.

So also—and here comes the analogy—there are various uses of language where language is used for a specific purpose, according to its own specified rules. So, for example, the language used by the quarterback in giving the signals in the huddle is not the same and does not fulfill the same purpose as the cheers of the spectators in the stands. In the huddle precise information is being communicated and the success of the play depends upon each player's having a precise understanding of his own peculiar assignment. The cheering crowd, however—except for the inevitable grandstand quarterback, yelling, "Pass! Pass!" when every possible receiver is covered like a blanket—is not intending to communicate information. All it is trying to do is stir up the adrenalin to greater efforts or give expression to joy or dismay. Or think of the difference between a squadron leader briefing his pilots on their mission or a surgeon giving directions to his assistants in a delicate brain operation and a preacher, proclaiming law and gospel to his congregation, or praying at a death-bed, or administering bread and wine to a kneeling congregation. It is important to understand this business about language at the start so that the peculiarity of the Christian's language and the purpose it serves will not be summarily ruled out of court because it does not serve the same purpose as that of the chemist or circus barker and is not played according to the same rules.

So the Christian's experiences are not "common human experiences"—they are experiences peculiar to Christians. Before anyone can understand words referring to those experiences it is necessary to have the experiences. We act as though the word "god" had a common, universally accepted and understood meaning. So we blithely ask, "Do you believe in God?" as though this were in itself an intelligible question, without a further classification of this "weasel" word which changes its color in different contexts. We ask, "Can you prove God's existence?" without a clear notion of what is to be understood by "proof" or by "existence" or by "God."

Only "Christians" know the "Christian" meaning of the word *God, the Father of our Lord Jesus Christ.* Only Christians understand words like *sin, grace, repentance, love, redemption, hope,* etc., because they have experienced them in a peculiar way. The same is true of "faith." A book called *Faiths Men Live By*[3] might describe the various *faiths* that claim the allegiance of men, from the most primitive faith in a fetish—for instance a rabbit's foot—to the Communist's faith in his party. And undoubtedly the word "faith" would designate something each has in common, such as all the games that are played with a ball. And yet, what the Christian means by faith is to be clearly distinguished from these other experiences. "Faith," for the Christian, refers to the Christian

7

experience and to nothing else. Therefore Gustaf Aulén defines faith as "the comprehensive expression for the *Christian* relationship between God and man."[4]

Ordinary Beliefs

Man believes many things, and could not get very far in life if he didn't. Most of these beliefs are sanely grounded. If they are not we call them superstitions. Such beliefs are arrived at by our own ingenuity. As human beings we have powers which are not granted to lower forms of life. (See pp. 61 ff.) One of these is the power to go beyond that of which we are immediately certain. If we only stopped to think we would come to the conclusion that there are very few things of which we are immediately and unconditionally certain. So, for example, as I sit in the sunshine surveying green meadows and encircling trees, and listening to birds singing and frogs croaking, I am immediately certain only of particular patches of color and sequences of sounds. That there are indeed trees, grasses, ponds, lilies, weeds, flowers, birds, and frogs "out there" accounting for my sensations is a matter of "rational belief" rather than immediate, incontrovertible (apodictic) certainty.[5]

Whatever else they may be—and I certainly believe they are something else—our minds are instruments, and very fine ones, given us by God and apparently developed through a long evolutionary process for the solving of problems. When we are in difficulty we do not have to proceed by actual trial and error to find our way out.

Our brains make preliminary trials and think out the possible consequences until a plausible or likely solution is found. Then an actual trial will reveal whether or not the proposed solution will work. If, for example, we are caught in a burning building, we do not really have to run around trying all the possible exits; rather, our brains will do the running for us, testing the various possibilities until we hit upon that which looks most likely. Then we say that we *believe* that this is the way out, although we are not yet certain, and only after we are actually out do we know that we were right. Such is the general pattern for all our reasonable *beliefs*. They are based upon the degree of probability which we establish for some guess of our own. Action upon our guess, no matter how well supported, always involves a risk. Usually no small degree of courage is required before we can find out whether or not we were right.

This is exactly what happened when Columbus *discovered* America. Columbus, you will recall, was intent upon discovering a new sea route to India after the old land route had been blocked by the Mohammedans. He "believed" that if he sailed west he would eventually get to India, inasmuch as he also *believed* that the world was round and not flat as commonly supposed. So he summoned the courage to act on his guess. He faced the ridicule of common opinion and the sneers of the best learning of his day. He overcame the superstitious fears of the mariners and his own recurring misgivings, and "sailed on and on" until he finally proved his point, even though he did not reach the goal he had set for himself. Columbus staked everything on his belief that the world was actually round.

We must bear in mind, however, that this guess or hypothesis of Columbus was not just a foolhardy shot in the dark. It was based on good evidence and sound reasoning. Before he set sail he established a sufficient degree of probability for his hypothesis to make it plausible. He gathered evidence that indicated to him that the world was round. He was convinced that he was right. Yet it took courage to act.

Let us take another example: Dostoevsky, in *The Brothers Karamazov,* tells us of the precocious lad, Kolya, who bet his companions that he would not be afraid to lie down between the rails and let the Moscow Express pass over him. The wager was taken, and Kolya calmly lay down between the tracks while his companions stood shivering as the train thundered by and passed over the prostrate body. After the train had passed, a few interminable moments intervened before Kolya arose unscathed, and whistling a merry tune walked disdainfully away from his awed companions with nary a word.

Courageous Kolya? Yes, indeed! But that is not the whole story. Kolya was no fool. Before he had made his wager he had done some investigating. The day before, as the Moscow Express stood in the station, he had examined it carefully from end to end to reassure himself that it would be possible for someone to lie down between the rails and let the train pass over him without any injury to himself. But it still took courage for the lad to lie there and let that thundering monster roll over him. There was always the possibility of something going wrong. The cowcatcher might have dropped down at the crucial moment or he himself might have raised his head too high. Then Dostoevsky adds a touch that puts a crimp into the glory of Kolya's deed. He explains that as Kolya had lain there, with the train rushing down upon him, he had "passed out cold," and that that was the reason he had not immediately arisen after the train had passed. It took a few moments for him to recover his senses. Perhaps Dostoevsky meant to indicate that, no matter how carefully we build up our degrees of probability, in actual life situations it is "Another" who mercifully holds us until the danger is past. Perhaps this will indicate the difference between "belief" in the ordinary sense and "faith."

In general, however, our beliefs do conform to the above pattern. We believe many things which have never been conclusively demonstrated to us, but for which we have what we regard as a sufficient degree of probability. We believe that the sun will rise tomorrow for another day; so we make our plans and calmly go to sleep. We believe that a certain bank is trustworthy; so we deposit our savings in it and don't worry about them, believing that when we need them they will be there with interest. All our great discoveries and inventions and advancements have been made by people who believed in their "hunches" and had the courage to act on them.

It is altogether reasonable to suppose that religious belief is just like that. All *religious* beliefs, as a matter of

11

fact, except those based on a direct revelation from God, *are*—from the Christian point of view—like that. Religions are man-made. They are man's more or less educated *guesses* by means of which he seeks to explain his world, give it meaning, and increase his own security and well-being. They are based on degrees of probability—good, bad, or indifferent. The savage, who thinks that a certain stone of unusual shape brought him luck on one hunt and will do so again, does not have a very well-grounded belief. Socrates, on the other hand, who denies the existence of the capricious and all-too-human gods of Olympus and supposes that what is good and true and beautiful would make a much better object of worship, has a much more reasonable belief. Yet all these religions are man-made. These gods are made in the image of man, and are therefore idols. Belief in them is no miracle but a perfectly sensible matter. In most cases, moreover, there is no personal relationship involved. We may speak of "belief" in entirely impersonal objects, as when we say that we believe in the curative powers of certain medicines. In the final analysis many of our ordinary beliefs do not really matter; they leave us quite cold and have no effect.

Christian Faith

When we come to the Christian concept of faith we must alter our whole mode of thinking. Here we are in a different world, and *faith* is something radically different from *belief,* although, to be sure, there are some elements common to both. (So both football and tennis

12

are played with a ball, while they are nevertheless radically different.)

In Christian faith, first of all, the direction is down and not up. In faith God approaches man; faith is not simply man's quest for God. This, to be sure, does not deny man's quest for God. Man's guesses and ventures and his self-made gods do form a basis upon which God reveals himself, and all this serves a purpose as we shall see later. But we must not confuse this quest of man for God with God's revelation of himself. God's self-revelation is just that; it is God revealing himself, taking the initiative, coming down and drawing the veil from himself and showing himself to man. And he does not just show himself to man. He gives himself to man; he enters into the most intimate personal relation. And that which happens *to* man and *within* man, when God thus comes to him and reveals himself and causes man to recognize, trust, and obey him, we designate as *faith*. Faith is, therefore, God's work in man. It is something that God does to man, without, however, treating man like a thing—a stick or a stone. In faith God deals with man person to person.

Faith a Personal Relationship

One thing must be quite clear: faith is a personal relationship, between two personal beings, in which one is active and the other responsive. We can find analogies, but we must remember that they are only analogies. Acknowledgment of utter dependence upon someone, trust, confidence, love, all these, as they are worked in us by another person, are included in what the Bible means by faith. You might think of your relationship to your parents, teachers, friends, or if you have progressed that far, your relationship to the person whom you have made or mean to make your life's partner. In the case of your mother it is quite clear that she has taken the initiative, for you were born into her love and through her pain. Your love for her is clearly your response to her, for she was there first and she first loved you. Without your being aware of it she inspired you with confidence, for she nursed you at her bosom and sheltered you with her care. Surely there is no question about the responsive nature of your love. Your love is brought to birth and inspired in you by her self-giving love. It would never occur to you to think that this was something you had brought forth in yourself. Nor would it occur to you to bring all this over into that other area of problem-solving of which we were speaking before. This has nothing to do with guesses and degrees of probability. A man does not line up all the young ladies of his acquaintance in a neat little row before him, proceed to figure out which one, in all probability, will make the best wife for him, and then promptly fall in love.[6] No, love simply takes possession of a man. One person is confronted by another who inspires him with love and confidence. This description of the responsive nature of faith ought not, however, to obscure faith's active character. Faith means obedience. It is obedience in trust. It is man's own audacious "yes" to God's "yes"—as we shall develop more fully later.

Perhaps we can see what is involved if we think again

14

of Kolya. Let us suppose that Kolya did not himself "cook up" the scene to impress his friends, and that he did not first make reasonably sure that it would work out without harm to himself. Let us suppose, rather, that this is what happened: One day Kolya's mother said to him, "Kolya, do you love me?" And Kolya, feeling a surge of love come over him, replied, "Yes, mother, you know that I love you." "Very well then," continued his mother, "if you really love and trust me, go lie down between the tracks and let the Moscow Express pass over you. Do not ask why, but do as I tell you. I will be with you." Kolya looked at his mother. How could this be? He took her hand, so tender and toil-worn with love, into his own hand. He was overwhelmed. He asked no more questions. He went out and did her bidding in "faith." Even so a sturdy fisherman, who knew the ways of fish and the laws of probability for catching them, was once persuaded by a calm voice to launch out into the deep and, counter to all good practice, let down the net. He went purely at the command of the Lord, and he took a draught of fishes so great that he was filled with fear and fell before his Lord and confessed, "Depart from me, for I am a sinful man, O Lord" (Luke 5:8). Afterwards he confessed, "Lord, you know everything; you know that I love you" (John 21:17), and in the strength of that love he followed his Lord even to death on a cross, where it was the Lord who held him until his faith was turned to sight.

Or think of the difference between Columbus and Abraham. Columbus was intent upon finding access to the riches of India and this fact impelled and motivated his courage. Man's quest for God has often been similarly selfishly motivated. He wants greater security, better crops, children in whom he may live on after his death, some assurance of riches far exceeding the wealth of the Indies as he moves toward that unseen, farther shore for which every man must some day set sail. For these things man fashions his gods and tries to compel them to do his bidding.

The story of Abraham is different (see Gen. 12:1 ff.). It begins abruptly with God's entrance into his life. It begins with God's command and Abraham's obedience, with God's promise and Abraham's confidence in that promise. The promise always runs counter to the evidence—the only guarantor of its fulfillment is God himself. Abraham is homeless and childless, a nameless wanderer upon the face of the earth. Yet he is to have a home; he is to be the father of a great nation; in him are all the families of the earth to be blessed. Abraham thinks of the arduous journey before him, of his advancing years, of Sarah's barren womb, of a thousand-and-one reasons that would cry folly to his trust. Yet he believes God, and it is counted to him for righteousness. Finally there comes the supreme and fearsome test. That God should make a request that caused him to appear more like an inhuman monster than like a loving father! "Take your son, your only son Isaac, whom you love . . . and offer him . . . as a burnt offering" (Gen. 22:2). And Abraham obeyed, trusting God: "The Lord will provide himself the lamb for a burnt offering" (Gen. 22:8). Here all the

evidence of faith

16

glory of *faith* is laid bare. Abraham is in very truth the *father of faith.*[7]

This is what it means to *have faith.* We stand beneath a cross on a hill that is called "the skull," a place of shame and defeat, of the triumph of all that is base and cruel and utterly wrong. "My God, my God, why hast thou forsaken me?" Yet this is the victory! This is the King of glory! This is he whom we love and trust and obey! "Lord, you know everything, you know that I love you" (John 21:17). This is what it means to *have faith.*

We stand in the darkness of this world and the sun hides its face; we are surrounded on all sides by the ravaging triumph of hatred and lust; ruthless hands suddenly tear our loved ones from us; sickness and pain convulse us. Where now is God? "Fear not, Abram, I am your shield; your reward shall be very great" (Gen. 15:1). "The Lord is my shepherd, I shall not want. . . . Even though I walk through the valley of the shadow of death, I fear no evil; for thou art with me" (Ps. 23). "I am the good shepherd. The good shepherd lays down his life for the sheep" (John 10:11). "I am the way, and the truth, and the life" (John 14:6). "Come to me, all who labor and are heavy-laden, and I will give you rest" (Matt. 23:28). "In my Father's house are many rooms; if it were not so, would I have told you that I go to prepare a place for you? And when I go . . . I will come again and will take you to myself, that where I am you may be also" (John 14:2 f.). "All authority in heaven and on earth has been given to me. . . . And lo, I am with you always, to the close of the age" (Matt. 28:18 ff.).

17

And so our anxious hearts are calmed, murmurings cease, confidence and love return, and with them obedience. "Lord, we will follow you wherever you go." The hand that leads us may be pierced, but it is the hand of love, and that is enough. This is what it means to *have faith*.

John the Baptist lies rotting in his prison and sends his half-doubting, half-defiant inquiry to the one to whom he had once pointed with such confidence: "Are you he who is to come, or shall we look for another?" There is pathos in the answer, "Go, and tell John what you have seen and heard: the blind receive their sight, the lame walk, lepers are cleansed, and the deaf hear, the dead are raised up, the poor have good news preached to them. *And blessed is he who takes no offense at me*" (Luke 7:18 ff.).

There is evidence enough of the healing touch of love, but what about "the occasion for stumbling"? If Jesus was really the one who was to come with healing, then why, after two thousand years, is the world troubled with anguish more than ever before? Were it not better to turn to other saviors? "Blessed is he who takes no offense at me." Others are freed from their prisons, others have health and sight, others are turned from death to life, but the head of John the Baptist is carried out on a platter at the whim of a jealous, vindictive Jezebel. "Blessed is he who takes no offense at me." This is what it means to *have faith*.

This is the story of faith as the Bible records it. God inspires men to trust and confidence in himself—no human achievement! God holds man, and man does not resist. Man does not himself bridge the gap between a high degree of probability and certainty with his own clever ingenuity and bold courage to act. God steps across the man-made breach that separates man from God. God gives man the courage to act—counter to all that is plausible and guaranteed by probabilities—when there is need for immediate action and no time for investigations.

In all this we must not forget that the approach is person-to-person. Faith is the reaction of a responsible being to God's initial action. God does not pick up man as he would a cheese and put him safely away on the shelf of salvation where the mice won't get him. No, he does address man and calls forth from him the response of love. But man is always free to resist and put his trust in other persons or things. He may choose to put his trust in himself, in his intellect with its fine-spun ideas about God, in a golden calf that he makes from the spoils of the Egyptians, or in the marvels that the scientist produces in his laboratory. He can clamor noisily for a sign; or take offense at the stumbling block and foolishness of the cross (1 Cor. 1:23). He can also err, not knowing the scriptures nor the power of God (Matt. 22:29). Or he may join the great multitude of those who have surrendered in *faith*.

The Place of Creeds and Confessions

We have discussed the nature of faith. Such faith spreads through the witness of those who have themselves been touched by it. Those who have been touched will always be constrained to confess their faith. Confessions are flags around which men rally as they separate themselves from others and band together marching toward a common objective. The first Christian confession was simply *"Jesus* is Lord"—not the emperor, for all his pomp and power; not some unknown god; but *Jesus,* who had lived and walked among them.

A *confession* is primarily a witness before men. A *creed,* on the other hand, is primarily a man's profession to God. The word *credo,* "I believe," indicates a personal expression of trust and confidence. It is, therefore, also a witness to the great things God has done. What is the Apostles' Creed but a witness to the glorious deeds of God in creation, redemption, and sanctification, deeds which form the basis of the Christian's trust? Strictly speaking, these facts are not the object of faith. The object of faith is God himself. But because men believe in God they also believe certain things. There is a distinction between "believing *in*" and "believing *that.*" Only "believing in" is faith. "Believing that" accompanies the "believing in." In order that men may make a confession before others, and clarify their stand, they try to state clearly what they believe. They do it so that they may instruct their children and new converts in the faith. They do it in conflict with others who hold different views. They do it to bring the diversified witness of the Bible into some kind of consistent whole around one central message. This is the inevitable origin of doctrines or teachings. Doctrines can never be formulated once and for all since they are always addressed to a specific situation which is usually one of conflict. They state, therefore, what Christians believe, at any given time and place of the church's history. And thus they need constant reformulation as situations change. In order to say the same thing in a new situation things must often be said differently. This is a human task in which men seek the guidance of the Holy Spirit. Care must always be taken: There must be no accommodation of the message to the sinful predilections of those to whom it is addressed. There must be fidelity to the message which sits in judgment on man's natural sinfulness. The good news, like all news, must be faithfully passed on without distortion or diminution. At the same time, however, that message must speak intelligibly to, and must meet the actual needs of, those to whom it is addressed.

All this should make it clear that faith is not just the holding of certain teachings to be true. A man is not saved from his predicament in existence by believing that there is someone wise enough to account for order in the world. This is what we have called a spectator-truth which does not involve the beholder. A man is *saved* only if he actually trusts, thanks, praises, and obeys the God of holy love who orders this world in accordance with his purpose.[8] A man is not *saved* because he believes that Jesus is both God and man but only because he actually lives under the lordship of Jesus as the Anointed One (Christ-Messiah) of God who is to him true man, as well as true God, and by whose suffering and victorious love he is redeemed.[9]

By the same token, faith is not deliberately forcing

21

yourself to hold something to be true when the evidence is insufficient, or even contradictory, as though the more impossible something is the more credit you would get for believing it. The White Queen in *Alice in Wonderland* tells Alice that she is "one hundred and one, five months and a day." When Alice protests that she can't believe that, the Red Queen gleefully announces: "That's just because you haven't tried. Now close your eyes tight, draw a long breath, and try again! Take me, I have gotten so by dint of much practice that I can believe as many as six impossible things *before breakfast.*"

There is a truth here, of course, that is of the very essence of *faith.* Faith *does* run counter to the evidence at hand, it runs counter to the common opinion, it does confront you with an obvious contradiction.[10] It is not, however, a kind of *tour de force* by which one achieves the impossible. Since faith is a personal relationship it means a firm reliance on the other person even when appearances are against him. Faith is trust in an unseen God who never shows his face, whose presence and action are always "hidden," but who nevertheless has revealed himself to men, acted on their behalf and who still comes to men today speaking his words of judgment and of grace.

Therefore, faith is not faith in one's own faith. This is perhaps the most common and most persistent and most natural of all the misunderstandings of faith. Faith in this case is regarded as a human achievement and those who say they are not saved by their good works but by their faith make faith a "good work" for which they want credit. To say that we are saved by faith can be very misleading. It is much better to say that *we are saved by God's grace, for Christ's sake, through faith, unto good works.* Faith is, as we said, the comprehensive name for the right God-relation and this includes a right relation to other men and to God's world. Then "whatsoever is not of faith is sin" makes some sense.

In these terms, what is commonly regarded as faith is of the very essence of sin, as, for example, when we hear a mother say, "I *believed* that my son would come back from the war and he came back." Believing is then something we do, something inside of us which if it is strong enough, will make things come true. This attitude is illustrated by the farmer who heard the pastor preach on the text, "If you have faith as a grain of mustard seed you will say to this mountain, 'Move hence to yonder place,' and it will move; and nothing will be impossible to you" (Matt. 17:20). In the course of the sermon the pastor mentioned that the prophet Elisha had, by his faith, made an ax head float on the water (2 Kings 6:1 ff.). After the service, the farmer went up to the preacher and said: "Rev'ner, if I throw my jackknife into the river and believe that it will float, will it float?" And the preacher said, "Yes, if you believe it." Whereupon the farmer replied: "O.K. Let's go down to the river and try it." Down to the river they went and the farmer threw his best jackknife far out across the water; it hit with a sorry little splash and went straight to the bottom. And the farmer said without blinking an eye, "That's just what I thought would happen."

So we laugh and conclude that the moral of the story is: Of course, *since he didn't believe that it would happen, it didn't, but if only he had believed that it would happen then it would have happened.* We make no mention of God or of trusting him to do something in line with his purposes. We laughed too soon. It is not faith in God to do that which he alone can do and for which we must trust him; rather, it is faith in our faith to accomplish something beyond ordinary methods of control. Ordinarily, of course, jackknives won't float on water, but if we believe strongly enough that they will, then our faith will be like an invisible hand that reaches out and keeps the jackknife from sinking. *But here we are still in control. We make something which suits our purposes to happen, because we will it.* This is nothing but mind over matter and there may be something to it. At Duke University experiments have shown that dice don't always roll according to the laws of chance and that apparently some people can, by willing it, make the seven come up more often than it should. Therefore it would seem that those who are saved by faith should be the best crapshooters in the outfit, but I, at least, have not found this to be so.

The whole cult of "faith in faith" reaches its nadir when its high priest recommends that you carry a little spring in your pocket to push whenever you are feeling low (when the doctor has just told you that you have incurable cancer and six months to live, or when, like Job, you have just received news that your six sons and your six daughters with all their children were wiped out in

24

an airplane crash, or when the newscast reports that an H-bomb has been dropped on New York and twelve million people have been pulverized); feeling it bounce back in your hand you would bounce back, too.

There are even more subtle ways of substituting faith in our faith for faith in the living God and his promises. For example, men put their faith in their conversion experience, the feeling of being saved which they once had in a crucial moment of their lives. It is from their conversion experience that they hope to live when doubts recur instead of listening again and again to God's sure word and letting *that* hold them. When seeming tragedy strikes, it is no good to remind myself how sure and certain I was in better days. Now I must hear again that sure and certain word that comes to me from outside myself stilling the storm and holding me above the seventy thousand fathoms.

Neither faith in our faith nor believing certain doctrines constitutes true faith; rather it is trust in the God who gives faith, whose word must be heard again and again. This present book means to set forth what those who make the Christian confession believe. But one thing must be clear. No one can become a Christian by reading about it and learning its teachings by heart, as he might become expert in mathematics by studying mathematics, or become a Democrat (or Republican) by reading Democratic (or Republican) propaganda that succeeds in selling a bill of goods. The only entrance into the Christian fellowship is through "repentance" and "faith." When the gospel (both the condemning law and the liberating good news) is proclaimed, it challenges us and calls us to decision so that we either *have faith in it* or *are offended by it.* The real stumbling block to becoming a believer is never anything but man's pride and his unwillingness to humble himself in trust and obedience, not to a stranger but to the true Lord of his life. "If any man's will is to do his [God's] will, he shall know whether the teaching is from God or whether I am speaking of my own authority" (John 7:17). God calls us to act, to take his *command of love* seriously, and to really set about trying to obey it instead of arguing and finding excuses. If we do this, we will discover our sin, our need of forgiveness and, casting ourselves upon God's mercy, we will through daily sorrow and repentence be enabled to live a true *life together in love.*

When the gospel is proclaimed, no matter by whom, it is the Lord who speaks. In the presence of the King of kings, the only proper attitude is that of worship, adoration, submission, and obedience. This is faith. Its origin is in the King himself. Here we cannot calculatingly ask for a sign. Here we cannot first sneak off to do some investigating, or to build up a tower of probabilities. Here the only thing that we can do is the Beloved's bidding. This is faith.

CHAPTER II

THE LIVING GOD

Knowing Ourselves

One of the ancients once said, and men have been repeating it ever since, that if an ox and a pig could think, they would fashion gods for themselves after their own image—glorified oxen and pigs. Some men conclude that there really is no God, and that man merely fashions his gods after his own image, bigger, more powerful, but after all simply glorified human beings with all human virtues and vices magnified.

There can be no doubt; men do fashion gods after their own image. This, as we have already noticed, and as shall be more fully developed later, is the story of man's religious quest outside the sphere of what we call revelation. But where God, instead of leaving man to search for him, shows or *reveals* himself to men, just the opposite is the case. It is revealed to man that he is made in the image of God instead of gods being made in the image of man. This means that man cannot understand himself and how he differs from the animal until it is revealed to him what the God, in whose image he is made, is like.

A Proper Understanding of Man

Perhaps you have heard the famous old Socratic maxim, "Know thyself." Socrates—he of the homely face and the shrewish wife, who went about the marketplace as the gadfly of Athens, deflating man's pretensions and showing them how little they knew—was of the opinion that if you really knew yourself you would solve the riddle of the universe and would know not only what all men are like but also what God is like. There is truth in what Socrates said, but what Socrates did not appreciate is that the only key to knowledge of self is knowledge of God.

You cannot come to know what people are like by studying others. If you want to know what makes a clock tick you take the clock apart. If you want to learn about the behavior of dogs you watch dogs under controlled conditions and discover why they behave this way and that. The same is true of some aspects of human behavior. Much of human behavior is like what happens inside a clock; or in the chemist's laboratory where chemicals are mixed and smells and explosions are bound to follow; or in the psychologist's laboratory where a touch will cause the reflex of a muscle, or the smell of cheese will change the rat's course through the maze. All such things can and must be studied "objectively," we say, in others. But if you want to understand jealousy, envy, love, hate, or fear, you need to understand not only all that the laboratory reveals but also all that goes on within yourself. And you will understand yourself—and this is the important thing—only if God has first revealed himself to you and shown you what it means to be created in his image. You will understand your motivations, why you act in certain ways, the hidden springs of your conduct, your self-deceptions, the way you "kid" yourself and build yourself up, what it is that makes you restless and afraid and guilty and aspiring, why you can climb so high and sink so low—you will understand all this only after the veil that hides your true self has been drawn away and you see yourself as a being who has been created in the image of God and then has fallen away from and distorted that image. But before you can understand the image you must know something about the original, you must have a picture of God himself.

Some Presuppositions

We have already said that we cannot of ourselves know what God is like. We know it only from God's self-revelation. The following statements are, therefore, all based on revelation, and what that involves will become clear only as we go along. At this point we cannot give a complete picture of God, but only enough information to help us understand what is meant by saying that we are made "in the image of God."

The Hidden God

Our predicament is that God never appears for all eyes to behold like a "very rare and tremendously large green bird, with a red beak, sitting in a tree on the mound, and perhaps even whistling in an unheard of manner" so that the captain of the hunt can shout out his presence.[1] To believe in a directly visible God is paganism. It makes God just another being among other beings, a part of this world of space and time, recognizable in some way by his unusual appearance, like the Greek god Pan, half-goat, half-man, known by his piping and betrayed by his smell. Such belief forgets that God as the creator of space and time is not himself in space and time and is therefore altogether different from the creatures who are bound to space and time. It forgets that as long as we exist in space and time we must live by faith and not by sight. The "naked God," as Luther said, never appears to man in his creaturely-sinful existence. "Man shall not see me and live," said God to Moses (Exod. 33:20). When God appears for all eyes to see the time of judgment is come. As C. S. Lewis has said, when the author comes out on the stage the play is over.

In the meantime God is present to many only in a "hidden" way, behind what Luther called a "mask," which, like the mask of the masquerader, hides the true identity of the wearer until the witching-hour strikes and the time for unmasking is come. Luther also uses the image of the "larvae," the unsightly cocoons from which come gorgeous butterflies. God is not way off somewhere; he is immediately present to man, closer than hands and feet, but always in a medium. Hence John Baillie uses the phrase a "mediated immediacy." God is present in his creation without being identified with it. He speaks through the prophet without being the prophet. He is effectively hidden in the man Jesus who nevertheless is

Immanuel (God with us). He judges and frees in the words of the preacher. He gives himself in the bread and wine of the sacrament. He is always, therefore—to use a much misunderstood Lutheran phrase—"in, with, and under" the earthly medium. Spatial imagery is unavoidable and yet it is used only to make clear that in God we do not deal with a spatial matter, either of "out there" beyond the curtain of the sky or of "in here" in some dimension of depth.[2]

This then is our burden: that the Lord of all never appears and that he can be seen only with the "eyes of faith." Every attempt at the kind of objectification which would make him visible, directly discernible to the senses of sight, sound, touch, taste, smell is to be rejected, as is every attempt by means of the unusual and astounding to guarantee his presence and action. God and his actions are perceived only in the inwardness of faith. That it is the God of holiness and love who is present and active is not ever apparent; it always remains "hidden."

This is what is basically involved in the legitimate aspect of Rudolf Bultmann's much debated program of "demythologization." He defines a myth very specifically as a presentation or objectification of that which lies beyond time and space as actually occurring within the realities of time and space. All such myths, therefore, need to be interpreted in order to bring out that which they are trying to express concerning the nature and action of the living God. This is quite different from the myth which is used to illustrate a timeless truth in the manner of a "visual aid" designed to help those who are

31

not clever enough to discern the truth without it.[3]

The "hiddenness" of God means, furthermore, that we know only as much of God as he has chosen to reveal to us. What God is like in and of himself apart from his relation to us, we do not know, nor can we know it until we see him face to face. And even then the distinction between Creator and creature will not be done away with but will rather be heightened as we become aware of the full glory of God. We shall not become God, as some people vainly and blasphemously imagine; rather, the ultimate I-Thou relation will be fulfilled in full face to face fellowship. Yet, even though we shall never know God in our existence as he is in and for himself, we have the full assurance that what he does reveal of himself is true. He may be more but he is certainly no less. What he reveals is his true heart and mind.

Finally, the "hiddenness" of God means not only that God is "hidden" in his revelation in the sense of the "mediated immediacy" we have described, but also that the revelation itself is a mystery which passes all our understanding. It is the *revealed* love that is itself unfathomable to us. The more we experience this love the more it amazes us and fills our hearts with awe. This does not mean that we are to do violence to our reason; it is our reason itself which tells us that here is something concerning which we understand that we do not understand it. The word "mystery" comes from the Greek word *mueo*, meaning to shut the mouth as when you say the letter "m." It therefore means that which closes your lips in all foolish attempts to explain. This mystery is not like that of the "who-dun-it" which disappears as the culprit is disclosed. When God discloses himself in his love, that is when the true mystery begins.

The Different Dimension of God

The "hiddenness" of God may perhaps be made intelligible to men of the twentieth century, if we think of God as living in a dimension different from ours. We live in the dimension of space and time and are caught up in its limitations. God lives in a dimension which includes, yet goes beyond, this limited dimension. We can to some extent understand what is meant by this when we think of a person who is blind and to whom the whole world of light and color is unknown. By way of contrast, the person with eyes lives in a different world, or better, in a different dimension of the same world. It is the same world, but the man with sight sees what the other cannot see. The best the seeing person can do is to try in some way to make clear to the sightless man what the world of light and color is like. Then, by means of the senses which he does have—by touching and hearing and smelling—the blind man will get some idea of what the world which is closed to him is like. But what a sorry substitute that is! Only when a blind man's eyes are opened can he see.

Contrast yourself with a lower animal. You live in a different dimension of the same world, a dimension which is, we say, "higher" than that of the animal. The world in which you live is closed to that of the animal. But the world of the animal is not—not so much at least—closed to you. You can understand the animal, but the animal cannot understand you. You can control and train the animal, but the animal cannot control and train you. You, therefore, are not a more highly trained animal, made in the image of the animal; rather, the animal is in some small way made in your image and is a sort of shadowy reflection of you. People who put it the other way around and think of humans as animals, are, therefore, just as much confused as those who think of God as a human being.

Man can in some small way open his world to those who are "below" him, while those "below" cannot in the same way, penetrate into his "higher" world. It is just so with God in his relation to man. He lives in a world "above" us, to which we by ourselves cannot obtain access. We cannot know what he is really like until we pass beyond the veil and meet him face to face. But in the meantime he can show us something of himself. This will be genuinely himself, although only as much as he wants us to know, and in the form in which he chooses to reveal it. And it will have to be apprehended with the understanding that we possess. This means that we will be confronted with a reality which will remain a mystery to our understanding. Our human terms will be inadequate to describe what we experience. Yet we are bound to make an attempt at description, always mindful of the fact that God is never quite like that which is within the realm of our ordinary experience. There is always a difference, and it is this difference which is revealed to us and which eludes our understanding, fills our hearts with awe, and brings us to our knees in worship and adoration. Keeping these things in mind, let us see what God is like as he has revealed himself, so that we may understand what is meant by "the image of God."

God Is a Personal Being

God, first of all, has revealed himself to us, when he spoke through the prophets and then himself entered into our world in the man Jesus, as a *personal being*. By that we mean he is not just a *force*, like electricity. He is not to be identified with the *energy* that pervades the world, but as the Creator and Source of that energy. He is not just a *principle* or *rule* or *law* according to which the world runs. Nor is he just an *idea*, like the imaginary picture we have in our minds of the perfect man of whom all men are but an imperfect copy. He is not like the *first cause* that got things started a long time ago—like the "bug" that causes typhoid fever. He is not like a huge *magnet* which sets things into motion and causes them to develop and grow by its attractive power. Men have seen him as all of these things. But he *is*, as we are, a *center of will and responsibility*.

The only beings we know of that can do things—that is, start something, initiate activity, and do so with the feeling of being responsible and not just of being pushed or pulled—are *personal beings*. In that sense God is a *personal God*. This does not mean that he is a person just like ourselves, with eyes and ears and hands and feet, although in speaking of the living God we can never get rid of these anthropomorphisms. What we mean is that he stands over against us, as we know ourselves to stand over against other people. Luther uses the expression that we stand *coram deo,* face to face with God. We cannot stand face to face with something which is less than personal. Just as we are aware of what is going on around us, and are affected by it and react to it, so also God.

God's Essence and Attributes — the Living God

The theologians used to *define* God as we define other objects of our experience. We assign things to a certain class and then we indicate those attributes or qualities which distinguish them from other members of the same class. In so doing we also distinguish the essence of a thing, that which makes a thing what it is and without which it could not be what it is, from the accidental qualities which are not "essential" and may therefore vary from individual to individual of the same class. So a chair is defined as an article of furniture made for one person to sit on, with legs and a support for the back. This gives you the so-called "essence" of "chairness," without which it would not be a chair. If more than one can sit on it —unless indeed they are lovers—it becomes a couch or a settee. If it has no back or legs but can be used for sitting we call it a hassock. So we arrive at what Plato called the eternal, unchangeable idea, or essence, of a chair. But such a chair also has many accidental attributes which may vary from individual to individual without affecting the essence. Chairs may be made of different materials: wood, iron, steel, stone, etc. They may have a variety of shapes and colors. But as long as you can still sit on it, however uncomfortably, its essence remains that of a chair.

God was defined in the same way. He was put into the class of beings and then differentiated as the "highest" or "supreme" being. Then his essence was given as "love" and a long list of attributes inherent in this essence was given. Most of us will recall at least the "omnis" of God—omniscient, omnipresent, omnipotent, together with eternal, spiritual (non-material), infinite, non-spatial, non-temporal. These were called the "metaphysical" attributes of God, because they were said to qualify him in his being beyond, *meta,* our "physical" being, without saying what he is like. To these "metaphysical attributes" were then added the "moral attributes," such as righteousness, truthfulness, faithfulness, goodness, mercy, grace, patience, long-suffering, all of which together constituted his holiness, the sum total of all moral virtues. God was, therefore, also called the perfect being, the embodiment of all possible virtues and powers to the highest degree.

These attributes—some of them at least—were actually considered separable from the "essence," as though they could be laid off and put on again as a man changes his clothes without changing himself. So, it was said, when God became man he kept the essence of his "god-hood" and divested himself of his powers, that is of omnipotence, omniscience, and omnipresence. Then when the man Jesus ascended into heaven even his "manhood" put on those same attributes, so as not to be confined to a

37

place above the sky but to be everywhere even as God is everywhere.

Now all this represents a human way of trying to do justice to the biblical revelation, and it once, no doubt, served its purpose. But it also put God far too much at man's disposal. We can define that which we control with our minds, but we cannot define the living God. Furthermore, we should recognize that all definition, with its distinctions between "essences" and "attributes," is only for purposes of clear talk, so we can communicate intelligibly. Actually not even the chemist can separate the essence of water from its attributes. Water can indeed be analyzed into H_2O but such water is always of a certain temperature, color, etc., in relation to us. It doesn't make sense to say that these attributes inhere in the essence and are separable from it. Actual water is not a stable, unchangeable essence—only our idea of water is. Actual water can be split into its components of hydrogen and oxygen, but then it ceases to be water. Hydrogen can itself be split as we know from the H-bomb; indeed, any atom can be split.

So everything is what it is only in certain relationships. This is crucially important for our speaking of God. We cannot neatly control God with our distinctions between essence and attributes. We know God only in his relationship to us and everything we say about him concerns this relationship. Let it be clear, however, that we do not make God dependent upon this relation. We also assert his separate, independent being, as the creative ground of all that is. We are dependent upon our relation to him, but he is not dependent upon us.

God Is Holy Love

On this basis, then, we affirm that what God basically is, what makes him what he is, can be summed up in the one word: *love*. Love includes it all, for "God is love" (1 John 4:16). He is, as Luther said, a fiery abyss of love that has no bottom (*"ein feuriger Abgrund der Liebe"*). Yet this needs qualification; it cannot simply be said in abstraction. Love implies an object which is loved. Love is the way God relates himself to us and our world and, therefore, love takes many different forms depending on the situation. Everything that is asserted about God will be an assertion about his love. Everything God does will be a manifestation of his love.

A further qualification of God's love is that it is *holy*. God's holiness has sometimes been confused with "moral perfection," the sum total of his virtues (cf. p. 37 above). Holiness in the Bible, however, is not a moral conception. As Gustaf Aulén says, it is the background against which God appears and it qualifies everything God is and does.[4] There is a dual root to the word "holiness." On the one hand, it means "otherness," "separateness," and thus indicates the profound difference between God and the world. In the history of religions the word indicates the completely unknown, the absolutely different which has in no way entered into the experience of man.[5] It is, therefore, called the *mysterium tremendum et fascinans*, the mystery which both attracts and repels. The awareness of the "holy" is the uncanny realization that there is something the nature of which is completely "hidden." It is like receiving a securely wrapped present with no hint of what is in it. You are both fascinated by it, eager to open it, yet filled with trembling, because you don't know what is in it. This is the general experience of the "holy" which any man may have as he contemplates the vastness of the night sky, the fury of the storm, the endless waves of the sea, the wild tumbling of Niagara Falls, the beauty of a sunset, or a baby's smile.

In the Bible, however, holiness has yet a second connotation, derived not from the awareness of the unknown, but from the encounter with the living God in his self-disclosure. The English word "holy" implies wholeness, soundness, health, freedom from disease or imperfection with nothing missing. So God is *whole* in his holiness. But this is something other than moral perfection. Not only is God *whole in himself,* but he will not tolerate a lack of wholeness in others. If he is confronted with it he must do something about it. He must get rid of it. Above all he will not tolerate rebellion. He puts a total claim upon his creatures. "I am the Lord, that is my name; my glory I give to no other, nor my praise to graven images" (Isa. 42:8). When Isaiah has a vision of the thrice-holy God in the temple, he cries out, "Woe is me! For I am lost; for I am a man of unclean lips, and I dwell in the midst of a people of unclean lips" (Isa. 6:5).

Hence, as will be developed more fully later, we cannot dispense with the notion of the "wrath of God." This is not like a peevish, human anger; it is the unalterable opposition of the holy God to sin. The Holy One could, of course, simply destroy that which is unclean, imperfect, rebellious. But to destroy the creatures whom he has made would not be *creative love*. He could, in contrast, purge out the uncleaness, make whole the unhealthy, win over the rebellious; he could recreate his creatures for proper communion with himself.

This is exactly what God's holy love prompts him to do. In his love he employs his holiness to achieve what his love desires, the well-being, the happiness, the blessedness of his creatures. In his holiness he employs his love to bring about that which his holiness demands, the "perfection" (in a very peculiar sense), the freedom from every spot and wrinkle, the *wholeness* of his creatures.

We see completely what God's love is like only in Jesus, the Christ, even though the same love is active in all creation and most particularly in the choice and guidance of the people of Israel. A full description of this love must therefore be postponed until later in our study. (This is the trouble with our procedure. We really should have begun with the revelation of God in Christ, but we can't have everything at the beginning.) It is sufficient at this time to point out the radical difference between our love and God's love. We love primarily because we are not sufficient unto ourselves. We love things and people that are lovable, because they have something to offer us to enrich and complete our lives. This is the desiring love which the Greeks called *eros* and which they said was the child of plenty and of want, the want of

41

one seeking its fulfillment in the plenty of the other. Such "erotic" love has its God-given place in our lives. We are not sufficient unto ourselves and must find satisfaction for our desires and needs—in food and sex and music and play and friends and in the God who alone is the fulfiller of all our needs. Augustine was right: "Thou hast made us Lord for thyself and our hearts are restless within us until they rest in Thee."

God's love for us, however, is different. For God there is nothing outside of himself which he needs for fulfillment. If there were, he would not be God. God's love, therefore, is creative and is wholly for the sake of those on whom it is spent. God does not find the objects of his love at hand as we do; he must first create them, in order that he may then spend his love on them for their sakes, and not for his own. God's love, therefore, is in no wise conditioned by the worthiness of its objects. His love is for the unlovely, the unlovable, the unworthy— even for the enemy. God's love is wholly unselfish and self-giving. This is its absolute miracle. It is designated in Greek as *agape* to distinguish it from *eros* and *filia* (the love of friendships) and the libido (the sex drive). It is this love of agape which God in Christ brings to us and creates in us by the Holy Spirit.[6]

The So-Called Qualities of God

Remembering now that we are not listing separable qualities but are rather describing God in his revelation to us, and remembering also that all we say is about the God who is love, we may nevertheless enumerate God's qualities. God is not limited as we are. Speaking humanly we may say that he sees everything and that he knows everything. This really has nothing to do with God's being able to tell you exactly how many flakes there are in all the packages of breakfast cereal in Pennsylvania on a given day or how many "burps" have been re-sounded by all the Eskimos who ever expressed their appreciation to their hosts in this fashion. Perhaps God could tell us if he wished. But if he is just a giant computer stored with useless information he cannot either judge or redeem us, make us tremble, or exalt us with joy unspeakable.

God is not in just one place at a time; he is present everywhere at all times with his whole being. He has never had a beginning nor will he ever have an end. There is no limit to his power. There is nothing that he could not do except those things he chooses not to do and which would go counter to his very nature. There is no point, then, in asking whether he can make an object so heavy he can't lift it or make a two-year-old calf in a minute. Precisely in this lies the limitlessness of his power: he can not only control others, which any buck sergeant can do, but he can control himself, and that is the biggest job of all. And equal to it is the power to make others free and then to respect their freedom. The lords of this earth exercise their power in taking freedom from men. Man, for all his genius, is unable to give freedom to his creations. The best man can do is make "gadgets" which he must control if they are not to turn upon him like a Frankenstein and destroy him. God alone can make free beings and preserve their freedom without at the same time losing control.

Furthermore, God does not depend, either for his being or his well-being, upon anybody or anything other than himself. He is his own ceaseless fountain of life. He is *absolutely independent and self-sufficient.* He does not need a world or human beings to be happy or to complete himself. He does not have to give an accounting of his actions to anyone. He does not have to be afraid of anyone nor does he need anyone to "kowtow" to him. He is the kind of person we would all like to be. But that is precisely what is basically wrong with us—we are not content to live within our limitations. We want to be like God. We want none to be over us. We want to do just as we please. We learn very unwillingly that we shall never have freedom until we learn to do as God pleases and make our wills conform to his. It is God who says: "If you want to get where you want to go, you will have to go my way."

God, moreover, *does not change.* Change implies imperfection of some kind. The plant grows and changes its form because it is not yet mature. Then when it has reached its full growth it begins to decay because it does not have everlasting life. All around us there is change and decay; there is only One who does not change. What he is, he is. We may rely upon his permanence. He is true to his word. He means what he says and sticks to it.

We have noted that everything to be said about God is a statement about his love. We must now apply this to the above. God's omnipotence, omniscience, independence, self-sufficiency, and changelessness are all that of his love. We can never abstract them from God's actions in specific situations. Nowhere is this better illustrated than in Psalm 139 where the psalmist speaks of his inability to escape from the loving care of God: "Whither shall I go from thy Spirit? Or whither shall I flee from thy presence? If I ascend to heaven, thou art there! If I make my bed in Sheol, thou art there! If I take the wings of the morning and dwell in the uttermost parts of the sea, even there thy hand shall lead me, and thy right hand shall hold me." So also, the omnipotence of God is the all-powerfulness of his love. It is love and not sheer force that finally conquers all things and wins the victory.

God Revealed in Actions

It may seem that this description of God is again manmade—that we have merely stripped from our idea of God all those human qualities which we think would be unworthy of God, and then have taken those human virtues which appeal to us and have magnified them to the nth degree and ascribed them to God. But this is not correct. *Every one of the elements in the description is given to us by revelation. Each has been revealed by an act of God.* We are not conjuring up an idea of God. This is a picture of God that unfolds before us in a tremendous drama of action. It is the drama of creation, of revelation, of redemption, of sanctification; of God choosing and guiding and delivering and chastising and buying back his people; of God's Son walking the earth,

45

healing the sick, feeding the multitudes, dying on the cross, rising again; of God's Holy Spirit founding a new community of love and endowing it with power from on high. God reveals himself through actions and not through the abstract thoughts of philosophers. Yet these actions need to be interpreted in words, for otherwise they are dumb and meaningless. Hence the real medium of revelation remains the *Word*—the Word become flesh in Jesus Christ.

The Holy Trinity

What clearly distinguishes the Christian faith from other monotheistic religions of the world is the doctrine of the Holy Trinity. It shows that when Christians use the word "God" they are using it in a unique sense. Christians worship the God who is the Father of their Lord, Jesus Christ, and they do so in the power of God the Holy Spirit. Without this confession there is no Christian life together in love.

We have said that God is a person as we are—in fact our full personhood derives from God's personhood. Yet he is not *just* a person as we are. That he is not and that we are unable to understand the mystery of his being is indicated by the doctrine of the Trinity. This is, however, not an intellectual conundrum—of three being one —which we must try to force ourselves to believe. Such a feat would in any case be impossible for our minds, and God respects the minds he gave us. The real mystery lies precisely in God's relations and actions toward us. One of the lessons appointed for the Festival of the Holy

Trinity says: "O the depth of the riches and wisdom and knowledge of God! How unsearchable are his judgments and how inscrutable his ways!" (Rom. 11:33). This is said not about "three persons in one essence," a formula not developed until centuries later; rather it is said of the wonder of God's dealings with men, of his choice of the people of Israel to be a mission to the world, of the grafting in of a strange olive branch until the fullness of the Gentiles has come and Israel, too, at last is saved.

The doctrine of the Trinity is not given in so many words in the Bible. It developed in its own peculiar way, as all doctrines do, as Christians developed, in terms of their particular situations, the implications of God's revelation of himself to them. It therefore bears the imprint of the Graeco-Roman world. When men came to believe that God had revealed himself in Jesus and in him acted decisively on their behalf they became convinced that God himself was present and active in Jesus. This could only mean that Jesus as the Christ (the Messiah, the Anointed One of God) was to them true God. Otherwise he would not really be directly revealing God, but would only be showing him in a kind of secondhand way. Moreover, if Jesus as the Christ by his death on the cross did what only God could do for man's redemption, then God must really be in him. "God was in Christ reconciling the world to himself" (2 Cor. 5:19). The whole development grew out of a "soteriological" (*soter* meaning savior) concern. That is to say, the issue at hand is the conviction that no one less than God himself, the

47

"very God of very God" of the Nicene Creed, could save man from his predicament—no intermediary being, however high; only he who is God in his very being (essence).

But if God was in Christ while he walked the earth, Christ must somehow be distinguished from the One who sent him. This already, speaking humanly, gives us the maximum number of one God plus two separate beings of whom we must affirm that they are both God. We must note, however, that the Latin word *persona* (three persons all of whom share in the essence of God) is not strictly speaking our word "person." The word "persona" in classical Latin designated the mask which an actor wore on the stage as he played a particular role. We may therefore think of God as playing three different roles—creator, redeemer, sanctifir—although this, too, must be regarded as an oversimplification. These three distinct activities must be allowed to penetrate into the very being of God, for he does not, like an actor, take turns playing different parts for the fun of it.

Furthermore, we remember Jesus' promise that the Comforter would lead men into the knowledge of all truth. This promise was fulfilled when the Holy Spirit came to the disciples on Pentecost and made them fearless witnesses to their Lord. It is the Holy Spirit whom the risen Christ and the Father sent, who lives and works in the church and leads men to faith and to "life together in love." If men are to believe in Christ, then the Holy Spirit must persuade and empower them to that faith. But this is not to say that the Father and the Son

48

are now up in heaven while the Holy Spirit alone is at work in the church. One God alone is active in all these works—creation, redemption, and sanctification. Yet to be created is not to be redeemed, although both are the work of the same God. And to be redeemed is not to be sanctified, though these, too, are the work of the same God.

Today these distinctions are often blurred and what belongs to the realm of creation is falsely ascribed to the realm of redemption. This happens when, for example, all the advances of science are somehow ascribed to Christ and themselves regarded as redemptive. Or there is further blurring when the mere coming of Christ into the world (the incarnation) is regarded as effecting a change in men and the world without the specific rebirth of the Holy Spirit. If these blurs were allowed to remain then the specific mission of the church as the redeemed and redeeming fellowship would drop away. It would be enough to be living A.D. rather than B.C., or, to push it further, it would be enough simply to be *created*.

This, then, is at least in part the meaning of the doctrine of the Trinity: (1) It is God himself who is the *revealer*, who takes the initiative and carries it through; it is God himself who is the *revelation*, who himself is fully present in the revelation; it is God himself who is the *revealedness*, who himself must persuade you that it is he, hold you in that persuasion, and unite you with himself.[7] (2) This is not only a "noetic" matter, that is, an intellectual matter of getting in on the true state of

49

affairs. There are actual events involved here, events which make a difference and which are rooted in the nature of God himself. The God of love has created us; the same God of love has done something very distinct in redeeming us; the same God of love now does something distinct in sanctifying us, that is in transforming us from sinners into saints and finally bringing us from faith to sight.[8]

The doctrine of the Trinity keeps us from reducing Christianity to the mere acceptance of certain ideas. Here God stands before us in the mystery, miracle, and glorious wonder of his revelation. Here it is apparent that God is not like a lesson in arithmetic or chemistry or even history, not a lesson we can learn by heart and then use to our own purpose. We do not control God, not even in our thoughts; but he continues in a personal way to control us. We become Christians in an experience, when something happens to us, when we are persuaded to love, trust, and obey the God who made and redeemed us, and who now draws us into his fellowship. This doctrine allows for a full, inclusive message; it does not stop with a unitarianism of the Father (the fatherhood of God and the brotherhood of man), or a unitarianism of the Son (ultimately failing to distinguish the law and the gospel), or a unitarianism of the Spirit (an *enthusiasm* which divorces the Spirit's activity from its anchorage in history and from specific means of grace).

It may seem that this presentation of the doctrine of the Trinity should come at the end of the book because it includes everything that we believe. However, we have made a fielder's choice and put it at the beginning because it must be clear from the start that the word *God* has a specific meaning for the Christian. When the Christian says *God* he means only the Triune God: that God who is the Father of our Lord Jesus Christ and who has sent and is sending his Holy Spirit to establish the Christian "community of life together in love."

The Creator of the World

It is of the utmost importance for us to understand that we are created "in the image of God." Man will not understand himself if he rates himself either too highly or too lowly. He must not identify himself with the animal, in spite of the obvious kinship, nor must he confuse himself with God, although he is rooted and grounded in him. In no sense is man God. He is the image, not the original. He reflects some of God's characteristics, but does not possess them in and of himself. This is clear only if we understand that man is *created* in the image of God.

We must first be clear about the notion of *creation,* another one of those words which has a meaning all its own in the Bible. To *create* is something which only God can do. It is therefore a real *miracle* and not just something *astonishing,* because by a miracle is meant *something which only God can do.* To create means to bring something forth out of nothing and that is manifestly humanly impossible, for *ex nihilo nihil fit* is axiomatic, "out of nothing nothing can be made," or "you cannot get something out of nothing."

We can make things but we cannot really create them. In order to make a coat, a tailor needs cloth from which to make it. But what of the designer? Doesn't he "create" the design in his imagination out of sheer nothingness? Just think of the newest "creations" in women's hats; are they really the "creation" of the designer? It may be perfectly true that we have never before seen anything just like these new hats, but that only shows us what they really are. They are not really new creations. They are combinations—new combinations perhaps—of old and familiar things, taken from the kitchen, the garden, the barnyard, the geometry book, etc. There they all are, combined into the latest woman's Easter bonnet by the so-called creative imagination of man. How lovely and intriguing! How able to cure the deep doldrums! That is precisely what happens when the heathen creates a god. He produces a monstrosity, combined of all the elements of his experience, in a vain effort to produce something which is indeed different from any existing creature. But he cannot succeed in making anything which is absolutely different.

It is quite another matter when God creates the world and man. Everything is his "idea," brand new and without precedent. Here is not just a new combination of old things, but a bringing forth of the genuinely new. In the sense in which we are now using the word, God alone is able to create.

Here is God, the only real creative genius, who first "thought up" the symmetry and harmony of geometry—circles, lines, and angles. He first "thought up" energy—

particles or waves of energy so tremendous that in one peanut shell there is enough power to blow a whole planet into smithereens or to drive a fleet of giant ships around the world. All this came from God, not from Oak Ridge, Tennessee. A ten-year-old friend of mine was holding our infant grandson in his hands, entranced by the wonder of him. When I said, "Quite an invention, isn't he?" the disdainful answer was, "You mean creation, don't you?"

Let us give credit where credit is due. It was the Creator who first "thought up" color that would combine into all the hues of a sunset, or a basket of summer fruit, or a spray of fall flowers, or the delicate tint of a baby's cheeks. What a creative artist! The towering mountain crags; the glistening snows stretching for miles; the seas, still as a mirror or whipped into the fury of a storm—all are his handiwork. "The heavens are telling the glory of God; and the firmament proclaims his handiwork."

What an inexhaustible imagination! The intricate designs of the snowflakes—billions and billions of them, with no two alike! The marvel of the human hand and brain! Each person a unique, distinctive individual, with no two of them alike either! The whole universe is God's canvass; it is his poem; it is his novel; it is his drama; it is his symphony.

All these "ideas," brand new! And they don't just stay ideas. It's like a fairy tale. God wants something. He thinks of it. And lo and behold, there it is! Just like that! Out of nowhere! And that is exactly where it would go, too—back where it came from, disappearing into nothingness—if God did not continue to sustain it. This is what the Bible means when it says, on the one hand, that everything was created through God's word (John 1:3), and, on the other hand, that all creatures depend on God for "in him we live, and move, and have our being" (Acts 17:28)—without, however, supposing that we are God, or that the dividing line between creator and creature is in any sense erased.

So the whole universe in space and time—"all the choir of heaven and the furniture of earth," everything that exists which is not God—is God's idea and miraculous creation. And the crown of this creation is man. He is no less the creation of God than all the rest of creation. There is no part of him which in and of itself is of the substance of God.

If this is what is meant by God's being the creator, nothing could be more disastrous than getting bogged down in a discussion as to whether or not the six-day account of creation in Genesis is true as opposed to the scientists' account of the origin of planetary systems and the evolutionary development on our planet over countless years. The Genesis account is the testimony of believers from within the covenant relation, believers who give glory to God for their origin and the origin of the world. And of course this account is all tied up with outmoded notions. We should in no way make of it a God-given "scientific explanation" to compete with man's reasonable hypotheses. The less we say about it the better. We are not concerned about what happened in the distant past. We are concerned about a *present* relationship brought about by God's own revelation of himself, the creator-creature relation. This is not a spectator-truth about which two individuals can hold different opinions as they speculate (*speculare* means "to behold") on various possibilities. This is a confession of faith which begins with the individual in the attitude of worship and praise, and extends from there to all the world. It is either made from the knees in faith or it is rejected *in offense*. Right now I acknowledge that all I have and am, including the whole universe, is owed to the loving Creator. It is all due to "fatherly divine goodness and mercy." Or else there is "offense" that man and his universe should be so utterly dependent that the whole "shebang" would drop into the abyss of nothingness from which it came if it were not for God's instant creative fiat: Let it be! He holds the whole wide world in the hollow of his hand. The prophet Isaiah says:

> Who has measured the waters in the hollow of his hand and marked off the heavens with a span, enclosed the dust of the earth in a measure and weighed the mountains in scales and the hills in a balance? . . . Behold, the nations are like a drop from a bucket, and are accounted as the dust on the scales. . . . All the nations are as nothing before him, they are accounted by him as less than nothing and emptiness. To whom then will you liken God, or what likeness compare with him? The idol! a workman casts it, and a goldsmith overlays it with gold, and casts for it silver chains. He who is impoverished chooses for an offering wood that will not rot; he seeks out a skilful craftsman to set up an image that will not move. Have you not known? Have you not heard? Has it not been told you from the beginning? Have you not

understood from the foundations of the earth? It is he who sits above the circle of the earth, and its inhabitants are like grasshoppers; who stretches out the heavens like a curtain, and spreads them like a tent to dwell in; who brings princes to nought, and makes the rulers of the earth as nothing (Isa. 40:12, 15, 17 ff.).[9]

St. Augustine is equally ecstatic.

Heaven and earth thus speak plainly that they did not make themselves: "We are, because we have been made; we did not exist before we came to be so that we could have made ourselves!" And the voice with which they speak is simply their visible presence. It was thou, O Lord, who madest these things. Thou art beautiful; thus they are beautiful. Thou art good, thus they are good. Thou art; thus they are. But they are not as beautiful, nor as good, nor as truly real as thou their Creator art. Compared with thee, they are neither beautiful nor good, nor do they even exist.[10]

And Martin Luther makes clear the "existential import" of all we have been trying to say in his explanation of the First Article of the Apostles' Creed.

I believe that God has created me and all that exists. He has given me and still preserves my body and soul with all their powers. He provides me with food and clothing, home and family, daily work, and all I need from day to day. God also protects me in time of danger and guards me from every evil. All this he does out of fatherly and divine goodness and mercy, though I do not deserve it. Therefore I surely ought to thank and praise, serve and obey him. This is most certainly true.

This is either confessed in "faith" or it is rejected in "offense."

CHAPTER III

THE IMAGE
OF GOD

Man and Creation

We ended the last chapter by noting that man, in his entirety, is a part of creation. But there is a difference between man and the rest of creation. When God made man he didn't just think up a new idea. When he made man he made him in his own image. In other words, the idea of what man would be like was there long before man appeared on the scene—it was there in the very being of God himself, and God made man to reflect himself.

Here we must be careful not to split man up into pieces and suppose that there is a part of him which is in the image of God while the other part is not. The whole person is created in God's image. We cannot, however, really understand what it means to be a person until we have revealed to us what God is like. We must, therefore, first keep in mind the picture of God received through revelation, and then see ourselves as some kind of reflection of God.

An "I" Over Against a "Thou"

Man is an "I" standing over against God as "Thou." Man, like God, is a center of activity and responsibility.

But he is responsible not only to himself but to God. God, we said, is responsible only to himself. He is the supreme "I," whose being is not constituted by his relation to a "Thou." Man, however, is a dependent "I," whose being is first constituted by his relation to a "Thou," in fact to many *thous—the Thou of God* and the *thous of his fellowmen.*

Man is responsible to God. He is a center of responsibility standing over against the Lord, his Maker. God set him over against himself so that he could talk to him; so that he could address him as "thou"; so that he could say to him: "Thou art free"; "thou are responsible"; "thou art to love me, and trust me, and obey me"; "thou shalt be happy." God gave man a name of his own, which set him apart from everyone else—John Jones, Maria Schmidt, Dimitri Korsakoff, Kung Fu, Selma Palonen— an unrepeated and unrepeatable center of responsibility, an *I* over against a *Thou*, not just an example of a species, like a rat, or a monkey. There are many rats and monkeys, but only one God and only one "you" and one "I."

Man a Unity

We said that we should not split up man, but regard him as a unity. This is important. We are, to be sure, in one sense two-sided beings. In the biblical account of creation we are told that God formed man of the dust and of the earth, and that he then breathed into his nostrils and man became a living soul. This is usually interpreted to mean that God made a soul, which is the real person, and that he then gave this soul a temporary home in a body, made of the dust of the earth.

Plato held that each soul was one, without parts. A chair comes into being when the carpenter puts it together and falls apart when the drunken sailor cracks it over his opponent's head. The soul, however, has no parts and therefore cannot come into being by the accumulation of parts or go out of being by their falling apart. It is, therefore, eternal and indestructible, without beginning and without end, not subject to the ravages of time and decay. Now if this idea were accurate the soul would itself be God, or as some say, a "spark of the divine"; God would not be necessary; he could die; the soul would go on living.

This, however, is a false dualism or twoness. The Bible does, as we shall see, speak of a twoness in man, that of the old, natural man and the new man in Christ. But this is quite different from a dualism of mind and matter or soul and body. Man is a unity.

All kinds of evils result from splitting up what belongs indissolubly together. In the first place it causes the body to be despised and neglected. The body may even come to be regarded as the source of evil, and it may be supposed that to get rid of the body would mean freedom from all sin and limitations. All the "things" which God made come to be depreciated along with the body, and all kinds of perverse notions of flight from the world develop. Instead of living normal lives in the world which God has made, delighting in clean bodies and beautiful things, because they are all the Creator's handiwork, people begin to torture their bodies, leaving them unwashed, refusing to marry, to eat, to be contaminated with the "material." These and many other evils result from splitting man up into a soul, apparently more godlike, and a body, which is worthless and fleeting. The whole person is of himself worthless and fleeting except as he is sustained and given worth by God. Man is a unity.

Another evil that results from this false duality or twoness is that we fail to see how intimately our bodies are influenced by what we think and feel and say and do. Note what medicine has discovered. The condition of a gland will influence not only a person's stature and his general health and vitality, but also influence his whole personality and disposition: whether he will be cheerful or pessimistic, whether he will be generous or a skinflint. On the other hand, the mind profoundly influences the body. Mind exerts a tremendous influence over matter, perhaps because in some sense mind and body are, in reality, one.

We are dealing with a unified being, a person, and not with something that is called a soul and which dwells in a house called the body, as though the body were just a tool for the soul to employ but not really a part of the person—as though you could divorce the look in a person's eyes, or the tone of his voice, or the pressure of his hand, from the real person. You may have your disembodied souls if you like; I'll take my family gathered about me at the table, with eyes and hands and words and laughter. Then I will try to remember that God is not the guest at this table, but the host. I will try to remember that this family does not stop with the narrow walls of my house, but extends down the street, and round the whole circle of the world. I will try to remember that this world family needs food and shelter and warmth, and that man does live first of all by bread, even though it is surely true that he does not live by bread alone. I will try to remember that I am also a part of and inexorably related to the whole subhuman creation. It is by no means romantic sentimentality to feel this kinship with rocks and rivers and "the sticky little leaves as they open in the spring."[1]

When God made man of the dust of the earth he breathed into his nostrils and the body became alive. Adam, an individual with a name, with a destiny, with powers and prerogatives that set him apart from all the rest of creation, came into being. To be sure he was of the dust of the earth. The same chemicals that constitute the rest of creation constituted him also. He was mostly water, plus some sulphur and iron and a few other chemicals—far too complicated for me to know much about, but no different in man than in all the stream of creation of which man is a part. This makes man part of a chain of cause and effect which he does not control. If he is pushed in front of a moving train he will be cut down. If he eats poison his blood will congeal, his heart will stop pumping, his breath will cease, he will die. The course of his life runs from birth through various stages to death just like that of any other living creature.

But even so man is not just a part of the stream of nature, being pushed and pulled along. He stands out from the order of nature somewhat in the way that God does, but not quite—that is the important thing, n*ot quite*. In fact, the difference is still so great that we might better say, *not at all* in the way God does.

Man's Prerogatives

Recently much light has been thrown on the biblical meaning of "the image of God." As we have said, it is no longer possible to say that it consists in man's rational soul.[2] In addition to bifurcating man, this puts a one-sided premium on man's rationality as that which makes him human and godlike. In the Old Testament the whole man, not exclusive of "the marvel of his bodily appearance," is in God's image.[3] The word in the Old Testament stands for a plastic image, such as those which kings erected of themselves to represent their sovereignty in places in which they did not personally appear; ". . . so man is placed upon earth in God's image as God's sovereign emblem. He is really only God's representative, summoned to maintain and enforce God's claim to dominion over the earth. The decisive thing about man's similarity to God is his function in the non-human world."[4]

This indicates man's decisive superiority over the rest of creation, which he is to conquer and put to God's purposes. Without placing all the emphasis on man's rationality or on his inherent dignity or moral worth, it indicates that man does have powers and prerogatives which lift him above the animal level and make him able to represent God. These powers and prerogatives in themselves do not make him God-like. It depends on how he uses them; it depends on his relationship to God. Strictly speaking, therefore, as the New Testament makes clear (Col. 3:1 ff.), man is not in God's image unless he is in the right relationship to God and can properly reflect God. It is like the moon which has no light of its own and can therefore shine only in reflected glory, when its relationship to the sun is right and there are no foreign bodies intervening. But since no man is ever completely out of a relationship to God every man has such powers and prerogatives which lift him above the animal and make him the kind of being with whom God can have face to face (I-Thou) fellowship.

In fact, man, like everything else in the universe, is constituted by his relations. Here we can learn a lesson from the physical world where nothing is stable. Water, for example, depending upon its relations, is either hot, cold, or warm; it is either vapor, steam, or ice, and it can be reduced to its components and cease being water entirely. So man, too, is what he is in terms of his relations (and this includes his mother-in-law), the chief of which, without which he could not be, is his relation to God. He is shaped by his relations from the time of his conception in the womb, by his relation to the physical world, his parents, siblings, teachers, friends, enemies. What is written indelibly in the genes of his heredity, as on the negative of a film, will not necessarily be developed. He is shaped ultimately by a combination of freedom (which is under his control) and destiny (which is not under his control).

There is, however, one great reservation attendent upon this matter of man's being constituted by his relations. Water, indeed everything in the physical universe, can be disintegrated so that nothing remains which even faintly resembles it. It is like peeling an onion until you have nothing left but the tears, not even a core which a shy Tom can give to his Becky. And in this way the atheistic existentialists and the orthodox Marxian Communists conceive of man. When the conditions that can sustain life change sufficiently there is nothing left. Man comes from nothing and he goes to nothing.

This is, however, not true of the Christian view of man, because in that view the factor basic to man's being is the God-relation which, once established, endures. When God addresses man as "Thou," man is by that address riveted fast to God forever. He can never escape God—not even by dying. If he only could! "It is appointed for men to die once, and after that comes judgment" (Heb. 9:27). There is, therefore, the immortality of the God-relationship, which is the Christian alternative to the immortality of the soul. Man has no indestructible core separable from the body, without beginning or end, able to survive death by its own inherent powers. But there is a center of responsibility, sustained forever by the God-relation.

Let us now enumerate the powers and prerogatives which constitute the image of God in man—powers and prerogatives which make man a unified being in the order of creation; make him a being who stands out from the rest of creation as a center of responsibility over against the Lord, his Maker; make him a created being, yet a different order of created being—the crown of creation.

We must keep in mind that not one of the characteristics of man can be understood apart from the others. They all form a unity and get their significance from each other. Thus, in defining self-consciousness we shall have to introduce other powers.

SELF-CONSCIOUSNESS, or self-awareness, is one of the characteristics of man. It is the ability to say "I" in a unique sense denied to animals. Just try a series of sentences like the following and you will know what is meant. "I was born in a little, leaky house in Sugar City, Colorado. I grew up in a country parsonage on the plains. I remember the first day I went to school. I was afraid one day when I stood at the window and watched the havoc of a passing tornado. I promised once at the altar that I would be faithful to my Lord; and I made another promise there together with the woman I love." So it goes. I did this and that. I initiated certain activities; I remember them; I judge them; I approve or disapprove; I set myself over against myself, and take a look at myself.

All this is part of self-consciousness—awareness of myself as a distinct being that persists through years of changes in the body; like a ship which, though it comes into port year after year for repairs until not a timber in it remains the same, is still the same ship. I am aware of the kind of being I am. An old teacher used to say that the only difference between a human jackass and another jackass is that the human jackass can say, "I am a jackass." In his better moments a man can recognize that he is making a fool of himself. His conscience, too, will tell him that he is doing what he ought not to do. Then when God addresses him in his revelation he will be most keenly aware of himself as the object of God's love and forgiveness. In the feeling of guilt, of having been unfaithful to a trust, of having offended against love, of having pierced the Savior's heart, he will at last be aware of himself for what he really is—a sinner redeemed by love.

SELF-DETERMINATION. In all this talk about self-consciousness there have been several presuppositions. One of these is self-determination. And this, in turn, presupposes a measure of freedom. Self-determination is the initiating of activity without being pushed or pulled by forces beyond one's control. I decide that I will become a doctor and I make my plans accordingly. I decide that I will help my neighbor in his distress, or, perhaps, that I will pass by on the other side. I decide that I will be faithful to a trust, or that I will not keep my promise. All these seem to be my decisions, and it is rather strange that it should be taken seriously that they are not. But doubts as to my freedom arise out of the fact that I recognize that I am not free to do just as I please. All around me in nature everything is determined by a strict and inviolable cause and effect relationship. Why should I be the exception? Chemicals in the laboratory always behave in the same way according to a predictable pattern, and I am nothing but a number of chemicals. Animals are guided by their instincts, their drives, hunger, sex, and I am nothing but an animal. *But this just is not true.* I am neither just a number of chemicals driven by necessity nor an animal guided by instincts.

Consider this example: All who can think can recognize what is meant by the word "ought" or its equivalent. All can feel that if friends really love them and mean well with them, then they ought not to repay their friends' love with hate. All can recognize that they ought not to take from another person what really belongs to that other person. The very fact that we become angry with the person who takes our things from us shows that we recognize this "ought." All can feel that they ought not to take another man's life. The very fact that there was a law of blood-revenge proves this feeling of "oughtness." This is what we mean by saying that people have consciences, even though the consciences of various people frequently function in contradictory ways. It is also what we mean when we say that the basic moral laws, the Ten Commandments, are written into the order of nature, that is, the order of creation, by the Creator himself.

What we want to notice now is that this feeling of "oughtness," which is in every human being, just could not be there in a meaningful way if man were not free, at least to some extent—free enough to make sense of "oughtness" and responsibility. If a person is pushed or pulled, he is clearly not responsible. Only if he acts deliberately is a man responsible, and in order to do anything deliberately a man must be free. A stone cannot deliberately get up and cast itself at a window. Little Johnny must deliberately pick it up and throw it at Toni's plate glass window in order to see the pieces fly, and Toni's temper with it. Those self-righteous scribes and Pharisees must deliberately pick up the stones to cast at the woman taken in adultery, and then of their own volition put them down again as something within them is touched to the quick. They, too, in their freedom, are guilty.

How strange and sad it is that men should insist on denying the glory and the awfulness of their freedom and their responsibility, and want to make themselves into stones and rats. It can only be because they are seeking to evade their responsibility, or else, perhaps, because they are trying to play god and control others like stones and rats. But this even God refuses to do. God made men free. He is great enough and good enough to respect man's freedom.

But now we have obviously overstated our case, which shows that the total picture must be seen before any final conclusions are drawn. Obviously there are definite limitations upon man's freedom. A man's destiny is inescapable. He does not choose his father and mother or the time and place into which he is born. He does not give himself his own heredity or environment. Man is part of the stream of nature. The so-called "behaviorists" or "determinists" who see man shaped entirely by factors beyond his control seem to have all the evidence on their side. It is really only by an act of will that atheistic existentialists like Jean Paul Sartre simply assert the dignity of man's freedom within the decided limitations of "the given." The Christian, however, is constrained to assert this freedom because he is aware of his responsibility to God. This literally means his response-ability; his ability to answer (respond) to God's word of address out of a free center of decision. The root of the word "response" is the Latin word for free will, *spons*. Only the all-seeing judge can know how much freedom man really has. God's judgment is not, therefore, like man's judgment.

Our conclusion, then, is that man is shaped, as Paul Tillich says, by a combination of freedom and destiny.[5] This will be elucidated further as we proceed.

SELF- AND WORLD-TRANSCENDENCE. Together with man's self-consciousness and self-determination and freedom there goes a certain amount of what we shall call *self- and world-transcendence*.

God as the Creator completely "transcends" his creation, that is, he stands completely outside of it, not in a spatial sense, but in the sense that he himself is not a part of his creation. He can, therefore, control that creation and do with it as he pleases. He is its absolute master. Man, on the other hand, while a part of the creation, can nevertheless "transcend," or rise above it. (To "transcend" means to go beyond.)

A simple analogy will serve to make clear what is involved. Let us imagine human life as a train running along endless tracks. The tracks must be endless, for we can set no limits to time or space. One fine day you and I find ourselves in a car of this train. We did not come into this train from somewhere else; rather, we originated in it. This is important, because we are not to suppose that our souls pre-existed and came from some other existence into this life. The only one who came from another existence into this life is the eternal Son of God who came down from heaven and was made man for our salvation. But we ourselves originated miraculously in the train of time when we were born of our parents. The train was started long before we got on it, and it will continue to travel on, we feel very sure, long after we get off. All this is beyond our control.

Here we are now, in a car of this train, moving along from day to day. We could be in a windowless car just being pushed or pulled along. Whether being pushed or pulled we would then never know, for we would have no way of finding out. Nor could we have the least idea whence we came or whither we were going. Whether we realized it or not, we would not be free; we would be strictly determined by forces beyond our control. We certainly could exercise no influence on the course of our life. This is the determinist's view of life—which we must reject.

In order to make man's real position clear let us consider what God would be like in this analogy. God would be completely outside the train, like a pilot controlling a robot from a distant base. At the same time, inasmuch as he is totally present everywhere, he would also be inside the train, though not confined by it. He would be free to come and go as he pleased, and he would not remove himself by going. This is what theologians have meant by saying that God is both "transcendent" (beyond) and "immanent" (within) and by resisting both the age-old Epicurean view that the gods do nothing but enjoy themselves in lordly isolation from the tragedies of the world, and the pantheism of a man like Spinoza for whom "God" and "nature" were interchangeable terms.

Now man is neither a being confined to a windowless car, pulled willy-nilly with nothing to say about his destiny, nor the complete master, like God. His status is in between. He is in the train, but he is not confined as described. He is more like the engineer who has mounted to the cabin with his orders in his hands. He can look out and back and ahead. He can control his train, too, within limits. He cannot make it fly, of course, or make it run cross country. There are limits, definite limits; limits, too, to what man can do with an airplane or with atomic energy or with the utmost increase of his powers, for he will stay the creature and will never be in absolute control.

This, then, is man's status. He is free, but only within limits. He is free, but not absolutely free. God might have made man so that he would be guided safely by his instincts. Then God would have had a busy beehive of a world, dripping with sticky sweetness. But he did not choose to make it so. Man can partially control his destiny, but not absolutely. By means of digging into the ground, and by means of the telescope and microscope, he can see part of the way back in the history of the world, but he cannot see back to the beginning. The road always has a final bend around which he cannot see. There is a horizon beyond which he cannot penetrate. The same is true of his vision into the future. He can see part of the way; he can make some predictions. But since he is in the train he cannot get out and see just where the tracks will end. God alone knows the beginning and the end, and man knows only as much as God reveals to him.

Thus man stands at the crossroads of time and eternity. If you imagine the line of time running along horizontally, and draw another line crossing it vertically to represent the dimension of God, then man is not exclusively in either the one or the other of these two. He is at the point where these two lines cross. This makes him part of the stream of time, part of the natural chain of cause and effect, subject to all its limitations; but at the same time, he is also in that vertical line, transcending or standing out from the present moment and the stream of time. He is aware of his eternal destiny; he has creative powers of freedom; he has power over the rest of creation. Yet, however high his prerogatives, there are limitations. It is the refusal to recognize these limitations which is man's undoing.

RATIONALITY AND POWER OF SPEECH. So far we have said nothing about man's reason, which is regarded by many as man's chief distinguishing feature. We have purposely left this until now in order to counteract the overemphasis on it. Man's reason, to be sure, is an essential part of his being, but it is not, as Aristotle imagined, the "end-all" and "be-all" of his being. The core of man's being is that he is a center of responsibility standing over against a sovereign and loving Lord. He could not be this if he did not possess those qualities we have already described. Nor could he be all this if he were not a rational being. The difference between a man and an animal is not only in the physical structure, let us say, of the hand, however important this may be. A monkey, for instance, does not have any hands, but only four feet, as you may see for yourself if you will watch him grasp a banana. He cannot juxtapose his thumb to his forefinger as a human being can. This simple difference makes impossible for the monkey all the delicate operations which man is able to perform with his hands.

Nor is the difference between a man and an animal due simply to the size of the brain; the fact is that a man's brain functions differently from the brain of an animal. Man has brain powers which differ qualitatively as well as quantitatively from those of the animal. Man possesses the power to form universals as opposed to particular things. Words like dog, cat, man, race, are all universals. They refer not to one particular thing but to a whole class of things. The same is true of words like love, hate, jealousy, ambition.

This power to form universals is, of course, also a major problem because the universal always abstracts (draws away) from the particular. And it is always the particular, the unique, that we care about. Plato affirmed the perfection of the idea, the universal archetype from which all particulars are pointed off. No particular embodiment, however, can ever be perfect because of the recalcitrance of the material, which then becomes the source of imperfection and evil. Only the non-material idea, according to Plato, is perfect. But this is a sorry state of affairs. Who wants a woman in general, no matter how perfect, without a particular embodiment?

Because man can form universals he can also make judgments. He knows not only that John Jones and Mary Smith died, but he generalizes that all men must die. He possesses the unique power of seeing implications. He can see that if certain things are true, then certain other things must also be true. He can see, for instance, that if all men are mortal, and John Jones is a man, it must follow that John Jones, too, is mortal.

This indicates that the power of speech is also part of man's prerogative, for without the "word" which reveals to another the real thoughts and intents of the heart no truly human I-Thou relationship would be possible and people would be like ships that pass each other in the night. It is also by speech that man conceals his true intent and deceives the other and undermines the human relationship. Speech, therefore, like all the powers and prerogatives which we have mentioned is not an unambiguous good. It is man's glory as well as his shame—as abundantly proved by the propagandists of the world. Without the spoken and the written word where would we be? Without words, i.e., without intelligible signs of some kind, we cannot communicate and without communication, we are clods; no life together in love is possible, no fidelity, no trust, no justice, no truth. Animals copulate with grunts and reproduce their kind. Man, too, insofar as he is one with the animal does the same. It is only the word of love and fidelity which raises the act of human sexual intercourse above that of the animal, when one "knows" the other and "is known" of him in the entirety of the being (not just the soul).

This, of course, is only a sketchy treatment of what is involved in man's rationality, but it will serve to illustrate that the ability to think is only one of the elements involved in being human. It pervades and colors and transforms all the other elements. Responsibility would be impossible without thinking, but thinking alone would not make man a responsible being. The brain would be just an instrument developed in the process of evolution as an instrument for problem solving which aids in survival. But love, fear, hatred, jealousy—as distinctly human qualities—presuppose much more than just an instrument for problem solving. They do, in fact, presuppose centers of responsibility standing over against one another and over against God and they presuppose the power of speech.

Another power which is part of man's prerogative is that of memory when seen in connection with self-identity. This is not simply the power to remember, a power which varies so greatly from individual to individual. That is something in which an animal, the elephant perhaps, might outdo a man. There are those with phenomenal memories, like Lord Macauley who is said on a bet to have memorized all of Milton's *Paradise Lost* overnight. There are those who can repeat all the numbers in succession on the cars of a freight train as it passes by.

And Freud has taught us that nothing that we have ever experienced is ever lost; it is rather stored in the great bottomless well of the subconscious which goes endlessly back into the history of the race.

All this has its importance and is related to what we are talking about. Someone who could remember nothing, but whose sensations, images, and thoughts followed in his mind like separate pictures without continuity, could scarcely be said to be human. What we are talking about in man, therefore, is related to self-consciousness, to an awareness of what we mean by "I." A person who suffers from amnesia has lost his self-identity. Persons with split personalities are sick. The sense of "I" is connected with memory and a chain of self-identity. If I say, "I did it with my little hatchet," there has to be an awareness of the continuity of the self that stretches from the past into the present. A sense of guilt and of sin (which are not the same) depend upon this continuity. I cannot do anything distinctively human without this memory and self-identity; I cannot love anyone or trust him or hate him or even address him as "thou." Above all I cannot trust, praise, and adore the God who made me and who loves me if I have no memory of what he has done for me in the past nor an anticipation of what he will do for me in the future (Cf. Psalm 103:1 ff.).

How could we, to choose an example, go to the table of the Lord, if there were not that long line of memory that stretches back to the night in which he was betrayed and to the cross on which he died, and to the tomb from which he rose victorious. Above all, when I come to see him, my Savior, face to face, I must remember and recognize that this is the same one who knew me in my sin and accepted me just as I was. The dissolution of true community in the anonymity of the mass will continue apace if this acute awareness of the discrete and separate "I" is not recovered. This was the burden of Kierkegaard's emphasis upon the *individual*.[6] Every man, in a sense, stands alone before God to answer only for himself. Every man, Luther says, must die his own death. It is, Kierkegaard says, like travelers ascending a mountain. First they walk abreast in joyful company, but as the climb continues, the path narrows and the travelers thin out, until the last steep ascent is made absolutely alone. And someone else: "We all die like amateurs, because none of us gets any practice." But here, too, we are unique in that we can anticipate our own death because we have the memory of others' dying, when suddenly and irrevocably—as far as we are concerned—we knew an I-Thou relation to be reduced to an I-It relation.

This emphasis upon individuality is, of course, not to obscure the necessity of the relation to others. Tillich speaks of the necessary polarity of individualization and participation. Man is from the start the man in community. Man and woman, in their uniqueness, are made to fulfill each other. They are not alike but different, not only physically (and, as the Frenchman says, *"Vive la différence!"*) but in a profound way that enables them to be companions and to join in a unique "one-flesh" rela-

77

tion. Life is from the start a life together in love and no one is a self-sufficient, lone Robinson Crusoe. Apart from his fellow men no one is human.

We will have to conclude, then, that all these powers combined—self-consciousness, self-determination, freedom, self- and world-transcendence, rationality and speech, memory, and self-identity—with the proper limitations placed upon them, constitute a person created in the image of God. And all this includes the body. A person can't think, for example, without a brain. It is really a survival of primitive superstition to believe that the soul is separable from the body and will go off wandering while a man sleeps, or come back and haunt others after he has died.

CAPACITY FOR COMMUNION WITH GOD. Finally, we must also say that the powers we have described give man the capacity for communion with God. That, in fact, is the purpose for which God created man—for fellowship, for *life together in love*. This is by no means to say that man, as he is now, is able of himself to enter into communion with God. All that we are saying is that all men, everywhere, and at all times—even now in fallen mankind —possess a certain form which fits them for communion with God in a way in which sticks and stones and animals are not fitted. Whatever we may still have to say about man's rebellion and about his incapacity to extricate himself from his bondage, this we must allow: that image of God which we have described and which distinguishes man from the animals was not lost through the fall, and all men therefore have a point of contact which God may utilize in order to bring them into the proper communion with himself.

Man as a dependent, limited creature, was made to take his life from God in trust and to return it in grateful obedience. This is the meaning of the biblical story of the Garden of Eden. Here is a man, the crown of creation, set to rule over the rest of creation, to conquer the earth and subdue it, but within the limitations which God has set. Of all the trees in the garden he may freely eat, even of the tree of life to sustain his life forever. But there are limitations. This is quite natural. The very nature of man as a dependent creature requires that he should trust and obey the one upon whom his happiness absolutely depends. Since God has not chosen to make man a robot, controlled by gadgets, or an animal guided by instincts, but rather a free, responsible being who nevertheless depends upon him for the fulfillment of his being, man must trust and obey God or perish. Every moment of a man's life, therefore, takes on decisive significance. In every moment he is called upon to decide for or against his Maker, for or against the fulfillment of his destiny. In every moment he will either realize or fail to realize that *life together in love* for which he was created.

And so we may summarize: Man, a center of responsibility standing over against a sovereign and loving Lord, was created to take his life from God in trust, and to give it back to him in grateful obedience of love. If he will not do that he will lose his paradise and eventually destroy himself.[7]

CHAPTER IV

THE REBEL

Original or Personal Sin

Perhaps the most unpopular Christian doctrine is that of *original* or *inherited* sin. The "learned" world has by and large given it up as an unhealthy, morbid, and even vicious superstition. People begin bristling with indignation at the thought of a God who holds men responsible for something they have not done. Their high-pitched indignation usually sounds off like an angry siren proclaiming a fire as they cry: "You mean to say that a long time ago two fantastic creatures were framed into eating a luscious-looking apple by a snake that could talk, and that now, as punishment for what they did, every last one of their descendants, including ourselves, is doomed to fry and burn endlessly over undying flames, unless he happens to be lucky enough to hear another equally fantastic story about a figure on a cross to which he needs only look up in order to be freed from this curse? That's monstrous! First we are blamed and punished for something which we did not do; and then we are offered a heaven which we neither deserve nor earn for ourselves. In both cases we are insulted and not treated in accordance with our dignity. When we confess that we are 'by nature sinful and unclean,' what we mean is that we are not as strong as we ought to be and that we sometimes fail to do all that we would like to do. Our arms aren't long enough to reach the ideal to which we aspire. But God understands this, and he is good enough to pardon it if we ask him. So we preserve our dignity, and God remains a gentleman. We are not blamed for something we did not do nor do we get something for nothing, because we really get only as much as we honestly work for and deserve."

What shall we say to this? Is it fair to the biblical account of the fall? Is it true to the human situation? That there is just complaint against the way in which the biblical doctrine is often put cannot be denied; but it does not follow that the doctrine is therefore false.

The World in Which We Live

Let us first of all take an honest, unbiased look at the world around us and within us. Here we find ourselves in a peculiar predicament. Before we can see the world and ourselves for what they are, we must come to faith in Christ. But before we can come to faith in Christ, we must see ourselves for what we are. How shall these seemingly impossible things ever be accomplished? Both must happen together. We must be confronted by Christ in his holiness and love, and in that meeting we must see ourselves for what we are at the same time that we believe in him. You will, therefore, understand the following presentation only if you have already been confronted by Christ and believe in him.

We have said that men were created "in the image of God" in order that in a "free" response to God's love they might take their lives from God in trust and give them back in loving obedience, and so live without fear and suspicion, without hatred or malice or envy, in a perfect love relationship with every other creature, including even the dumb creatures and the inanimate creation. Now is this really the way men live? Is this the spontaneous inclination and outflowing of their hearts? Do they live and breathe in this kind of an atmosphere? Can we even go so far as to say that this is really what they always intend in the bottom of their hearts, even though they sometimes get mixed up? Do they sometimes get their wires crossed and think they are loving God when they really love only an idol? And when you show them their mistake does their true, basic love for God blossom forth? Is this really the true human situation? Is sin reducible to ignorance and imperfection and "cultural lag"?

The Course of History

The statements above do not seem true when we survey the course of history. What a bloody, gruesome, shameful story! The first brother repudiates his responsibility as his brother's keeper, and is a murderer. Soon the whole earth is covered with wickedness—so much so that we are told that God was sorry he had made man. God decides that he will destroy all the wicked and save only the righteous Noah. But after this effort to rid the world of evil by killing off the so-called evil and saving only the so-called good, God sets his rainbow in the sky as the sign of an everlasting covenant that he will never again send such a visitation upon the earth; "For," said he, "the imagination of man's heart is evil from his youth" (Gen. 9:21). The seeds of evil are within each heart, and a purge is not the cure.

There is so much evidence of evil that we have come to learn our history in terms of its wars. The wars are the high spots that dwarf the peaceful years in between. They are the pegs along the wall of time that help us keep events in proper sequence. And what are these wars but the story of intrigue, deceit, treachery, and lust for power? Wars are the eruption points, where the turmoil that seethes within individual hearts breaks forth and manifests itself like a volcano spewing its destructive fires over the earth. Here all the evils of which the human heart is capable, from a delight in a show of superiority and unrestrained adventure to the most degraded sadism, come to the marketplace and have their heyday. Here *life together in love* is really destroyed.

War is not entirely negative; it has its positive, constructive side; its witness, like that of all history, is ambiguous. Some wars have been against the agressor; some have been in self-defense; some have been "the power of the sword" manifesting itself on a giant scale in the keeping of order and in the restraining of the criminal. But even then Sherman's dictum remains true, "War is hell," and the fact that there is something desperately wrong with mankind that such drastic measures become necessary is only confirmed. Can wars and all the attendant evils be explained simply by saying that men are ignorant? Or by saying that men revert to the animals from whom they have evolved? Are animals really capable of all the subtle deviltries of war?

The History of Religions

We have cited the example of war in order to show that men themselves destroy the *life together in love* for which they were created, that something is desperately wrong, and that men are indeed living in contradiction to their origin. The history of religions, and its story of fear and superstition, is equally revealing. Instead of trusting the unseen God, men make idols which they hope to control by their prayers and sacrifices. After Yahweh, the God who rules all the forces of nature, had led the people out of their bondage with a mighty hand, the people made a golden calf out of the enemy's gold and silver, and fashioned it in the very likeness of those forces of nature which had been so ignominiously defeated. This is but a symbol of what men do everywhere. They will acknowledge their dependence upon the sun, and will harness its energy; they will admit that they depend upon the wind and the rain, and will set about controlling them to their will. Windmills, turbines, dams, irrigation ditches, chemical laboratories, nuclear bombs —these are the golden calves in which men really put their trust. They replace the living God whose gifts all these things are. It is not that men should not employ the marvels of science, but that they should acknowledge the Giver.

The World Within

We have looked at the world about us, but we shall never know what men are like unless we look within—

84

unless each one of us honestly examines himself to see what he is like. Ask yourself: Who, quite naturally and spontaneously, is the center of your life? Of whom do you think first, for example, when lives are endangered or when there is the promise of some good? Does your concern for others come only upon second thought? We make much of our spontaneous sympathy with the sufferings of others. Ask yourself why you are so sympathetic. Is it because the sight of suffering in others makes you uncomfortable? Does it give you butterflies in your stomach when you don't like butterflies in your stomach? Even much of what we are pleased to call sympathy for others is based upon our own self-interest.

We may feel squeamish about seeing a rabbit in a trap or, more realistically, at the sight, sound, and smell of a slaughterhouse, but we soon lose our squeamishness when our stomachs begin to growl. Or what dries up a man's compassion for his neighbor? What was it that made Ahab pout with discontent when he could not have Naboth's vineyard in addition to all that he already possessed? (See 1 Kings 21) Where now was his natural sympathy for Naboth who justly prized the inheritance of his fathers? When one who has hurt you deeply must in turn suffer, do you naturally sympathize with him, or do you have to struggle against the tendency to be glad that he is reaping what he sowed?

Do you really take your life from God in trust, and give it back to him in obedience? Think of Luther's explanation of the First Article of the Creed—complete acknowledgment that everything you have and are comes from God, purely because of his divine goodness and mercy, without any merit or worthiness in you. Ah, to be able to say this, and to be thankful even when you do not have sufficient means to live! To be able to say it when you have worked hard from early dawn until late at night, year after year, in order to provide yourself with a measure of security—to say it and then to live in such a way as to prove you realize fully that there is no security anywhere except in God! Does it really come naturally to a man to do all this? What does man usually do? He thumps his chest in pride; he says, "I built these machines, these bridges, these skyscrapers, these airplanes, these atom bombs. I am the captain of my soul and the master of my fate." This seems to come most naturally to man. This is how he lives out of himself and for himself. In anything—in his fine brain, in his blue blood, in his hard work, in the money he accumulates, in the regularity of the order of nature, in the fountain of youth once located on a fabulous isle but now in some chemist's laboratory, in armies and stockpiles of atom bombs, in the microscope, in the telescope, in the astrologer down the street—in anything whatsoever, even to a rabbit's foot in his back pocket, will a man put his trust rather than in the living but hidden God.

Let us go a step further and recall the true nature of love as God reveals it—love which does not seek its own good but only the good of the beloved, and which extends even to the enemy. Where is this kind of love found in the natural human heart? Does not the very fact that we must be commanded to love prove that something is wrong? He who really loves and trusts certainly does not have to be commanded to do so. It is only when something is wrong with us that we must be told to breathe—otherwise we breathe naturally. Similarly it is only because something is wrong that we must be commanded to love. Our obedience is not at all the spontaneous, joyful obedience of a loving son, but the slow, dragging, servile obedience of the slave, whipped out of us by fear of punishment and lured out of us by hope of reward. We are always double-minded. One eye is cocked toward the punishment and the other toward the reward, and we are never quite able to focus our undivided attention on the good for itself alone.

How can we account for this situation? Let us go back to the biblical story of the Fall, and, with it, to the very beginning of human history, whenever or wherever that may have been. The date and place are unimportant here. This is not just a fable which, like Aesop's fable of the fox and the sour grapes, is meant merely to present a moral. Nor is it like one of the myths which Plato used to illustrate a universal truth, as when, for example, the nature of *eros* is made clear by the myth of the union of Want and Plenty in the begetting of the child Eros. Plato is not saying that a boy named Plenty and a girl named Want actually once met in a garden and begot the baby Eros. It is a little different with the Fall in the Genesis account which does refer to an actual event although the setting, of course, is "mythological" and needs interpretation. Here is the true account of man's encounter with God, when man first rose up in rebellion against God. This is the first man's story; it is Adam's story. But it is also the second man's story, and the third's, and the fourth's; in fact, it is every man's story; it is yours and mine.

The Biblical Account of the Fall

Let us recall the situation in which the Fall occurs, remembering that while this, correctly understood, is really history and not just fable, it does have to be interpreted. It is to be taken literally but not literalistically. It is to be understood in the sense in which it was intended by the writers and in the total biblical context. It is not to be made into an allegory or a parable or into an ace reporter's account of what he might have witnessed had he been there. This is to be read as part of the "testimony literature" of the Bible, witnessing to God's dealings with men, dealings which are seen only with the eye of faith. It witnesses to the purpose for which God created men and how man frustrated that purpose. It does not follow that man actually lived in a state of integrity (wholeness, sinlessness) over an extended period of time, either of hours, days, or years. Martin Luther, being a child of his time, did believe in such an actual historical state but he was convinced that it did not last very long. He *speculated* that if man was created on the morning of the sixth day, then before the sun had set, perhaps even by noon, he had already been tempted, sinned, and lost his paradise. It is not clear just what happened to the seventh day on which God rested if that interpretation is to be taken literalistically.

In any case, the point is that the state of integrity for which man was created not only did not last very long, but it never was actualized. If it had been, then Adam, who is supposed to be the father of the human race and its true representative, would be the only one who is not really a part of the race, standing fantastically outside of it.[1] He would be the only one who, under the conditions of existence, did not have to live by faith trusting a "hidden" God; he would have been privileged to see God face to face and to enjoy unclouded communion with him. If that had happened it is difficult to see how Adam could ever have rejected God. Of course, he still might have asserted himself in his pride and refused to trust and take the God who had given him his paradise at his word. The story is obviously set up so as to make clear man's full responsibility for his fallenness, which he can in no way blame upon God. God was not unfair to him; God did not stack the cards against him.

Nevertheless it is necessary, for a variety of reasons, to reject the notion of an actual historical state of integrity. It comes into unnecessary conflict with the reasonable hypothesis of man's evolutionary development from a sub-human ancestor. This conflict is unnecessary not because man's own notions should have priority over God's revelation, but rather for the sake of not confusing that which is subject to investigation and reasonable hypothesis with that which man cannot discover for himself. And the fact that all men are from the very beginning of their history involved in alienation from and rebellion against

God is not a fact that can be explained. If it could, we could also escape our involvement in it. Putting the blame on Adam as the first man with a better chance than the rest of us, puts the "offense" at the wrong place and justifies the objection that we bear the brunt of something in which we had no part. It obscures the fact that the situation in existence is the same for all men and it is in those very conditions of existence that man inevitably but not necessarily[2] falls into sin.

This means that all human history begins with the Fall and no one—particularly not Adam who is the representative human being—can get behind it to a state of integrity. Human history and the Fall begin together. We all live "east of Eden," "after the Fall" as is made so poignantly clear by Arthur Miller's *After the Fall* (much more so than by Steinbeck's *East of Eden*). Arthur Miller sees no hope of man's escaping his predicament by himself, intimating that only Jesus is the resurrection and the life. Steinbeck, however, naively suggests that man is able by some kind of self-assertion to rule over his sin.

Adam and Eve are placed in a garden which they are to dress and keep. They are the crown of creation, and all the rest of creation is at their service. Adam is able to name the animals, thus discerning their nature and evidencing his superiority over them. Adam and Eve are not surrounded by a million and one restrictions. All the good things around them are for their use, benefit, and enjoyment. God did not put all those tempting-looking fruits within their reach and then forbid them to touch them. They even have access to the tree of life, so that

90

they may continue to enjoy their paradise forever. This is the purpose for which they were created: the happiness of being sustained by the bounty of God, the happiness of conquest and proper rule over the rest of creation, the happiness of unclouded communion with God.

But there was a condition attached to all this happiness. The condition was trust, faith, obedience, love; the condition was that they accept certain limitations or restrictions. These were not burdensome or unfair; they were simply necessary for man's own good since he was the dependent creature and could have freedom only in the acknowledgment of his dependence. There was one tree, and one tree only, of which they were not allowed to eat. This one tree, significantly enough, was called the tree of the knowledge of good and evil. There are many who think that since this was the case it was a good thing that man did eat of the tree. They talk of it therefore as a "fall up" when man in his moral development became aware of the distinction between good and evil. But this is the worst kind of reinterpretation and misunderstanding. It is true that today we know good and evil by their contrast with each other; but this is only because of the Fall. We can say, moreover, that if man had never mistrusted God he would never have known evil and he would have known the good for itself alone, and not just by way of contrast with evil. Just what this would be like we do not know, but we have no good reason for saying that it would be impossible. Why should it be impossible for a creature of God who trusted him completely to have only the positive experience of good and unclouded happiness without any knowledge whatsoever of evil? Such, we are led to believe, is the state of the angels in heaven, who willingly do God's bidding and joyfully acknowledge his lordship. Such hypothesis with respect to man is, however, contrary to fact, and therefore pointless. Man did not, as the biblical account makes clear, so trust God.

The Tempter

One other element in the story must be noted at the outset: the presence of a tempter. This is not in order to enable man to push the blame on someone else. Part of man's rebellion, in fact, is that he does try to push the blame on someone else. The presence of a tempter, however, makes it clear that when man sins he is not simply following his own devices; he is being possessed. He is being ruled, or more accurately, he gives himself over to the rule of another. Here, in the presence of the tempter, it is made clear that rampant in God's world—and it does remain God's world—is a will which would not let us hallow God's name nor let his kingdom come, a will opposed to the will of God and into whose power we may by our own decision come, and by which we may eventually be ruled to our complete and utter destruction.

This is not to suggest that the writer of Genesis 3 actually thought of the serpent as Satan or the devil. The notion of Satan is actually a much later importation into the Bible from the Zoroastrians, although in the Bible the notion undergoes a radical transformation.[3] It was then introduced simply to excuse God himself from being the cause of evil.[4] In the Book of Job this is enlarged upon so that Satan appears as God's adversary, a sort of attorney for the prosecution in behalf of man against God. Only in the totality of the biblical witness does the notion of "the Evil One" emerge in all its profundity. It is, therefore, not to be rejected at the outset as a naive survival of superstition. Perhaps the one who denies this profoundest of mysteries is the one who is unspeakably naive, like the farmer who goes to the zoo and greets his first sight of a camel with the words, "Hell, there ain't no such animal." But in the Genesis account the serpent only represents the cleverness that naturally makes its seductive suggestions, for "the serpent was more subtle than any other wild creature that the Lord God had made" (Gen. 3:1). This, too, in its context has something very profound to say. It is the voice of cleverness that prompts man to mistrust and doubt and suspicion.

Steps of the Fall

Follow in detail, now, the steps of the fall into sin. The voice of the tempter speaks, so the temptation may be said to arise not merely from within but also from the objective situation in which a man finds himself. The way the tempter's question is put is important, even to the tone of the voice: Did God *really* say that you were not to eat of any of the trees in the garden? This is, first of all, a purely objective matter; the question is simply whether or not Eve remembers the Lord's command. Does she know what God expects of her, and what her limitations are? On this score there is no hesitation. She knows very well what God had said, and she also knows that it was for their own welfare. So far so good! This makes it clear that the fault does not lie in ignorance. It is not the fact that men do not know what the will of God is that makes them sin, although it often causes them to err. But erring and sinning are not the same thing. To err is human and therefore excusable; but to sin is rebellion and therefore not excusable. The law of God is either written into the heart or revealed in a special way: "Therefore you have no excuse, O man" (Rom. 2:1).

Now pay a little closer attention to the inflection of the tempter's words and get its subtle insinuation: Do you mean to tell me that God put you into the midst of all these fruits and then said, "No, no, do not touch!"? Here the seed of suspicion is being sown; here is the first intimation of unfairness; here is the suggestion that God is like some bloated ogre in a fairy story, who puts a little boy in a garden of sugarplum trees and then says with a leer, "Look, but do not touch!" This is the strategy. First a subtle insinuation, and then a forthright accusation: You will not die. For God knows that when you eat of it your eyes will be opened, and you will be like God, knowing good and evil. There it was, blurted right out: "So you trust this God of yours? You think he loves you? But can't you see through his design? You think that he has put this restriction on you for your own good, but that is just where you are being duped. He is looking out for himself, not for you. He is jealous of his own rights. He doesn't want you 'horning in' on his private domain. He is withholding something you really have a right to possess." It is as though it were suggested to the little boy in his sugarplum paradise: "Don't be fooled by the old skinflint's seeming concern. What if he did say you could eat up to five plums, and that if you ate more than that you would get a stomachache? He doesn't care about your stomach; he just doesn't want you to have all his plums." So the little boy looks at the plums and starts drooling. And down go the plums. Finally the awakening comes, and he begins to rub his stomach. Even then he is still suspicious of the castor oil offered him for his own good.

Let us not be deceived by the simplicity of this story, and its even more simple analogy. What does it all mean?

Keep in mind all that we have said about the image of God in man. God did not make man to be guided safely by instinct, but gave him the freedom of decision within definite limits. Here man is now in this freedom, confronted by the unknown future, and limited in other ways. He is neither all-knowing, nor all-seeing, nor all-powerful. The future lies hidden before him. A few steps he can figure out, on the basis of past experience; but he can never be quite sure. In the end it all trails off into uncertainty. So there arises *anxiety* or *dread* in view of this uncertainty of the future. There is the anxious thought for the morrow.

This same "dread" accompanies an ethical or moral decision. A certain action is forbidden because it is destructive of life and happiness. Yet it is a restriction upon freedom, and it seems an unjust restriction. This is man's situation because he is free, and yet not absolutely free;

because as a creature there are necessary limitations to his powers, and as a responsible, moral being there are necessary limitations upon what is and what is not allowed.

A little more needs to be said about *anxiety* or *dread* as the necessary concomitant of man's limited freedom.[5] These words are used as synonyms. Anxiety brings to mind the suffering involved in angina pectoris and the desperate struggle for breath. Dread, on the other hand, has the connotation of a nameless fear, "uncanny" because the object of it is not known.

Our age is characterized as an age of anxiety, as though this were a peculiar phenomenon of our day.[6] Anxiety, however, in the sense in which we are using it here, is the inescapable accompaniment of human existence and really should have been treated in the previous chapter as part of the description of man's creation in God's image. It is treated here because it should help us to understand the perennial human situation in which sin arises. It is not itself sin, although there is also a *sinful* anxiety. It is rather the psychological state out of which both man's creativity and his sin arise. It does not explain sin but may help us to see its inevitability alongside our inability to absolve ourselves of responsibility.

Such anxiety or dread is, first of all, not to be equated with fear. Fear is always of a specific object, even when the object is unknown. Fear is really a God-given, sort of built-in protective device which helps both the sub-human animal and the human animal to survive. Human infants, for example, have no fears except those of falling and of loud noises. All the rest are learned. Some are ungrounded and silly of course, others develop into phobias, but some continue to help man to survive. When on a dark night we are passing a cemetery and suddenly hear an unearthly moan we run first, and only afterwards do we feel the surge of fear. In other words, the physical reaction precedes the emotional one. Such ambiguous and intermittent fears, which we can learn to use or to conquer, are not to be equated with the anxiety or dread which always accompanies our being human. Furthermore, we are not dealing with the various neurotic anxieties of which the psychologists speak, because these too come and go and can be handled more or less.

The anxiety or dread of which we are speaking is different from fear in that it has no specific object. It is a nameless dread. It results from the possibility of being able to act in freedom without being completely free. There are only two possibilities for the absence of anxiety or dread. The one is in God, or a being who is absolutely free, completely in charge, with no limitations, no impenetrable veil of the future before him or dark well of the past behind him. The other is in the security of the womb where there is no freedom whatsoever and all wants are supplied and no decisions have to be made. Anxiety or dread, however, rises in the inbetween situation of man's *limited* freedom. Man must act in freedom. He does so to overcome his limitations and this is his creativity. At the same time he overreaches himself and this is his sin. All his free, creative activity as well as his sinfulness arises out of the state of dread which continues

97

to accompany all activity like an organ pedal which is stuck and continues to drone on as an undertone to whatever other music man makes.

This should help make clear why there is not an actual historical state of integrity in which man lives and acts without being a sinner. Prior to man's free act of decision there is only the state of what Kierkegaard calls "innocence."[7] As soon as man acts he has lost his innocence and is guilty. So sinfulness stands at the beginning of all human history. Sin always presupposes itself. Sin comes into the world by a sin. Therefore it is better called "original" sin or "personal" sin than "inherited" sin because all men are "originally" and "personally" involved.

We can see that, ideally, when man acts within his limitations there is always the possibility that he should rely in trust on his Maker. He should simply "accept" his dependence and his limitations and live within them. When he must act in the situation of dread before the uncertainty of the future he should not overreach himself but be content to walk by faith; he should not be resentful of limitations; he should not be suspicious of the motives that might have caused these limitations; he should, within all the limitations, take his life from God in trust and give it back to him in loving obedience.

That is what every man should do. But that is also precisely what every man does not do. He does exactly what Adam and Eve did in the garden. In his anxiety he grasps for what is near at hand; he seeks his own devices; he regards any limitation as a repression meant to deprive him of some happiness. He is, in fact, a rebel in the father's house. It is pride which is at the root of his undoing; it is his unwillingness to have a lord over him; it is his desire to be his own and complete lord; it is self-sufficiency. Sin, therefore, is best defined, not simply as a violation of God's law—which undoubtedly it is—but as a set of the whole personality in rebellion against the Lord. Man does not just commit sins, but is a sinner, a proud rebel against his origin.

Sinful Humanity

Adam's story must be seen to be the common human story. It says simply that every one of us is born of sinful parents and is, therefore, already in a sinful state at birth. What is born of flesh is flesh. Sinners can only beget sinners. The whole human race is a sinful race which is incapable of producing men and women who are in the right relationship to God. If you or I were the first human beings, sin would come into the world through us. But we are by no means the first. Sin already has a long history into which we are born as part of our destiny. What we do inherit therefore is the consequences of past sin. In this sense the sins of the fathers are visited "upon the children to the third and fourth generation of those who hate me" (Exod. 20:5). All men are, as the Augsburg Confession states, born "without fear of God, . . . without trust in God, and [they] are concupiscent."[8] They have turned away from God and turned in upon themselves. It is like the view of the world which was common before Copernicus. But he learned that not the earth, but the sun is the center around which all the planets revolve. Not man, but God is the center around which all things inevitably revolve, whether men recognize it or not. Man's sin is that he makes himself and not the Lord his Maker the center of his world.

We must grasp the full import of the First Commandment as Luther explains it: "Thou shalt fear, love and trust God above all things," and we must see this commandment fulfilled in the life of perfect obedience lived by the Son of Man before we can see the inner contradiction of our nature.

We have now said that we are "by nature sinful," and yet we bear the full responsibility for sin. How can this possibly make sense? In one way it will never make sense. All we can do is hold it to be realistic, and face the facts. Adam's story is our story. We cannot, therefore, blame Adam for our plight, because if we had been in Adam's place we would have done the same thing. As a matter of fact we *are* in Adam's place. There is no compulsion about our mistrust. *When we turn to our own devices we are not just the victims of forces beyond our control.* We do not do so with the same kind of necessity that rules the chemicals in the laboratory. We do so because we will not take refuge from our anxiety in a Lord above us, and we think it is much safer to trust to our own wisdom and devices. This is what we all invariably do. This is simply a fact. And if we will not assume full responsibility for it, then we are only blaming God or saying that, after all, it isn't so bad—and so we give fresh evidence of our sinfulness. There is no recourse but to admit that we are by nature sinful, while yet taking the full blame. We admit that we are part of a sinful humanity—all of us together in the same fix, with nobody pushing the blame on the next fellow, all of us together and each of us individually admitting that this is something which we have brought and are continuing to bring upon ourselves.

This should make clear that we cannot recognize our sinfulness in mere spectator fashion or by being convinced by argument. The fact that we are alienated from our origin (God), our true selves, and from our neighbor is an irrational fact. It is like a surd, or irrational number, which does not fit into a system. We understand only that we do not understand it. What is called for, actually, is not understanding but repentance. As Kierkegaard says[9] it is not to be the subject of psychology but of ethics. Its proper place is the sermon. We are convicted of sin by the Holy Spirit working in us. "And when he [the Holy Spirit, the Counselor] comes, he will convince the world of sin and of righteousness and of judgment: of sin, because they do not believe in me; of righteousness because I go to the Father, and you will see me no more; of judgment, because the ruler of this world is judged" (John 16:8 ff.). The realization that we are sinners is the beginning of our salvation. The same one who alone can make the diagnosis is also the one who alone can provide the cure.

CARL A. RUDISILL LIBRARY
LENOIR RHYNE COLLEGE

CHAPTER V

GOD REVEALED

Knowing God

The very heart of our existence on this earth is that we should acknowledge God's lordship, trusting, loving, and obeying him, and so have life. But to what extent can we know God and his will? Obviously he cannot be seen. He does not come to talk with us in the cool of the day and make known to us his heart and will. Where then shall he be found?

Original Revelation and the Revelation in Christ

A distinction has traditionally been made between a general and a special revelation. By the general revelation was meant God's revelation of himself in nature and in the human heart, while special revelation referred to his revelation first in the prophets who spoke for him, and finally in the Son in whom the fullness of the Godhead dwelled bodily. This distinction is essential, but in order to avoid confusion it is better to speak of the former as the *self-disclosure of God in nature* or as the *witness* of God present in the creation for all men to perceive. Then the term *revelation* can be reserved for that special activity of God in which his heart and will are made known in a qualitatively different way. Or we could also differentiate between an "original" revelation to all men and the specific revelation in Jesus, the Christ.

God's Witness in Creation as Personal Encounter

In making this distinction we must, however, not forget that in both cases God encounters or meets man personally at a time and place. The trouble with the old distinction between a general and special revelation is that it seems to imply that in the former God is not really present to man but far off in his heaven, while only in the latter does he condescend to come down to earth. This is, however, a misunderstanding of the inescapability of God's presence to all men everywhere. This is all that was intended by the use of the word "general." It affirms that at every time and place God is present to man in his very existence, putting his claim upon him and calling him to gratitude and worship so that he is without excuse. There is no one who is not so encountered. If this is remembered then the mistake will be avoided of regarding as revelation all discovery of general truths even though God is not encountered with his personal claim and call to surrender. It will be seen that arguments for God's existence which remove him from the immediate encounter destroy the living God and only produce idols. As we said above, God is the creator and not the first cause of the universe. Arguments in which we infer the existence of some kind of god from certain other facts are, therefore, wrong in principle. The living God is met directly and personally or he is not the living God.

When we, however, say that God is met directly, we must remember that such meeting is never face to face. We said above that God is the "hidden God." This means that what Luther called the "naked God," God in all his glory, is never visible to men as long as they live in the time of decision and of faith. God in his glory will be beheld only when the time for decision is over and the time of the judgment and the fulfillment is come. In the meantime, as we have already said (pp. 29 f.), God "appears" to men only through a "medium" or behind what Luther called a "mask," which like the mask of the masquerader both hides and reveals. The masquerader is immediately present but his true identity is hidden by the mask. So it is with the presence of God. He is immediately present to us everywhere, as close as he can get, closer than hands and feet, but never directly visible to our sense. We "see" him only with the eyes of faith, and his presence may, therefore, always be denied or misinterpreted. We may, therefore, speak of his presence as a "mediated immediacy." God is immediately present, but in a medium. The medium itself is not God. The creature must never be confused with the Creator. But neither must God be removed from the medium. He is present, as Luther said of the presence of Christ in the Sacrament, "in, with, and under" the earthly medium. This is true of the presence of God in nature as well as of his presence in the man Jesus, the carpenter of Nazareth, for the fact that God was present on the earth in him was certainly not directly discernible. In nature the masks are the sun, the moon, the good earth itself, the clouds, the rain, and all the forces of nature, as well as human beings themselves—father, mother, children, brothers and sisters, the neighbors near or far. In all of these God is present, blessing men and calling them to gratitude, surrender, and service. God both blesses men in and through these masks and gives them the opportunity to serve him in and through them. He gives us light and life through the sun, the rain, the crops of the field, the parents, the farmer, and all the workers of the world. In the neighbor in his need, whether this be some member of our own family or the stranger fallen among thieves by the wayside, it is God himself who confronts us and calls us to be the instrument of his love to meet that neighbor in his need. "As you did it to one of the least of these my brethren, you did it to me," Jesus said (Matt. 25:40), for in him God was present in a unique and special way, as we shall see.

St. Paul's Testimony to God's Presence

When St. Paul wanted to emphasize that all men are without excuse in their failure to acknowledge the lordship of God, he wrote: "What can be known about God is plain to them, because God has shown it to them. Ever since the creation of the world his invisible nature, namely, his eternal power and deity, has been clearly perceived in the things that have been made. So they are without excuse" (Rom. 1:19 f.).

Paul means that all men can see the order of nature —the sun, moon, and stars; trees and flowers; the mystery and rhythm of life and growth; the family relationship;

the moral sense within every man—and all these bear testimony to the presence of an invisible power and wisdom in and behind them. God is inescapably present everywhere; yet not openly; he is immediately present in the medium, in the "masks" or "wrappings" that both hide and reveal.

Let us use an analogy, remembering that every analogy has its faults. Suppose that one day you find yourself in a confined area, together with many other people. Not one of you knows how he got there. But there you are, for better or for worse. After many vain attempts you discover that you cannot get out. High walls surround you. Nevertheless, there are some in the group who just won't give up trying to scale them.

You discover, however, that it is not such an unpleasant place to be after all. Naturally you are interested in finding out who your host is. You begin questioning and you discover that none of your associates is the host, though some of them would like to be and even pretend to be. They are all guests. It never occurs to you, of course, to suppose that there is no host, no real owner, no one in control. You just aren't made that way. Well, if one of those with you is not the owner, who is, and what is he like? Are there no clues? You may not be a Sherlock Holmes, yet some elementary deductions will be possible. Whoever your host is, he must have brains and power. Overwhelming evidence is all around you.

Wisdom and power are qualities of your host, you inevitably conclude, and it would be quite natural for you to acknowledge this in some way. You might write a poem about it. You might simply pour out a libation, a drink offering, to your hidden host as a gesture on your part, an acknowledgment, a thank offering.

We must add another detail to our imaginary picture. Scattered here and there are signs: "Do not trespass!" "Speed limit 70 miles per hour!" "Poison! Not good for food!" "This way to the Supermarket!" You discover upon inquiry that no one present has put up those signs. Apparently they came with the place. They were put up by the management, and it's not a bad management at that. Concern for the well-being of the guests is apparent, as well as order. You can't just do as you please. Wisdom and power and a will to be obeyed! There is not one in the group who would not reach such conclusions about the hidden host. Ought not, then, each also honor the host?

Yet it is not quite as simple as that. So far only one part of the picture has been presented. Wisdom, power, and a will to be obeyed! Yes, but every day all kinds of disturbing things happen that would make you think your hidden host, though clever enough, must be a fiend at heart. One day the finest building in the whole resort collapses, and hundreds are killed. Indeed, so overwhelming is the piled-up evidence that it becomes difficult to believe in the goodness of the hidden host, for, you see, this is not a matter of numbers, of being satisfied with a balance on the black side of the ledger. Human suffering is terrible. Is a host who builds the contentment of nine hundred ninety-nine of his guests on the undeserved and unrequited suffering of even one a host to be trusted and worshiped and obeyed? If you were to sit down in a banquet hall with rich dainties spread before you, and the sweetest music to enchant you, you would soon lose your appetite if you got a glimpse of the slaves in the pit below—the toilers, the sufferers, who must produce these riches and whose cries of agony are converted into that deceptive music.

Or suppose what you see happening to others around you strikes you personally. You now begin to have grave doubts about your hidden host. The witness to himself is far too ambiguous for calm assurance. After all his true heart and will toward you are not revealed. It is a revelation of God's wisdom and his power rather than of his love (Rom. 1:20). Yet, if you have any sense of what is proper and right you will acknowledge his wisdom and power, and you will find some things for which to give him thanks.

To complete our analogy, one thing remains. We would have to allow that in the final analysis the guests do not properly acknowledge their hidden host. Granted that the testimony concerning him is inadequate and ambiguous, it is still enough to demand proper recognition. Honest observation, however, reveals the pride and willfulness of the guests. They act as though they were the proprietors and not the guests. They take things for granted. They forget completely to give thanks. Their recognition of their absolute dependence upon the host is always qualified by their confidence in themselves. They betray their self-sufficiency. They give their host to understand that they are pretty good guests to have around and that he is indebted to them too. They complain secretly to the management that they are not really getting all that they are paying for. In the most subtle and self-deceiving ways they really insult their host even when they seem to be honoring him. They take the credit to themselves even in their most flattering oratory. They continually break the rules. Even though past experience should give them adequate warning, they always figure they can get by this time. They are all guilty and without excuse.

This is our analogy. God witnesses to himself in his creation and discloses himself in it. This witness is sufficient so that from it men ought to acknowledge his power and wisdom. In this witness God calls men to surrender, thanksgiving, worship. Yet man in his pride always misreads and disastrously perverts that witness. There is always a confusion between the Creator and the creature. A review of the religions of the world will show that confusion not only in the crude idols of wood and stone but particularly in the gods of the philosophers. No matter whether, with the ancient Greeks, they glorify man's reason as essentially divine; or, with the orientals, they identify God with the universe; or, with so many moderns, they make of God a well-meaning but helpless adventurer who needs their cooperation if he is going to get anywhere; the confusion is always the same. The strict dividing line between the absolute Creator and the dependent creature is not maintained. And you need not go to the learned tomes of the philosophers to discover that this is so. Walk down Main Street of any

Middletown, and talk with the truck driver, the grocery clerk, the banker, the lawyer, the actor, and the others you meet. Each in his own way will dethrone God and put an idol in his stead. Look into your own heart and you will find that you do the same. It is for this cause that God's wrath manifests itself and terrible evils befall mankind. This self-disclosure of God, therefore, remains a revelation of wrath. It is the law rather than the gospel. It does not reveal the gracious God who accepts man as he is in his sin. It does not proclaim forgiveness. It does not reveal the God who in Jesus Christ took upon himself the sins of the world and atoned for them.

All this needs to be read in St. Paul's own devastating words. He wrote his letter to the Romans as a sort of prophylactic in advance of his coming, setting forth the content of his gospel so that there might be no misunderstanding such as he had encountered elsewhere. He states as his theme that he is "not ashamed of the gospel: it is the power of God for salvation to every one who has faith, to the Jew first and also to the Greek. For in it the righteousness of God is revealed through faith for faith; as it is written, 'He who through faith is righteous shall live'" (Rom. 1:16 f.). Then he develops the thesis that *all* men lack a righteousness in which they can stand in God's judgment. They are all equally sinful and their righteousness is before God but as filthy rags. Therefore, their only escape from God's wrath and just condemnation is in the active righteousness that comes from God himself to cover their unrighteousness.

If, however, *all* men are under judgment this means

that to *all* of them God must have disclosed himself in such a way that they are without excuse. God had spoken to the Jews and made himself known through Moses and the prophets. They clearly, then, have no excuse for not having responded and obeyed. But what about the Gentiles (the non-Jews)? They too are without excuse, for to them, too, God has sufficiently disclosed himself. Read Paul's own indictment:

> Now the holy anger of God is disclosed from Heaven against the godlessness and evil of those men who render truth dumb and inoperative by their wickedness. It is not that they do not know the truth about God: indeed he has made it quite plain to them. For since the beginning of the world the invisible attributes of God, for example, his eternal power and divinity, have been plainly discernible through things which he has made and which are commonly seen and known, thus leaving these men without a rag of excuse. They knew all the time there is a God, yet they refused to acknowledge him as such, or to thank him for what he is or does. Thus they became fatuous in their argumentations, and plunged their silly minds still further into the dark. Behind a façade of "wisdom" they became just fools, fools who would exchange the glory of the eternal God for an imitation image of a mortal man, or of creatures that run or fly or crawl. They gave up God: and therefore God gave them up—to be playthings of their own foul desires in dishonoring their own bodies.
>
> These men deliberately forfeited the Truth of God and accepted a lie, paying homage and giving service to the creature instead of to the Creator, who alone is worthy to be worshiped for ever and ever, Amen. God therefore handed them over to disgraceful passions. Their women

111

exchanged the normal practices of sexual intercourse for something which is abnormal and unnatural. Similarly the men, turning from natural intercourse with women, were swept into lustful passions for one another. Men with men performed these shameful horrors, receiving, of course, in their own personalities the consequences of sexual perversity.

Moreover, since they considered themselves too high and mighty to acknowledge God, he allowed them to become the slaves of their degenerate minds, and to perform unmentionable deeds. They became filled with wickedness, rottenness, greed and malice: their minds became steeped in envy, murder, quarrelsomeness, deceitfulness and spite. They became whisperers-behind-doors, stabbers-in-the-back, God-haters; they overflowed with insolent pride and boastfulness, and their minds teemed with diabolical invention. They scoffed at duty to parents; they mocked at learning, recognized no obligations of honor, lost all natural affection, and had no use for mercy. More than this—being well aware of God's pronouncement that all who do these things deserve to die, they not only continued their own practices, but did not hesitate to give their thorough approval to others who did the same.

Now if you feel inclined to set yourself up as a judge of those who sin, let me assure you, whoever you are, that you are in no position to do so. For at whatever point you condemn others you automatically condemn yourself, since you, the judge, commit the same sins (Rom. 1:18-2:1).[1]

Orders of Creation and Civil Righteousness

We would not be doing justice to the witness of himself that God has left in creation if we did not refer to the specific orders or structures within which God has arranged that men should live, nor if we did not call attention to the degree of righteousness and the measure of community to which men, in spite of St. Paul's fearful indictment, can attain in those orders.

Among the orders of creation are the family, the state, the economic order, and the community of culture. It is sometimes held that these are simply human institutions which men have developed in the struggle for existence. For instance, in order to procreate, male and female mate, sometimes monogamously, sometimes polygamously, depending upon circumstances. Which is proper—so it is claimed—can never be determined except on the basis of how it happens to work out.

The claim is also made that men discovered that if they are to live together and hold their own against the hostile forces of nature, and against one another's rapacity, they must recognize some kind of authority, and thus the state came into being. So also with the economic order. As soon as men lived together in some sort of community and began to specialize in their work, they recognized that they must carry on business with one another. They must exchange labor for food; they must recognize property, possessions, and the like. So a certain kind of economic order came into being. Only experience can decide which is the best one. Or men felt an urge to know, just for the sake of knowing; to create beautiful things—pictures, sculpture, music—just for their beauty; and to associate with one another in pleasant ways, in games and in friendly intercourse. And who is to say what is legitimate and what is not?

But these are not merely human institutions; they are

definite structures given in creation in which, moreover, God's love is manifested, for the God of redemption and the God of creation are the same God. Society does have a unit which came not by mere chance, or because it happened to work out best, but because God so ordered the world. This unit of society is the monogamous family, and every departure from it is a violation of the order of creation. While it would be contradicted by many, it is possible to show from a review of the course of history that the societies in which the monogamous family was the unit have been the most healthy and stable. One of the signs of a disintegrating society is the disintegration of the basic social unit, the family.

So also with the order that we call the state. Government—that is, an authority with power to enforce order —is not just a human institution. The powers that be, as St. Paul says, are ordained of God (Rom. 13:1). This does not mean, of course, that all existing governments are as such divinely ordained. They may be godless and tyrannical and in direct contradiction to God's order when they do not maintain justice and order, the purpose for which they are ordained. It is to say, however, simply that governmental authority is itself a divine institution. That is, it is in the order of creation that some should rule and others be ruled; that there should be laws to be obeyed, and penalties for the violators. In this way God's love takes the form of law and it would not be love if it did not do so. An ideal state, where everybody does just as he pleases, is an empty pipe dream unsuited for a world of sinful men. Furthermore, there is a certain basic

114

pattern to which a government must conform if it is not to violate the order of creation. The state must promote justice, give to each man his due, preserve order, maintain individual freedoms and rights, all of which are written into the order of creation.

Or consider the economic order. Whether you have a right to the fruits of your own labor or not, whether you shall eat even if you willfully refuse work, whether labor with the hands is to be considered inferior or superior to mental work—all such things are written into the order of nature. Men can build a relatively just economic order only on the basis of them. This is not to advocate the classical Protestant work ethic. In an economy of abundance, with automation making many forms of work obsolete, work will have to take other forms than physical labor or debilitating drudgery. There is no premium on toil for the sake of toil. Our point is simply that all who are able must contribute in some way to the economic order. To this end there is a God-given community of work in which men depend on each other's gifts, for the production and just distribution of the goods necessary for human life is a God-given necessity!

And as far as cultural pursuits are concerned, their relative independence must also be recognized. They can be kept from becoming idols only if viewed in the order of creation.

What we are saying is this: Since this is God's world and God witnesses to himself in the order of creation, it is possible for men even outside the sphere of special revelation to live together in community with a semblance of stability and a measure of happiness. It is not true that outside the sphere of special revelation all is confusion, chaos, gross immorality. The ancient Teutons with their stable family life, the Golden Age of Greece, the best days of the Roman Empire, the civilizations of ancient Egypt and of the Far East have had many things to commend them. It is not true that apart from Christ a man would be an atheist. It is not true, either, that apart from Christ all men sink equally into depths of depravity. There are always some who meet responsibility in accordance with the light that is granted them. They read the law written in their hearts, and do by nature the things contained in the law, and are, therefore, a law unto themselves (see Rom. 2:14 f.).

Here we return to what was meant when, in discussing the doctrine of the Trinity, we stressed the importance of keeping creation separate from redemption and not ascribing to the redeemer what is the work of the creator. All the advances of science which have brought us to the dawn of the space age with its untold possibilities for both good and evil are not the result of Christ's coming into the world as redeemer and reconciler. They are simply the result of the fact that God gave man his brains. They, therefore, should be claimed for God under the first article and not the second. That they belong to the first article and are not strictly speaking redemptive can be clearly seen from their ambiguity; they have dual possibilities and may be used for evil as well as for good. The hand God gave man may be used for healing or for smiting on the cheek and if the hand is extended by the invention of a tool, then Cain can use it either to till the soil or kill his brother. The drug may be used to assuage pain or to enslave a man hopelessly. And so it is with the splitting of the atom—it is not the devil's work, but God's. But it can be put into the service of the enemy of God; man can distort and demonize what God has given. He can claim as his own to do with as he pleases that which he only holds in trust. "What have you that you did not receive? If then you received it, why do you boast as if it were not a gift?" (1 Cor. 4:7).

But it would be a mistake to conclude that the special revelation culminating in Christ has little to add to the above. In one sense, to be sure, it has nothing to add, for this is not a quantitative matter, as though to the nine-tenths which natural man already possesses only another tenth needs to be added. It is not that something must be added, but that the whole personality, the basic orientation, the whole world-outlook of the natural man must be transformed by that radical cure: Christianity. In this sense Christianity has everything to add.

Some, particularly traditional Roman Catholics, believe that what the "natural" man is able to perceive of God and is able to do in the way of "good works," needs only quantitative supplementation from the supernatural revelation in Christ. When man fell into sin he lost only certain superadded powers which went beyond his natural abilities. Before the Fall he was able to see God clearly in his true nature and he was able to practice the highest virtues. After the Fall his vision was dimmed and his picture of God clouded. With his natural reason man

117

can now conclude certain truths about God which are true enough as far as they go. He can conclude that there is a perfect being, who is the first cause of all, the orderer of the universe. But the triune nature of God he is unable to discern. This is revealed to him in Christ and mediated to him through the church. Once when we were driving down Broad Street in Philadelphia with the late Father Gustav Weigle he pointed to a billboard in the distance on which the "ad" was not yet clearly visible, although we were sure there was something there, a bottle and a tall glass. This, he said, was like the natural man's vision of God. Then as we approached the billboard the vision cleared and we could see clearly the Ballantine three-ring sign. This is the way, the Jesuit facetiously explained, in which revelation clears up the vision of the Trinity. By quantitative supplementation, by the church's infusions of grace, the power is given to practice the supernatural virtues along with the natural ones. In this way man makes the climb up to the beatific vision of God, a vision which is vouchsafed to him only at the point of perfection. If, therefore, such perfection (saint-hood) is not by God's grace achieved in this life the process must continue in purgatory until the soul is worthy of seeing God face to face. There is no realization in this view of the basic rebellion of the "natural" man which makes of him a self-centered sinner in all he does and which always turns his god into an idol. It is simply that something is lacking: the natural man does not know enough and his powers are not great enough.

By way of contrast, Luther felt that the trouble with man was not simply that man in the Fall had lost certain powers. The trouble was his *incurvatus in se,* his being curved in upon himself, which causes him to seek himself in all he does and makes him an inveterate idol-worshiper. The purpose of the act of God in Christ, therefore, is not just to clear up man's vision and make new powers available to him in a process of purification. It is to drive the idols from his heart, to convert him, to cure him of his disastrous curvature of the spine, and make a righteous, upright man of him, facing up to God and out to the neighbor. He does not achieve the beatific vision by the practice of virtues, but he is assured of life and salvation by the forgiveness of his sins, for "where there is forgiveness of sins there is life and salvation." By this act he is made a new man for only a good tree can bring forth good fruit. By it he is freed from his frantic efforts to save himself and for service of the neighbor.

The Fullness of Time

In the foregoing analogy it is clear that the only way we could get really to know our hidden host and his true will and disposition toward us would be if he paid us a special kind of visit. This is what actually happened when God sent his Son into the world in the fullness of time, heralding his coming by messengers sent beforehand. "In many and various ways God spoke of old to our fathers by the prophets; but in these last days he has spoken to us by a Son" (Heb. 1:1 f.).

119

A Period of Preparation

There was a long period of preparation before the time was ripe for the coming of the Son. If it seems strange to us that so many years should have passed before this crowning event, it will do no harm to admit that the reason is hidden in part in the eternal counsels of God (see Eph. 1). When considering God's providential guidance of the course of history, St. Paul writes: "O the depth of the riches and wisdom and knowledge of God! How unsearchable are his judgments and how inscrutable his ways!" (Rom. 11:33). On the other hand we can discern how the world was being prepared both positively and negatively for the new aeon that was to be ushered in. Centuries of history were making clear the malady and the need. One chosen nation was being schooled for the approaching day. It was not on account of their own so-called religious genius that the Israelites were selected to participate in these events of history, but because God spoke to them through the prophets, guided, sheltered, blessed, and punished them, built a fence around them, and kept their hopes focused on a future great day.

There are two divergent lines of prophecy. On the one hand it is a son of David who is to be the deliverer; on the other hand it is the Lord himself. These two lines meet in the Incarnate One. The law is the "schoolmaster" to lead men to Christ. That is to say, the law is like the slave in the ancient Greek household, the pedagogue, whose business it was to lead the child to the real teacher. So the law was, and still is, intended to teach men their need of the Savior. The temple with its sacrifices, the one great Day of Atonement when the high priest entered behind the veil with the blood of a lamb without blemish to plead at the mercy seat, the Passover with its meal of communion, all contribute to keeping alive the sense of the divine holiness that both repels and attracts, the sense of sin, the need for forgiveness, the necessity of a Mediator.

The world was being prepared for that coming into history of the Savior who would set the captives free. That deliverance is symbolized by the exodus from Egypt. The Lord appears to Moses and tells him his name, "Yahweh," "I am that I am," "The Eternal." He tells him that he is not a god who is far away, shining discouragingly far up in the sky for men to grope after. He is not just an eternal, unchanging ideal. He is not a god who has forgotten the plight of his people or who is powerless before the gods of the Egyptians and the forces of nature. He is "Yahweh," the eternally Active One, both willing and able to help, coming from eternity into time, manifesting his superiority over all the forces of nature, winning the victory over all enemies, leading his peoples out of bondage through a miracle of waters piled high to the right and the left, accompanying them, guiding them, feeding them throughout their long pilgrimage, until at last they pass the Jordan into the Promised Land.

The Incarnate One

That which was symbolized beforehand is fulfilled in the Incarnate One, "Jesus Christ . . . conceived by the

121

Holy Ghost, born of the Virgin Mary." Here is a birth that is different. We need not ask ourselves whether men ever are or will be born of virgins. The virgin birth of a man is not the issue. Here we are dealing with a real miracle which only God can perform: the real issue is the coming of the Son of God into the flesh. Nor must we suppose that it is the absence of sexual relationship which guarantees the uniqueness and sinlessness of Jesus. That would be to make the sexual act itself a sinful act, for which there is no warrant. Nor can we say that the fact that Jesus had no earthly father frees him from the taint of original sin, for unless we posit the immaculate conception of the Virgin Mary there would still be contact with a sinful humanity.

We must simply contrast this birth with our own birth. We are born of our parents, at their initiative, through the process of procreation. We have absolutely no pre-existence. We derive our life from our parents and the long stream of our ancestors. At the same time that center of responsibility which each of us essentially is, is creatively brought forth out of nothing, without any pre-existence. We derive our life from our parents and the this side of the Great Divide, without any crossing over.

How different is the birth of Jesus. This is the crossing of the Great Divide! Matthew is very careful to trace his genealogy back to Abraham; he is the promised seed. Luke on the other hand goes all the way back to Adam; he is a true son of man, one with all the stream of mankind. As such he is carried beneath his mother's heart, drawing his life from hers just like any other human child. But what a difference! The life stirring within her did not come from any human initiative. This is an act of God, the prototype of all God's gracious dealings with men, where God implants himself and himself enters into the course of history. This act of God involves God himself. This is the coming of God himself. This is *the miracle*. It is not simply something stupendous or amazing or unusual. This is the coming of God himself, the one who pervades all the world, imprisoned for love in the form of a servant, wrapped in swaddling clothes, laid in a manger. The life stirring within the Virgin's womb is from above. "In the beginning was the Word, and the Word was with God, and the Word was God" (John 1:1). There never was a time when he was not. He shared the Father's glory from eternity: "And now, Father, glorify thou me in thy own presence with the glory which I had with thee before the world was made" (John 17:5). At the creation he was there, not just with the spectators, shouting for joy, but sharing in the creative power: "Without him was not anything made that was made" (John 1:3). He was a king upon a royal throne, who gave up his throne for love. And when he gave it up he really gave it up. He really became a commoner. It was not just pretense. He was not just traveling incognito, with a beggar's cloak thrown over his royal habiliments, which a vagrant breeze might reveal. In this way he established the only true equality of love with all men, even the humblest.[2] Though he was in the form of God he did not think that this was something to which he should cling as a soldier clings to his booty; but he emptied himself; he poured out all his glory and took upon himself the form of a servant, and being found in fashion as a man he humbled himself and became obedient unto death, even the death on the cross (Phil. 2:6 ff., paraphrase).

The King became a true commoner, and yet he could not deny his kingly blood or the kingly love that prompted his descent to our earth. This is the mystery of the Incarnation: Jesus Christ, true God and true man, our brother, stands with us on our side of the Great Divide to share with us all our human weaknesses, temptations, and sufferings, and yet at the same time he is our Lord, who stands over against us as the One to whom we owe absolutely all—our Deliverer, our Judge, our King. There is no more wonderful expression of it than is found in the great *Te Deum:*

> Thou art the King of Glory O Christ;
> Thou art the everlasting Son of the Father.
> When thou tookest upon thee to deliver man:
> Thou didst humble thyself to be born of a Virgin.
> When Thou hadst overcome the sharpness of death:
> Thou didst open the kingdom of heaven to all believers.

No wonder it cuts the heart of a believer to the quick when this one, our brother and our blessed Lord, is thought of only as the Master, who merely excels the rest of us in our spiritual evolution and who is divine only in the same sense that we are all divine. No! He differs qualitatively and not just quantitatively from all other beings. There is a qualitative difference between cotton and silk. Increase a pile of cotton until it is a mile

124

high; it will never become silk. Or vary it from the cheapest cheesecloth to the finest muslin; it is still no closer to being silk. Silk has a different beauty. So it is with him, "very God of very God," "Who for us men, and for our salvation, came down from heaven, and was incarnate by the Holy Ghost of the Virgin Mary." If you catch the full import of this miracle of condescending love, then you will want at this point to make a deep and reverent bow, not only of the knees, but of your whole being.

"The Word became flesh and dwelt among us, full of grace and truth; we have beheld his glory, glory as of the only Son from the Father" (John 1:14). But this true glory was discernible only to the eyes of faith. The Son of God walked the earth in the true form of a servant, and this servant form is still reflected in word and Sacrament, and blessed is he who is not offended by them.

We said at the start that a man is not saved by believing that Jesus is both true God and true man any more than he is saved by believing that there are three persons in one essence. Such intellectual feats are in any case quite impossible, as we have already noted. We are saved by what God himself does for us and in us through Jesus, the Christ. To end the so-called Christological controversy of the fourth and fifth centuries, which followed inevitably upon the Trinitarian controversy, the Council of Chalcedon, 451 A.D., developed the formula that there were "two natures" *inseparably* and *indivisibly*, yet *unconfusedly* and *unchangeably* united in the one person of Christ. This necessitated the assertion of two wills in only one so-called *person*. By person, however, they did not understand exactly what we understand today; they meant a being who is able to stand on his own (*hypostasis*). It was, I suppose, as much as to say that the personality of Jesus was not split. He functioned as a unified whole.

This was asserted out of a "soteriological" concern, because, as we noted in connection with the doctrine of the Trinity, only one who is "very God of very God" is sufficient to effect man's redemption. At the same time to bring the Savior actually into the sphere of human history it is necessary that he be flesh of our flesh and bone of our bone, sharing our full humanity (Heb. 4:15).

So far so good. But if we now try to figure out just how these two natures, so radically different, are united in one person, we really have one "doozy" of a problem on our hands, as many a bright-eyed child in Sunday school has pointed out. Do these two natures converse with one another in one consciousness as we sometimes do when we talk to ourselves? Does the one nature know everything, fully aware of its godhood, while the other is limited in knowledge and power like any true human being? When the man Jesus gets tired, sleeps, and is subject to all the infirmities of the flesh, is the divine in him always buoyantly alert and serenely unaffected by all this? When the man Jesus faces the death of the cross, does the divine nature in him know that there is an ace up his sleeve and that the whole ordeal is only for three days? Could the weakness of the one nature draw at will on the strength of the other and give a show of omnipotence whenever it so pleased?

You have to read the history of Christian thought to see how subtly the learned doctors tried to deal with these difficulties. It is an amazing story! They began with the separable attributes of God and man which were supposed to be communicated from one nature to the other or from either nature to the one person. Then, in order to account for the limitations, some thought up the so-called "kenotic theory" which is really a "hairy" one. The name comes from the Greek word *kenoō* which means to empty out. It is based upon the great early Christian hymn cited by Paul (Phil. 2:5 ff.) on the words put into the mouth of Jesus by the fourth evangelist, in the high-priestly prayer, "And now, Father, glorify thou me in thy own presence with the glory which I had with thee before the world was made" (John 17:5), and on the words of Paul, "Though he was rich, yet for your sake he became poor, so that by his poverty you might become rich" (2 Cor. 8:9). These passages in their context all speak in wonder of the humility of the Lord in taking on the servant form. They indicate "the shape of the deed of God," which is from the highest heights to the lowest depths in order that there might be an elevation again to the highest heights. The earthly state of Jesus was therefore referred to as the "state of humiliation." It begins with the conception in the womb and ends with the cry of victory, "It is finished," on the cross. After that, Jesus as the Christ is in the "state of exaltation," sharing the Father's power and reign. Paul particularly, in the Philippians passage, uses this "shape of the deed of

God" as an exhortation to his readers that they, too, should genuinely humble themselves as the price for true life: "Have this mind among yourselves, which you have also in Christ Jesus, who . . ." (quoted above in full, p. 123). It echoes Jesus' own exhortations: "Whoever exalts himself will be humbled, and whoever humbles himself will be exalted" (Matt. 23:12); "He who finds his life will lose it, and he who loses his life for my sake will find it" (Matt. 10:39); "You know that the rulers of the Gentiles lord it over them, and their great men exercise authority over them. It shall not be so among you; but whoever would be great among you must be your servant, and whoever would be first among you must be your slave; even as the Son of man came not to be served but to serve, and to give his life as a ransom for many" (Matt. 20:25 ff.). So he, in the night he was betrayed, took a towel and girded himself and washed his disciples' feet (John 13).

This is not to be interpreted as a shrewd and calculating way to get to the top, feigning and courting humility, while all the while the eye is on the reward. No! "Purify your hearts, you men of double mind" (Jas. 4:8). Purity of heart is to will one thing: the good.[3] None of this cock-eyed business of one eye quivering in the direction of the punishment, with the other eye bulging in the direction of the reward. This is what makes this so difficult, because one is confidently to trust in the reward as he acts purely out of loving concern for the neighbor and not for the sake of the reward. This requires trust, taking God at his word, for the reward is not promised in this life. So there is to be no "theology of glory." The church, that is, the fellowship of believers, is never to assume earthly rule, power, ostentation, or glory—it is to retain the servant form to the end of time itself, even as our Lord retained it to the end. Only then will the church be highly exalted as the bride of him who was given a name above every other name.

Now we seem to have wandered far afield from the "kenotic" theory, which we called a "hairy" one. But this was done on purpose. The whole story of the incarnation is a story of necessary and inevitable "kenosis." But this is a far cry from those masterpieces of rationalization which attempt to figure out just how the divine and the human could be side by side in the one person of Jesus.[4] It is held, for example, that at the moment of incarnation the divine attributes (those separable qualities of omnipresence, omniscience, etc.) were communicated to the human nature, so as to make a genuine incarnation. The infinite God really enters into the finite and he does not divest himself of any of his glory before he enters into the flesh. But after the incarnation the "emptying out" (the kenosis) takes place; then the king does lay off all the royal habiliments and assumes the servant form. And after the death on the cross he once more takes up those qualities which he had laid off and in which the human nature had been made to share. This gets even more subtle, if you have the taste and the time for such subtleties, because even in the state of humiliation, the divine nature did not really give up its glory, but only the divine-human person according to one mode of his existence. It's time we stopped here, before we get all bollixed up again.

We must return to our starting point. Luther explains the Second Article of the Creed simply by saying, "I believe that Jesus Christ, true God, begotten of the Father from eternity, and also true man, born of the virgin Mary,[5] *is my Lord,* who . . ." and then he goes on to describe what this Lord has done to make us his own and live under him in his kingdom. Jesus, the Christ, therefore, *is* what he *does,* as God *is* what he *does,* or anything living and active, for that matter, *is* what it *does.* This is what is known as a *functional Christology:* Jesus is the Christ because of the function which he performs. This, however, is not to be understood in such a way as to have this functioning up in the air. Something cannot function up in the air without there being something to function. Whatever functions as man must *be* a man and whatever functions as God must *be* God or we are being hoodwinked. Here an "as if" is not enough.

The question remains whether this kind of "high" Christology can be supported from the New Testament. Scholars are now certain that there is not one but many Christologies in the New Testament.[6] This has led some to throw in the sponge and to say that no consistent message or gospel is to be found in the New Testament, only diverse and conflicting messages.

Let us grant that there is not one but several different Christologies in the New Testament. That is natural, for each grows out of a particular form. Yet all of them have the same intention, all point to the same crucial event in which God himself acted decisively. It would go far beyond the scope of this brief presentation to give an adequate analysis, and a mere listing would serve only to confuse. If the reader is interested he can pursue the cited references. It is enough to say that out of the New Testament witness in all its multiplicity there did develop a consistent Christology, however time-bound the form of its expression. The formation of doctrine within the Christian community performed its function of unifying this message, of guarding against heresy, of putting into a confession what constituted the faith of the church, of formulating what could be recited in praise of God and taught to children and converts. It was the "mystery" of God's act in Christ which the church celebrated. Without a so-called "high" Christology the whole pattern of Christian worship in the triune name, particularly the celebration of the Lord's Supper, makes not a modicum of sense.

Throughout the history of the Christian Church—even in the New Testament itself—the pendulum has swung from one extreme to the other. Either Jesus was held to be God in such a way that he only appeared to be a man (docetism) or else he was just a man like everyone else, the highest and best, to be sure, but just a man who by his life showed what God was like and exemplified God-like living. Some tried to avoid both these interpretations by erasing the difference between God and man and saying that the God-man Jesus only illustrates the basic divine-human unity. Then Jesus on the cross only serves as a visual aid for the dullards in the class who haven't the wit to see into the true state of affairs without any of this "bloody" prompting.

There have been some, however, for whom the mystery has remained. Of course in the light of everything that has been said[7] about our no longer believing in a three-story universe from which a heavenly being could "come down" to earth (including a further "descent" into the bowels of the earth) and "ascend" again from whence he came, we do have to be clear about the human, anthropomorphic language we are using. We do have to interpret in terms that will not come into conflict with the kind of boundless universe in which we know we are living. We must not suppose that the real wonder and mystery of the incarnation was ever really that of one of three heavenly beings making a space journey to the planet Earth from some near or distant celestial abode, while the other two awaited his return while sitting on their hands until they too would get into the act. The giant theologians of the past, as well as the simple believers, were not so naive. What happened was, by its very nature, the one incomprehensible and unrepeatable event, of God himself becoming involved in his world and acting decisively in a man who was the true man, "the man for others."

Marc Connelly in his *Green Pastures* succeeds in making us feel, through the experience of a simple but faithful people, the full pattern of what is involved. God is pictured as having done all he intended to do for his faithless children. At last he loses patience when he sees how his people have succumbed to temptation:

. . . I helped Adam, I helped Noah, I helped Moses, an' I helped David. What's de grain dat grew out of de seed? Sin! Nothin' but sin throughout de whole world. I've given you ev'y chance. I sent you warriors and prophets. I've given you laws and commandments, an' you betrayed my trust. Ev'ything I've given you, you've defiled. Ev'y time I've fo'given you, you've mocked me. . . . Listen, you chillun of darkness, yo' Lawd is tired. I'm tired of de struggle to make you worthy of de breath I gave you. I put you in bondage ag'in to cure you an' yo' worse dan you was amongst de flesh pots of Egypt. So I renounce you. Listen to the words of yo' Lawd God Jehovah, for dey is de last words yo' ever hear from me. I repent of dese people dat I have made and I will deliver dem no more.[8]

But the Lord God is unable to go through with it. Constantly, for hundreds of years, he is assailed by the voices of the fathers, Abraham, Isaac, Jacob, and Moses. And before the door of his celestial office there never ceases to pace the patient figure of the prophet, Hosea, who has not given up on his harlot wife, Gomer. Then he sees for himself the confidence of those who defend the Lord's city against Herod's desecrations. He is assured that the only way Hosea or anyone else found mercy was through suffering.

So the fable ends with this conversation between Gabriel and the Lord God:

Gabriel

You look a little pensive, Lawd. [God nods his head.] Have a seegar, Lawd?

God

No thanks, Gabriel.

[Gabriel goes to the table, accepts a cup of custard;

chats with the angel behind the table for a moment as he sips, puts the cup down and returns to the side of God.]

Gabriel

You look awful pensive, Lawd. You been sittin' yere, lookin' dis way, an awful long time. Is it somethin' serious, Lawd?

God

Very serious, Gabriel.

Gabriel

[Awed by His tone.] Lawd, is de time come for me to blow?

God

Not yet, Gabriel. I'm just thinkin'.

Gabriel

What about, Lawd? [Puts up hand. Singing stops.]

God

'Bout somethin' de boy tol' me. Somethin' 'bout Hosea, and himself. How dey foun' somethin'.

Gabriel

What, Lawd?

God

Mercy. [A pause.] Through *sufferin'*, he said.

Gabriel

Yes, Lawd.

God

I'm tryin' to find it, too. It's awful impo'tant. It's awful impo'tant to all de people on my earth. Did he mean dat even God must suffer?

[God continues to look out over the audience for a moment and then a look of surprise comes into his face. He sighs. In the distance a voice cries.]

The Voice

Oh, look at him! Oh, look, dey goin' to make him carry

it up dat high hill! Dey goin' to nail him to it! Oh, dat's a terrible burden for one man to carry!

[God rises and murmurs "Yes!" as if in recognition. The heavenly beings have been watching him closely, and now, seeing him smile gently, draw back relieved. All the angels burst into "Hallelujah, King Jesus." God continues to smile as the lights fade away. The singing becomes fortissimo.]

Curtain.[9]

CHAPTER VI

THE TRUE MAN

God's Purpose

God's purpose is the establishment of the Christian pattern of life, which we are calling *life together in love*. In this *life together in love* men are to live in the right relationship to God and to each other. In the establishment of such a community it is impossible to separate what Christ is from what he does. God reveals himself to us by what he does when he creates the world, when he chooses and guides the children of Israel, and when he sends his only begotten Son into the world for its redemption.

This Son came to do something and not just to sit around and talk. That which he came to do was really to make a difference. "God was in Christ reconciling the world to himself" (2 Cor. 5:19). We must presuppose the breach and the disturbed relationship of which we have been speaking. We must presuppose that what is wrong with man is something other than just weakness, ignorance, or finitude. Christ's work is the healing of the breach, the reestablishment of the right relationship, the restoration of communion. It all culminates in what happened on the cross of Calvary; but we must not too narrowly center our attention only on that cross. We must view the entire life of Jesus as a cross. The whole life from the cradle to the grave is one of suffering and victorious love and the cross is the culmination point.

The Subjective View of the Atonement

There are views of the atonement based on the assumption that man's only trouble is his weakness and his ignorance. The only thing that was necessary, therefore, was that something should happen within the mind of man, subjectively. The reasoning runs something like this: Men in their ignorance have false notions of God. Above all they always tend to be afraid of God as some kind of ogre or malevolent being whom they must appease with gifts of one kind or another. They just can't know, of themselves, how different, how loving, kind, and willing to pardon God really is. So God appeared in Jesus Christ to show men his true nature, which is *love*. He didn't just talk about love, but he also practiced it, and finally gave his life upon the cross as the conclusive demonstration of his love. When men are confronted by this love a change takes place in their hearts; the scales drop from their eyes; their ignorance is removed. They are no longer at enmity with God but are reconciled to him. Nothing, therefore, happened through the cross which effected any kind of change either in God or in the relation between man and God. The only change is that which results from man's change of attitude.

The trouble with this view is that it begins with the wrong premises. It does not reckon with the fact that man is basically in revolt against God not through ignorance but through pride, and that, therefore, something other is needed than the mere removal of a certain mis-apprehension about God.

The trouble lies not so much in what is said, as in what is not said, and in the fact that what is said appears in the wrong context. It is true that when men are confronted by the cross an inner change takes place, but this is not what we are now talking about. We are not talking about what happens today, in the twentieth century, when a man comes to faith in Christ, but about what happened over nineteen hundred years ago when Jesus was crucified. Something happened then which is quite independent of what happens today. What happened on Calvary is decisive, unrepeatable, irrevocable, having happened once and for all. There a real battle was fought and won, and because it was fought and won men today are free—unless they choose to be slaves. What happened there was not just something to reveal to men a true state of affairs of which they were ignorant, but what happened was an actual liberation. Men were in need of a real emancipator and not just a teacher.

Christ For Us, and Christ In Us

If we are to do justice to the work of Christ we must speak both of a *Christ for us* and a *Christ in us*. The Christ for us has a temporal and logical priority over the Christ in us. It is only because Christ has done something, not only on our behalf or for our benefit, but actually in our stead, that he can now also enter into our lives and change them. But we must not suppose that we can really reap the benefit of what he has done in our place unless that inner change also occurs in our life. The two are inseparable, like the convex and concave surfaces of a sphere.

Jesus, the Second Adam, the True Man, the "Man for Others"

What then did Christ *do for us?* In the first place, as the second Adam, that is, as the founder of a reborn race, he fulfilled for us the whole will and law of God. It would be a mistake to regard Christ merely as the flowering of all manhood, who prematurely attained the goal which all humankind will some day attain. He was not the high point of human evolution. In him God entered into human history and if it was really human history then Jesus was the true man in whom the purpose of all creation was fulfilled.

True Humanity

Jesus' manhood must thus be taken seriously. This means that we must take his temptations seriously. He was subjected to all the conditions of our existence, our finitude, our limitations, and yet he did not succumb to them.[1] He was in all points tempted like we are. Furthermore, we must be clear about what the basic temptation is. The basic temptation is the temptation not to trust and love God completely. Man was made to take his life from God in trust, and to give it back to him in grateful obedience. This is what the first Adam and every man after him failed to do. It was precisely this which Jesus did, which makes him the second Adam and the true man. His whole life was one of obedience to the heavenly Father's will. This was symbolized by the fact that when he was twelve years old and assumed his manhood, he said, "Did you not know that I must be in my Father's house?" and again when he later went down into the waters of the Jordan to be baptized of John. Immediately thereafter he withstood the temptations of Satan, and again and again he withstood those same temptations until at last that moment arrived when he was able to say, "It is finished!"

A More Excellent Righteousness

In the Sermon on the Mount Jesus demanded a right-eousness that would exceed the righteousness of the scribes and Pharisees. What is demanded is nothing other than utter purity of heart in the sense of absolute single-mindedness. When we think of purity of heart we are apt to think merely of purity in sexual matters. Purity of heart is something much more basic than that kind of purity. He who is absolutely pure of heart and single-minded has only one purpose, one desire, one motivation, one goal: to do the good, to do the will of God, to glorify God's holy name. He really has a one-track mind. Only one thing matters: the good, God himself. As soon as any other consideration enters in—fear of punishment, or hope of reward—then the purity, the single-mindedness, is gone.

It is this kind of purity which was demanded by Jesus and which was also demonstrated by him. All the injunctions of the Sermon on the Mount are thus reduced to one: to seek first the kingdom of God and his righteousness. No angry thought, no lustful glance, no shadow of hypocrisy, no compromise with evil, no judging of others, no ostentatious praying or fasting, no worry about the morrow, but genuineness, sincerity, positive helpfulness, unrestricted love even of the enemy, calm confidence, and trust—these constitute purity of heart.

It is sometimes held that the injunctions of the Sermon on the Mount are not to be taken literally, since Jesus was only exaggerating for the sake of emphasis. This would be the worst kind of misunderstanding. To be sure, Jesus himself burned with indignation when he drove the money changers from the temple and when he inveighed against the hypocritical scribes and Pharisees, but this was nothing but holy zeal and righteous indignation, not in any way adulterating his purity of heart. It was quite different from what we are also pleased to call righteous indignation and zeal for the Lord, with its mixture of irritation, offended pride, envy, jealousy, secret ambition, self-righteousness, vindictiveness, outright vengeance, ill-disguised sadism.

If we contemplate the life and death of Jesus we will know what is meant. If we see him genuinely concerned for all, not resisting the malevolence of his captors, allowing himself to be reviled and spit upon and beaten without the slightest tremor of bitterness in his heart—we will know what is meant. We will know that Jesus did not in any way tone down his high demands when he himself kept them or when he said: "A new commandment I give to you, that you love one another; even as I have loved you" (John 13:34). We will also know that Jesus is the only selfless one, the all-loving one who gave his life for his enemies. He is the second Adam.

As the second Adam Jesus lived a life of perfect *obedience in trust*. He fulfilled the First Commandment in a life of uninterrupted fellowship with God, in faith escaping every anxiety. He actually lived like the birds of the air and the lilies of the field, except that their natural unconcern was in him a joyful commitment. And the Second Commandment, which is like the first, he also kept. All men were equally dear to him—the grasping publicans, the abandoned harlots, the straitlaced Pharisees, the ambitious high priests, the uneasy Pontius Pilate, the timid Nicodemus, the suspicious Samaritan woman with her unsavory past—he loved them all equally. He did not resort to the subterfuge to which we sometimes turn when we say that he did not love them for what they were but for what they might become, or when we make a distinction between liking and loving and say that we are under no obligation to like all men, even though we are obligated to love them. These are evasions and we know it. All the smelly, disgusting, self-centered, obnoxious, mean, petty, ungrateful, licentious, boasting, shoving, leering, babbling, boring, sniveling, whining, cowardly, bombastic, strutting, cold men and women: each one was singled out and for each his love was infinite, and for each without distinction he gave his life.

It is easy to speak unrealistically about the sinlessness of Jesus, to go far beyond what we can pretend to know.

142

Perhaps we have produced what must appear to be but the pale shadow of a man, the haloed Jesus with the marcelled hair, the soulful eyes, the spotless garment of white—not the carpenter from Galilee with knotted hands and the fearless spirit of Amos, the herdsman of Tekoah. Perhaps it is enough to say that he himself lived in the radical obedience and trust which he demanded of others,[2] without trying to spell this out in such a way that the whole life gets phony. According to one legend he was born of the virgin without any pain. He just popped out from a closed womb that never opened, just as he later arose from a closed tomb. If this were so, then the whole life would be as unreal as the birth—void of the pain and joy, the tension, the bitterness, the woe of real life. How can we say that he was a true man, one of us, if all our passions, irritations, moods, and vagaries did not stir in him? All we can really say is that he was subjected to *all* the conditions of our existence in finitude without succumbing to them, without even at the darkest hour losing his trust in God because he took refuge in the faithfulness of God, without losing his love for his fellow men, really living *for them* and not in some ill-disguised way for himself. We must think of sin, therefore, not in terms of breaches of the laws, for apparently he, too, broke the laws, and was accounted a glutton and a wine bibber. As we have said, we have to think of sin as a wrong relationship and of faith as the right relationship. He lived in faith and therefore he had no sin, for "whatsoever is not of faith is sin."

In any case what should most concern us now is to

avoid making Jesus but the pale shadow of a man. God revealed himself in our history just as it is, and not in some hothouse segment of it; he did so particularly in the history of the man Jesus, whom none of his contemporaries—not even his disciples—ever took for a God walking the earth. There was nothing to betray his divinity; he did not wear a halo, nor did he glow in the dark like a fluorescent shirt. If he had lived in the twentieth century instead of the first century, we, too, would have said, "Is this not the carpenter from up-country?" For his contemporaries he was from Nazareth and they all knew his father and mother, brothers and sisters. It was only to faith that he was born in Bethlehem in fulfillment of ancient prophecy. At his birth the heavens did not open for *all* to see and hear the angel voices—but only for the eyes and ears of faith. It is significant, therefore, that later legends—as of how as a child he made birds out of mud which flew away when he clapped his hands— are absent from the New Testament. We do not have to make of him an Apollo or a milksop or an unkempt boor. What did he look like? As a matter of fact there are conflicting legends as to his appearance. According to one he was a beautiful specimen of manhood, justifying the hymn "Beautiful Savior, King of Creation." According to another he was as ugly as Socrates so that he could, like Socrates, say that it was not because of the attraction of his face or form that anyone followed him. He is to each how he imagines him, just so he does not lose his true humanity and cease to be our true brother. To the white he is white, to the black he is black, to the

144

yellow he is yellow. He is the universal man because he was a particular man. He possesses, as Paul Tillich has said, absolute universality and absolute particularity. He is for all men because he was the true man, who lived our life, was subjected to all the conditions of our human existence, and yet did not in pride and lovelessness succumb to them. Therefore, he judges us as well as redeems us.

This was the second Adam: this was God's beloved Son with whom he was well pleased. In a sinful world it was inevitable that his life should antagonize men and so end in seeming tragedy. Selfish, sinful men cannot endure such a purity of heart which constantly points its accusing finger at them and shines like a light into the dark crevices of their lives, revealing all the hidden faults. Therefore Jesus' obedience led him to the cross. He came into the world in order to suffer and to die.

Vicarious or Substitutionary Obedience

Jesus was the second Adam who fulfilled the whole will and law of God. This sets the pattern for our lives, not indeed in the sense that we must actually follow in his footsteps, doing the things that he did, for then we could not take up a profession, we could not assume any of the responsibilities of our God-given calling in the world but would have to die on the cross. We should therefore not speak of the *imitation* of Christ but rather of *conformity* to the shape of his life. Jesus set the pattern for us in the sense that we must be motivated by his spirit and his love, so that we will do what is the will of God for us, just as Jesus did what was the will of God for him. We, therefore, should not ask when we face a decision, "What would Jesus do in this situation?" but rather "What would Jesus have us do in our situation?" The will of God for Jesus was that he should give his life for the sins of the world. The obedience that he rendered, the death that he died, and the punishment that he bore, were therefore vicarious or substitutionary.

Jesus Our Substitute

The notion that Jesus was our substitute is being bitterly contested in our age, as it has been so often in the past. This is quite natural, and in a sense even commendable, for we must take seriously the matter of our own responsibility. If we are really under obligation to do something, then no one else can fulfill our obligation.

There are some situations in which we have no difficulty with the idea of substitution. Let us suppose that there is a refuse heap to be shoveled. It is unsightly and must be removed. Who does it is not important, as long as the pile is cleared away. In such a case I could readily find a substitute to do my share of the work. Or in case some were negligent, others could do more than their share, and so the work would get done. In such a case substitution is entirely possible.

It is not quite like this, however, in relation to God. The problem is not simply that the refuse heap of sin should be removed, or that the Augean stables of the world should be cleaned, no matter who does it. The problem here is that each individual should clean up his own pile.

So, even if I should get someone else to do my share I still could not be said to have fulfilled my obligation. To mix the metaphor, this is a nontransferable ticket. I am the one who is under orders. I am the one who is supposed to do the loving, and loving is not something which another can do for me. No one can borrow his brother's love for the Savior.

If there are five children in a family every single one of them is obligated to love his parents and return their faithfulness. If there is one ingrate among the five then the others cannot shoulder his burden. If a certain sum of money were to be raised then one could assume the other's share. But the obligation of personal obedience and love is different. If a son does not love his father and does not do his will then no one can do it by substitution. Love simply is not something which you can borrow or substitute any more than responsibility and guilt are. It may be true that all society shares in the guilt of a criminal, but that is only because each one in a particular way is guilty for himself. In the God-relationship each individual is strictly responsible for his own attitude, behavior, and guilt, and he can push the responsibility off on no one else. The moral order makes no sense on any other basis. If all this is true, what sense does it make to speak of the substitutionary obedience and atonement of Christ? How can he be our substitute?

The Miracle of Forgiveness

It is precisely here that the wonder of forgiveness is apparent. How can God forgive, really forgive, the guilty

147

person? How is any forgiveness just? We think we understand this only when we misunderstand it by substituting ignorance for sin and excusing for forgiving. Certainly, if we really did not mean to do something, if it was at the bottom unintentional, then it is only just that we should be excused. Sin is ignorance then, and God is a gentleman who knows his parlor manners. But what if it is intentional, as so many moderns are loathe to admit? What if, as in Shakespeare's *Othello*, Iago really meant to hurt Othello to the quick because Othello had been preferred before him and won the woman he loved? What if proud Iago was offended by Othello's black skin and courtly ways, without the possibility of tracing this back to some wrong upbringing, some repression of childhood, some fault of society? Can you still say that Iago ought to be forgiven, that it is just that Othello should love him for his deed? All our sense of justice rises up against Iago's cruelly planned revenge. How now can Iago go scot-free? how can he be forgiven simply because he comes sniveling? The publicans, the harlots, the thief on the cross in the eleventh hour, Peter after his denial, John with his vain ambitions—how can these records simply be wiped out? Yes, how? But they were. And that is precisely the miracle of *forgiving love*.

Forgiveness is the wiping out of an unrepayable debt. Think of the parable in which the debtor owed his lord the tidy sum of one hundred million dollars and had not a red cent with which to pay, and his master canceled the whole debt (Matt. 18:23). But here it is more than that, for forgiveness is more than the canceling of a debt.

It is the erasing of the ineradicable; it is the covering up of that which cannot be covered; it is the silencing of that which continues to cry out; it is *a miracle*.

If we should be inclined to balk at the idea of a substitution, of the fulfillment of an untransferable obligation by someone else, we had better think twice, for then we ought to balk at forgiveness too. We must balk, too, at what is the very essence of God's love and grace; his love for those who have in no wise deserved it. Then it must be that we are still proud enough to think that we can make ourselves worthy of heaven.

Of course forgiveness goes counter to what we think is just. This is the very meaning of God's love: it breaks through the order of justice. It is precisely so with the idea of substitution. We must recognize the meaning of humility, of forgiveness, of love, before we are ready to allow that Christ fulfilled the whole will and law of God in our place and as our substitute. Our pride must really be broken before we will let another carry that burden which we are strictly obliged to carry ourselves.

Inclusive Substitution

Without meaning to detract in the least from the sheer miracle of it, without meaning to tone it down in any way, there is nevertheless something to be said for the idea of a substitutionary obedience and bearing of punishment. Let us think of it in this way: We are back again with the family of which we spoke before. The father asks each of his children to clean up his own room in his absence and have everything neat and tidy for his return. But all the children go out to play except one. He stays and does the work. And why does he do it? He does it not because he wants to stand well with his father; he does it simply because he loves his father, and because he loves his brothers and sisters. As he does their work he is thinking only of them; he wants to draw them into the same obedience and love. Somehow, by doing their work, he hopes to make them repentant and henceforth obedient too. He cannot fulfill their obligation; he cannot do their loving; but he can by his love draw forth their love and obedience. And when the father comes home and the children face a well-deserved punishment for willful disobedience, then again the only obedient one can step forward and offer to take that punishment, a punishment he did not deserve but which he gladly bears for love, because he knows that only such vicarious suffering has the power to break a willful, disobedient heart.

Such is the vicarious obedience and suffering of Christ —for men, in their place, in order to draw them into the same obedience. This is the only justification which can be offered for the idea of substitution. Like love and grace, it is sheer miracle which cannot be eliminated from Christianity without removing the heart of the gospel. There are many today who ride this particular issue, and they judge a man's Christianity by whether or not he believes in the vicarious atonement. There is both a decided danger and something commendable about this. The decided danger lies in a wrong emphasis upon the acceptance of a doctrine. The acceptance of a doctrine of the atonement can save no one. Only actually being drawn into the right God-relationship matters, and that can happen even without the acceptance of some doctrine. The other side, however, is that men too often see Jesus as merely a teacher; they see God as only a kindly Father whose business it is to pardon; they see neither God's holiness nor his love in their proper immensity; they reinterpret all references to sacrifice and substitution as remnants of an outmoded and false conception of God. Against such views the idea of substitution cannot be emphasized forcefully enough. Jesus is the Lamb of God that takes away the sins of the world. He actually did fulfill for us the whole will and law of God, and bear our punishment that we might go free.

CHAPTER VII

THE RECONCILER

A Mystery?

Some people act as though the atonement and reconciliation were such a mystery that we cannot even talk intelligently about them—as though it all is something we feel but cannot put into words. This is shallow sentimentality. Very often it is a cover-up for indifference. Usually, in the very effort to avoid setting up a definite theory, a very definite theory is actually set up—sometimes a superficial one which is pleasing to man's pride and leaves out the stumbling block and foolishness of the cross.

We must think about the atonement and reconciliation and try to understand their mystery. Men have employed many parables, analogies, and pictures for this purpose. None is complete, but three of these analogies will be considered in the present chapter. We will focus attention upon the courtroom analogy, the sacrifice analogy, and the dramatic struggle analogy.

The Forensic or Courtroom Analogy

The first picture is one that is taken from the court of law. The prisoner is arraigned before the bar of justice, with nothing to plead but his guilt, and no excuse to offer. Not only is there an advocate to plead his cause, but there is one to take the condemned prisoner's place. The guilty one goes free; the innocent one pays the penalty.

Men have used the picture of a court of law in an attempt to give the semblance of justice to the mystery, for that is the business of a court: to see that strict and impartial justice is done. This is what Anselm, the arch medieval rationalist, tried to do. First he argued that a perfect being unquestionably exists. It is as certain as any demonstration in geometry behind which you write "Q.E.D." The very notion of a perfect being implies that such a being also *is*. Otherwise, of course, it would not be perfect, for what is perfection which has no "embodiment"? Since, then, it is impossible to call the exist-ence of the perfect being into question the rest of Anselm's argument follows by valid implication as in any valid syllogism. There is absolute certainty all along the way for all who have the wit to follow the argument. There is no break in the chain. It's like any problem in mathematics. Once you accept the premise you no longer argue; you just check the figures.

Since there is the perfect being, Anselm argued, he expressed himself in a perfect celestial creation—for how could perfection produce imperfection? Perfection thus created a perfect number of angels. But then, unfortunately, a certain number of these angels fell, destroying the perfect symmetry. So to restore the perfection the perfect being had then to create a world and provide the necessary number of created beings. No sooner said, or even thought, than done! But now—unfortunately and again without rational explanation—the newly created being, listening to the voice of the already fallen angels, also fell. So the perfect thinking-machine goes into action again and grinds out its further valid implications and conclusions. Perfection now dictates why God had to become a man (*Cur deus homo?*). The reasoning is this: The perfect being is also infinite. Any offense or rebellion against an infinite being is, on the basis of strict justice (an aspect of perfection), also infinite. Man, each individual man and mankind as a whole, therefore owes God an infinite debt, which he, being finite, can never repay. You simply cannot get a finite number to cover an infinite one, without having an infinitude left over. Man is therefore wholly lost and must spend the rest of infinity in the debtors prison without a ghost of a chance —unless, of course, the infinite God, once more to restore perfection, does something about it. So God himself becomes a man in order to pay back the infinite debt man owes from man's side. God becomes a man in Jesus Christ and, as a man, he is obedient and he fulfills the whole will and law of God. This is his so-called "active obedience." There is *in this case* no infinite offense against an infinite being and so all is even. Since, however, this is what man owed to God in the first place nothing is left over to apply to the rest of sinful mankind. So Christ innocently suffers a punishment he did not deserve. This is his "passive obedience," his "suffering obedience." At this point the whole medieval idea of merit enters in, particularly the notion of merits of "supererogation," that is, of merits earned over and above what is due. Christ's suffering and death thus supply a treasury of such merits which are to be applied as needed. This is where the arithmetic is important. Since Christ is God, and therefore, infinite, his "passive obedience" (his suffering and death) is also itself infinite. The treasury of merits is infinite and inexhaustible and therefore covers each man's and all mankind's infinite debt. On the scales of justice a balance is struck. At the same time, since Christ is also man, the debt is actually paid from man's side to God. So God's justice is satisfied, perfection is restored, the symmetry is maintained. *Cur deus homo?* Q.E.D.

What a neat rationalization! Is there any truth in it? If, of course, the argument were valid in the way in which Anselm thought, we would be spared all the agony of believing; we would simply be certain without any possibility of doubt. There is, however, a great difference between simply pursuing the rational cogency of an argument of abstract ideas and actually having to trust an unseen God and take him at his word. Moreover, nowhere in the Bible, as we have already pointed out, is God dealt with as a "perfect being." He is the God of holy love. Now Anselm's whole notion of "perfection" was no doubt colored by this and here we get the real clue as to what may after all be valid in Anselm's noble attempt at apology. He begins his so-called "ontological proof" (proving the existence of a perfect being) with the prayer to the living God of his fathers that he might, to his glory, be able to carry off the argument successfully. He, therefore, begins with faith. So also in his *Cur deus homo?* his burden is that of the greatness of man's offense against the God of holy love—an offense which makes man's case hopeless unless indeed God himself does something about it.

"Have you not considered how ponderous (how unbearable, how crushing) is the burden of man's sin?" This is the real biblical premise from which Anselm operates. Christian piety, from Peter and Paul on down, has always felt this: "You know that you were ransomed from the futile ways inherited from your fathers, not with perishable things such as silver or gold, but with the precious blood of Christ, like that of a lamb without blemish or spot" (1 Pet. 1:18 f.). "While we were yet helpless, at the right time Christ died for the ungodly. Why, one will hardly die for a righteous man—though perhaps for a good man one will dare even to die. But God shows his love for us in that while we were yet sinners Christ died for us. Since, therefore, we are now justified by his blood, much more shall we be saved by him from the wrath of God" (Rom. 5:6 ff.). "He has redeemed me, a lost and condemned person, saved me at great cost from sin, death, and the power of the devil —not with silver or gold, but with his holy and precious blood and his innocent suffering and death" (Martin Luther in the Small Catechism).[1]

God did have to become involved, he did have to "become a man." But the constraint upon him was love and not merely justice. Only God was sufficient in his love to conquer and appease his own wrath. Only God could take the punishment man deserved upon himself. Only God could really by his own suffering make it right. But, if we stick to the courtroom analogy, we see how this springs all the bounds of justice. No just court (as we said above, p. 126), will allow that the innocent suffer for the guilty. Therefore, it is not justice that has now been done. No! The seriousness of man's sin has been maintained, *while love has been triumphant!*

The Sacrifice Analogy

A second picture is that from the Old Testament ceremonial of sacrifice. By means of continued sacrifices the sense of guilt and the need of constant forgiveness were kept alive. A perfect lamb, without spot or blemish, is offered to God. It is a perfect life, dedicated wholly to God, that is represented by the blood poured out. So fortified, the high priest, the mediator, enters into the holy place and sprinkles the blood upon the mercy seat. It is a perfect substitute which lays down its innocent life for a guilty people. This sacrifice was fulfilled in Christ, the one, pure, true, immortal Sacrifice.

But who brings the sacrifice, and what is the sacrifice? It is never man, from his side, offering up a sacrifice to God in order to appease him or cause him to be favorably disposed. This is the difference between the pagan sacrifices which man offered to God in appeasement and those sacrifices which God always himself provided. It is, as we sing in the Communion hymn, "Offered was He for greatest and for least, Himself the Victim and Himself the Priest." This is altogether God's doing, from beginning to end. It is God atoning, God making it good again, God suffering, God bringing and being the sacrifice.

When it is said that this sacrifice analogy does not speak to men today I disagree. Of course, our situation is not the same as that of biblical times. We are not surrounded by pagan altars on every high hill. Some of us scarcely "know" any sheep, goats, or oxen from "personal" acquaintance, other than as they appear on our dinner plates all aromatic and "drool arousing." We do not ever bother to have our squeamish stomachs overturned by a visit to the monstrosity of a slaughterhouse. But this does not mean that we, the great moderns, have no appreciation of sacrifice and, precisely, of the sacrifice of the innocent in the place of the guilty for the sake of a greater good. Our whole life is woven of the warp and woof of vicarious sacrifice. Mothers and fathers sacrifice themselves for their children. Each one of us is born of a mother's pain (or was until they invented caudal anesthesia). The pride of every nation's youth is sacrificed in times of war for the sake of peace with justice, while the rest, as Thomas Wolfe says, "batten on their brothers' blood." We live and laugh and eat and sing only by the toil and sweat of others—that is, if we are fortunate enough to be among those who can live and laugh and eat and sing. While we sleep or play or just sit in the sunshine and dream, there are thousands who go on toiling, not only risking, but giving their lives, in mines and tunnels beneath the earth, on the high seas, in torrid desert heat, on the frigid, snowswept wastes, all over the earth and sea and sky, building bridges, keeping watch, fighting fires, wars, pestilence, hunger, death. Men are constantly giving their lives that others may live. *This is for real, man!*[2] The innocent suffer vicariously for the guilty! Is then "the lamb of God, slain for the sins of the world" such an impossible and unintelligible symbol —even for twentieth-century man? Even he knows how defenseless, how harmless, a lamb is, and how it does not cry out when it is brought to the slaughter. Are Isaiah's words not intelligible?

> Surely he has borne our griefs and carried our sorrows; yet we esteemed him stricken, smitten by God, and afflicted. But he was wounded for our transgressions, he was bruised for our iniquities; upon him was the chastisement that made us whole, and with his stripes we are healed. All we like sheep have gone astray; we have turned every one to his own way; and the Lord has laid on him the iniquity of us all. He was oppressed, and he was afflicted, yet he opened not his mouth; like a lamb that is led to the slaughter, and like a sheep that before its shearers is dumb, so he opened not his mouth (Isa. 53:4 ff.).

The Dramatic Struggle Analogy

The third picture is that of a dramatic struggle between good and evil, between God and Satan, between God and all his enemies. The death of Christ is the great victory in this battle. It is as though an impregnable fort had been stormed and the prisoners within set free. If we remember the humanness of the analogy we may say this: Every man is vulnerable because of his sin. Each has his Achilles' heel which the river Styx did not touch, and where a fatal weapon may penetrate. Or, like Siegfried in the German saga, each has a spot on his back into which a treacherous Hagan may plunge his spear.

159

Such men cannot be liberators. If, however, there were someone really invulnerable, he would be able to take even the strongest fortress and nothing could stop him, not even an atom bomb. Such an invulnerable one was the one who knew no sin and yet was made sin for us, that we might be made the *righteousness of God in him*.

This third analogy is claimed by many to be the basic New Testament one which prevailed throughout the early centuries of the church.[3] It was then followed by the forensic or courtroom analogy as the medieval idea of merit took over. Finally, it was reemphasized by Luther at the time of the Reformation. The analogy itself has been presented in all kinds of queer forms. For example, Jesus' humanity was once regarded as the bait God used to lure the Devil on. But when the Devil snapped he was caught on the hidden hook of Jesus' divinity. And Luther's use of this analogy was always in terms which appear to us to be brutally, almost crudely, realistic. No one had quite such an appreciation of the awful, mysterious power of the Evil One, the Devil, whose subtle wiles and overwhelming power should never be underestimated. Hence Luther saw all of life as a bitter struggle between God and the forces of evil. The prize in this struggle was man himself and the battle never ended as long as life lasted. We have already quoted Luther as saying, "Man always worships either God or an idol." That is because, as he also said, "either God or the Devil always rides man." But in this battle, one which will go on until the end of time, the decisive victory has already been won. There has been a crucial turning point and the eventual outcome is no longer in doubt. It is like the battle of Gettysburg in the Civil War, the struggle that marked the decisive turning point. Although there were many bitterly contested battles and the toll of the dead continued, the issue was once and for all decided. So it is with the cross of Christ. There the decisive, once-and-for-all victory has been won. Therefore the Devil, though he still "prowls around like a roaring lion seeking some one to devour" (1 Pet. 5:8), *has had it.* The usual English translation of Luther's explanation of the second article of the Creed is misleading when it is made to say that our Lord "has purchased and won us from all sins, from death, and from the power of the Devil." This sounds as though it were nothing but a calm transaction over the bargain counter. Nothing could be further from the truth. The German is *erworben und gewonnen* meaning "earned and won" with all the overtones of a mighty, bitter struggle. The victory was not accomplished with silver or gold at the bargain counter, but only on the battlefield, where innocence was constantly assailed without giving in, and where the victory was achieved only at the price of the last full measure of devotion.

Keeping in mind the above three pictures, with the third as the dominant one, let us now look at the doctrine of the atonement in more detail.

The Propitiation

The basis of the atonement is Christ's vicarious (substitutionary) obedience. This obedience is the propitiation for man's sin. This word *propitiation* means "covering up" and is really only a synonym for forgiveness. Christ's obedience covers man's disobedience; in fact, it covers the sins of all the world so that they can no longer be seen of God. The psalmist speaks of all his righteousness as but filthy rags in the sight of God. Here is a different sort of righteousness, the righteousness of Christ, which is sufficient to cover all our filthy rags.

Recall Jesus' parable of the wedding garment. At the feast provided by the king there was one guest who did not have on a wedding garment and he was summarily cast out. When guests were invited to an Oriental wedding not only was the food provided, but wedding garments as well. All who sat at the feast must be fittingly arrayed and none must mar its beauty or say that he was there by anything but the king's bounty and largess. But here was one guest who had disdained that wedding garment. Perhaps he had said to himself: "I will go just the way I am, and if the king doesn't like it he can lump it. Besides, I would look funny in that borrowed finery." So men insist on appearing before God in their own righteousness. Just listen to them and you will hear how disdainful they are of having to appear before God in borrowed finery when they have all that finery of their own —all the nice things they have said and done. Yet, there is only one proper wedding garment:

> Jesus, Thy Blood and righteousness
> My beauty are, my glorious dress;
> Midst flaming worlds, in these arrayed,
> With joy shall I lift up my head.

We should take special note of the peculiar biblical meaning of the words "propitiation" and "righteousness." When we hear the word "propitiate" we tend to think of it in the pagan sense of man doing something in order to "placate," "soothe the displeasure of," "win the favor of" the gods. We think of sacrifices of all kinds from the first fruits of the field, the "burnt offerings of calves a year old . . . thousands of rams . . . ten thousands of rivers of oil . . . , [to the] first-born, the fruit of [the] body, for the sin of [the] soul" (Mic. 6:6 f.). This is at best a futile gesture on the part of man to give expression to his dependence and thankfulness; at worst it is a desperate effort to twist God's arm, to win his favor and manipulate him to our desires. In the Old Testament, however, the Hebrew equivalent of the word "propitiate" means "to cover up" and, significantly, it is God who does the covering up, not man. As was pointed out in connection with the notion of sacrifice, it is God who provides the sacrifice, whose blood hides the sin. We must remember that it is not the blood itself, which in some magic way, possesses this efficacy. How many million gallons of blood would it take to cover the sins of the world? The life is in the blood. It is the life that is given unselfishly for others which has the blotting out quality. "We have an advocate with the Father, Jesus Christ the righteous; and he is the expiation [propitiation] for our sins, and not for ours only but also for the sins of the whole world" (1 John 2:1 f.).

The same caution must be repeated concerning the term "righteousness," so that it is understood in its peculiarly biblical (Pauline) sense. Usually we think of "righteousness" as a quality or characteristic of a person, in virtue of which he himself is righteous, upright, just, free of blame. So the "righteousness of God," of which Paul speaks in Romans (1:17) tends also to be thought of as a characteristic of God, in virtue of which he, above all, is righteous in himself. This, of course, is true. However, Paul means more than that. He means God's outgoing righteousness which proceeds from him and makes others righteous. The "propitiation" and the "righteousness" must therefore be held together. It is the active, outgoing righteousness of God manifested in Jesus, the Christ, which is the propitiation, that is, the covering, for the sins of the world.

Satisfaction

This propitiation, then, covers man's sins and the sins of all the world in the obedience of Christ. Now, properly understood, both God's holiness and his love are satisfied. We ought not to split God's holiness from his love and yet, if we are to discuss them at all, we cannot avoid doing so. God's holiness can brook no sin. It is like a consuming fire; it must devour all impurities like chaff. Where, however, the obedience of Christ covers the sins of men, there God's holiness is satisfied. There are no impurities now to be consumed, there is only righteousness; the holy God need not have fellowship with sin, for the sin is seen no more, it is covered. And so God's love, which desires nothing but the salvation of the sinner and union with him, is also satisfied. Both holiness and love are triumphant, for each has attained its objective. Sin is purged and the sinner is saved. In order to achieve the end of his holiness, which is to get rid of sin, God has employed his love; and in order to achieve the end of his love, which is to unite himself with the sinner, God has employed his holiness. The one has been employed by the other as the means to its end.

The whole is therefore a work of love. We have said that we can never say anything about God in abstraction, apart from his relation to us. God's love manifests itself in different ways, in the form of a creative bringing forth, or of ordering law, or of wrath at man's disobedience, or of saving righteousness. Again this must qualify and enlarge our neat division of the chores between God's holiness and love. The oneness of God's act must not be split up; the work of atonement, reconciliation, and redemption is one continuous act of the one God.

A vicarious obedience, which serves as a covering for sin and thereby satisfies God's holiness and love! That is the foundation. The result is twofold. There is one result for man's relationship to God, and another result for man's relationship to those powers to which God has abandoned him on account of his sin.

Reconciliation

Let us consider first the God-relationship. Because man's sins are covered there is a change in the relationship between God and man, for the word reconciliation means a *change*. It is significant that the change is in the *relationship*, not in either God or man. We must be most careful not to allow foreign notions, characteristic of so much religion, to creep in. Above all, the direction is from God to man, and not from man to God. If there is any change it is because God, not man, brings it about. The heathen mean to propitiate (appease) their gods by the sacrifices which they bring or the good works which they perform. With these they mean to change the god's mind or attitude. The god is angry or indifferent, so the heathen makes quite an impression on him with his performance until the god finally breaks down and gives the successful suppliant what he wants. So the priests of Baal hoped to bring fire down from heaven with their frenzied shouts and bloody slashings. Elijah, however, simply left it up to God whether he would vindicate himself or not. Elijah did not think that he had power to coerce God, not even by "faith."

It is both impossible and unnecessary for God to change. God cannot change. That would be contrary to his nature, and we have already said that the greatest demonstration of omnipotence lies in being able to be true to yourself. God need not change, moreover, because God *is love* and need not first be brought around to loving. It was *love* that prompted the whole act of redemption in the first place, and so we can hardly say that the carrying out of it would result in a change of heart.

As far as man is concerned, it is impossible for him to change himself. If man could change his heart, if he could make himself into the kind of creature that he ought to be, then an act of atonement would not be necessary. But this is precisely what man cannot do. The change which takes place is therefore a change in the relationship between God and man. God and man are reconciled, that is to say, *the wrath-relationship is changed into a peace-relationship.* "You, who once were estranged . . . he has now reconciled. . . ." (Col. 1:21 f.).

We can say that though a father loves his son uninterruptedly, nevertheless, because of the son's willful disobedience a real wrath-relationship may prevail between the two. Authority has been defied; a rightful order has been violated; honor has been besmirched; the relationship is not right. So it is in the relationship between God and man. His supreme authority has been defied; his holy name has been besmirched; his boundless love has been spurned; the relationship just is not right. Instead of running joyfully to meet his Lord, Adam cries out in fear: "I heard the sound of thee in the garden, and I was afraid . . . and I hid myself." Instead of unclouded communion there are the terrors of a guilty conscience and the frantic efforts to make amends. But where, for Christ's sake, God has forgiven man and has accepted him in love, all this is changed. There is peace.

Redemption

The second result of the covering of sin is redemption, the freeing from those powers to which God himself has abandoned man because of his guilt. Redemption means literally release as the result of the payment of a ransom. The act of redemption may be the act of the one who pays the ransom, or it may be the act of the one who receives the ransom and then sets the prisoner free. In this case it is the act of the one who pays the ransom as well as the act of the one who receives the ransom, for curiously enough, this is the same person. In both instances it is God.

Men have sometimes said that the ransom was paid to the Devil, and that it was therefore the Devil who had to set men free. This rests upon a complete misunderstanding, for the Devil could have no power over man unless it were given him of God. God has not abdicated his absolute sovereignty over all the world. Even the Devil and all his angels are under God's rule and domain. The ransom money, therefore, was paid by God, so to speak, to himself, and then he himself set the prisoners free. This may seem to be a very curious, illogical sort of transaction, but it is no more curious and illogical than the love and grace of God. They are the miracle, and our theories about them can only serve to establish that fact. The ransom money that was paid was, of course, not gold or silver, but Jesus' holy and precious blood, and his innocent suffering and death. So even the ransom itself is God. We should therefore keep in mind the analogy of the dramatic struggle, the storming of the fortress by the invulnerable one, and not just that of a ransom being paid. Through this ransom and victory we are delivered from the guilt and power of sin.

From the Guilt of Sin

Guilt is a peculiar thing. It is the feeling of having failed in a responsibility, with the anguished certainty that it can never be made right. If money were stolen, it could be repaid; if property were smashed, it could be rebuilt, even if it took a billion years. But what of the fact that you were once unfaithful to a trust, that you once hated when you should have loved, that you once repaid a kindness with bitterness? How will you erase such facts? The billion years will not help now. Every effort to make amends is only a fresh confession of guilt. And it is not primarily a matter of individual acts of the past; it is above all a matter of a present sinful state from which a man cannot extricate himself. Only Jesus' victory, his obedience, his love, have the miraculous power to take away the guilt. The good news is therefore all caught up, in those liberating words, "Your sins are forgiven you." This gets rid of all the hidden, festering garbage, with one thorough cleansing. This is not just a piecemeal matter of this sin or that. It is the whole guilty, sinful being who is forgiven, counted clean and whole, and accepted. It is other than just the assurance, "So you accept me, slob that I am." All the slobbishness is itself washed away. A man is what he knows he should be and wants to be: clean, whole, upright!

From the Power of Sin

We are freed not only from the guilt of sin, but also from its power. Man does remain a sinner throughout life. But when man comes to faith in Christ a new man is born in him, a man who is actually a sinner no longer. We are always at the same time righteous and a sinner.

This is one of the insights which Luther restored to Christianity, but which was so quickly lost again. Men either simply rested in the thought of the divine forgiveness and the fact that they were clothed with Christ's righteousness, or else, realizing that a change had come over them, forgot that they were sinners still.

With the victory of Christ a new era has begun. God has started his mankind anew from the second Adam. Those who are born anew in him are new creatures (2 Cor. 5:17). What Christ was, they have now become also. He who is a reborn child of God really loves his father with an unfeigned and unselfish love. He does do what the first Adam failed to do, and what the old Adam within him still fails to do. He is straightened out. The direction of his life is no longer away from God and toward the world and the self, but toward God and his kingdom. Everything that we said before about the old sinful nature is true no longer of this nature. The power of selfishness is broken; the selfless love of Christ himself lives in the reborn child of God. The heart once turned in upon itself has found its proper center outside of itself. A man has been restored to true *life together in love*. This is the Christ in us. But, as we will develop further, the old Adam is also still there and the lifelong struggle between the old and the new continues.

From the Curse of the Law

The law is a cruel taskmaster, a heartless, relentless tyrant. The demands of the law are inexorable, driving a man from one task to the next, never satisfied that he has done enough. Luther experienced this in its full rigor. This drove him into the monastery and caused him to fast and scourge himself in vain efforts to fulfill the demands of the law. What troubled Luther was that he knew that he did not love his fellow monks as God's law demanded. He felt the power of pride and envy and a hot temper, and try as he might he could not win a complete victory over the stirrings within him. God himself appeared monstrous to him, whipping him with the scourge of the law, demanding of him the impossible. Luther would not tone down the demands; he would not let a few *pater nosters,* hastily murmured, take the place of real love.

One of the most magnificent scenes in John Osborne's *Luther*[4] is that of the monks confessing their petty sins—how they had cheated on the count of their *pater nosters,* or failed to fast, or reneged at their turn with the begging bowl, and other trivial externalities. And then Luther groans out his awful, "I am a worm and no man," and he falls prostrate, absolutely rigid in one of his catatonic fits. What bothered him was not the trivial, external omissions. Contrary to popular opinion it was not the pull of sexual passion either, normal as this no doubt was for a man of his age and temper. What bothered him was that he knew he was supposed to love those sniveling, surly, evil-smelling, jealous, self-seeking, back-biting, cowardly, mercenary, vile, wretched fellow monks of his, with their pious posings and hypocritical fawning. He was supposed to love them and he hated their stinking guts. And he was supposed to trust God and take him at his word and yet he didn't and couldn't. He hated the God who demanded impossible things of him even more than he hated those stinking monks. So he cried out, like St. Paul, "The evil I do not want is what I do. . . . Who will deliver me from this body of death?" (Rom. 7:19, 24). So he increased his efforts, prayed more earnestly, fasted more rigorously, abused himself to the very point of death. No wonder that he could see the law only as an enemy and never as a friend. *Lex semper accusat:* the law always accuses. Only the gospel comforts and gives peace. The gospel must never be made into a new law and the relentless rigor of the law must never be diminished if everything is not to go wrong. Peace came only when Luther realized that Jesus, by fulfilling the law, had freed him from its tyranny. Where there is forgiveness for Christ's sake the law is no longer in force.

The Christian is a free man subject to no one. The law's demands have been fulfilled and God can therefore call off the hounds that pursue the poor sinner. This is again the *Christ for us.* But there is also the *Christ in us.* Those who are in Christ are ruled by love and not by law. They freely do God's bidding.

Freedom from the law is a fact insofar as a man is reborn. But we dare never forget the Christian's predicament. The old Adam is still within him, and insofar as that old Adam is still there a man is still under law; the law must still be his schoolmaster to bring him to Christ in daily repentance; it is still the big stick which must restrain him from the path of evil and self-destruction through fear of punishment; it still is the rule by which he must guide his life in order that love may not be merely a pious sentiment. Wherever men live together they must be under rules whether this be for work or for play. These rules must be just and fair and must be obeyed whether one is inclined to do so or not. Otherwise no living or playing together is possible. This goes for the Christian as well as the non-Christian. It is true of the home, the school, and every area of human relations. The more intimate and personal the relation, of course, the more one can dispense with rules, but even in the most intimate and personal relation, let us say the marriage relation, there have to be rules to be obeyed, just because the sinful human being cannot be trusted always to be just and fair to the other's rights and needs without this coercion of the rule. Such rules are always connected with coercion, in however subtle a form; it need not be the razor strop in the woodshed or an atom bomb, but rules are always connected with fear and punishment of some sort. These rules should never be confused with love (*agape*), which is free and spontaneous, uncoerced, and unconcerned about reward or punishment. They are, however, the necessary form which love (*agape*) must take under certain circumstances. In that sense the law, although it will not redeem a man, is good and can be the believer's delight: "I delight in thy law. . . . The law of thy mouth is better to me than thousands of gold and silver pieces" (Ps. 119:70 ff.). No Christian, however, should suppose that he can fulfill the whole will and law of God by being obedient to a set of rules. With these rules he must begin, but love springs all rules and does what in each moment is for the fulfillment of that moment's real needs. So, for the Christian the Sermon on the Mount does not give a new set of rules or principles but the paradigms of love, only examples of how love behaves under certain circumstances. We shall have more to say about this later.

From the Power of Death

Again we must proceed from the right premises. If we see death merely as an incident in a process of evolution from the lower to the higher, merely a moment of transition when the immortal soul is released from its prison, the body, then Christ's victory over death is nothing. At best it can be only the demonstration that the soul is immortal and that every person survives death and decay. But there can be small comfort in that, if the judgment is still to be faced. No! We must first see death as the wages of sin. This, however, is not to say that sin is the *cause* of death. Death is caused by all kinds of things, old age, a lethal germ, an accident, etc. Death is part of all finitude. It is every living being's destiny. To say that "death is the wages of sin" is not a physiological statement but a theological one. Death is what man has earned and deserves because of his sin. "We are consumed by thy wrath" (Ps. 90:7). Each man for himself must face death as the last enemy into whose power God himself has given him on account of his sin. Death is the intruder in God's world as the fruit of disobedience. Death is foulness, decay, the opposite of life and health; and human death is willed by God in his world in order

174

to make clear God's answer to sin. Whenever men sin they are in revolt against God; they are saying that they can have access to the tree of life, that they can have life apart from God; that they can take their lives from themselves and from the world instead of from God. But God says, "No!" He puts an end to man's proud pretensions. "In the day that you eat of it you shall die." That is God's judgment upon sin. "We bear about us our mortality, the witness of our sin" (St. Augustine).

It is not a remnant of outmoded superstition to speak of the terrors of death. The people who admit they are afraid to die are more honest than those who smother graves with flowers and act as though death were beautiful. There is no argument, no scientific observation, and no advance or inside knowledge available about death, as is claimed by longhaired yogis whom silly women follow. "We all die like amateurs, because none of us gets any practice." Jesus did not come just to give us inside information about life after death, though he did say that there are many mansions in the Father's house. Jesus came, first of all, to win a victory over death. He did so in that moment when, burdened with all the sins of humanity, he felt himself abandoned, and yet he clung in confidence to his heavenly Father. It is on this basis that death loses its terrors.

He who trusts in Christ no longer fears death. Yet it is a constant struggle. Ever and again God's love must break through the manifestations of his wrath; ever and again man's love for God must triumph over his fear of him and his just condemnation. There is no still, untroubled sea; there is always only the calm after the storm. Or better, while the waves on the surface are continually tossed about, deep down below the waters lie absolutely still and unruffled. This is the peace of God that passes all understanding.

From the Power of Satan

Whether we are dealing in biblical categories or have substituted some neat little scheme of our own which our minds can handle will become apparent at this point. There is in God's world the mystery of the evil one, the personal adversary of God. Each of these words is said advisedly. Here is a mystery which remains for us unsolved in this life, and the more we know about life the greater the mystery becomes. It is "the evil one," because, without reducing the Devil to a hideous monster with tails and horns and red asbestos underwear, we can conceive of any active power only in personal terms, granting the full mystery that remains even when we use this term. And this evil one is God's unequivocal, final enemy who contends with him for mastery of the world.

This is God's world. He is its omnipotent ruler. He has never abdicated to the prince of this world. No matter how strong the forces of evil in the world they are still under God's control and he turns them to his purposes. God has not called up a Frankenstein monster which has gotten out of control. Whatever power Satan has, therefore, he has only because God permits him to have it, as the instrument of his punishment. The greatest mystery now lies in the fact that at the cross Satan was utterly and completely routed. Here that proud enemy of God, who will not let God be God, went down in defeat before that One who did in all earnestness let God be God. When Satan appears before God's throne he contends that there is no one who will serve God for naught. But there is One, and before him Satan went down in defeat. Christ contended with the tempter, who used all his wiles to get Christ, too, to revolt, but Christ was victor in the strife. This is a human way of speaking about the final conquest of evil.

But here is the mystery. In eternity the victory is won; in time the struggle goes on and will go on until the end of time. This is nothing other than to say that it is only in faith that we are victors. "This is the victory that overcomes the world, our faith" (1 John 5:4). In faith I know that I am a child of God, translated from the kingdom of darkness into that of marvelous light, freed from sin, death, and the power of the Devil. In faith I know that there is a resurrection on the other side of death, and a complete fulfillment in a new heaven and a new earth. But the struggle nevertheless goes on, otherwise there would be no occasion for faith. The Devil still goes about as a roaring lion seeking whom he may devour. Very real forces of evil are still being continually released, and I must fight if I would win; I must resist unto blood if I would live; I must be faithful unto death if I would receive the crown. Yet in all this struggle I have peace, for the victory has been won, and in faith I am already beyond the battle. I have arrived.

177

Summary

Without meaning to reduce the reconciliation and redemption to a neat rational scheme, we may set up this scheme to represent what Christ has done for us in reconciling us to God and redeeming us: God was in Jesus, the Christ, and as a true man this Jesus rendered perfect obedience unto God, thereby covering the sins of the world and satisfying both God's holiness and love. The result is that with respect to man's relationship to God there is reconciliation, and the wrath-relationship is changed into one of peace. With respect to those powers which God has delivered man on account of his sin, there is redemption; man is redeemed from sin, as well as from the curse of the law, from death, and from the power of the Devil. Upon all this the resurrection is the seal. It is God's stamp of approval upon the work of redemption. Because Christ lives we too shall live.

The Resurrection of Our Lord

Without the resurrection of the Lord all that we have said would be meaningless; the cross would be a tragedy and not the victory we have acclaimed it. Without a risen, living Lord, the church of Jesus Christ, worshiping him as Lord, celebrating his presence, awaiting his coming again in glory, is unthinkable. Today, as often before in the church's history, the resurrection is being bitterly contested. Some say that it never happened as an actual event. It only testifies to the meaning of the crucifixion. The notion of a body rising from the tomb and leaving

178

it empty is pious legend. It is an attempt at "objectifica-tion," that is, of making obvious to the senses what can be seen only with the "eyes of faith." Others, in contrast, insist that there was an actual physical resurrection, that the corpse was resuscitated and walked about on the earth until it was taken up from the earth back to heaven.

The question is whether or not these represent the only possible alternatives: On the one hand, the whole notion of a preexistent being who comes down to earth from a heaven above the sky, lives on it for a while, dies on the cross, rises on the third day leaving the tomb empty, appears to sundry individuals, eats and drinks with them to prove his corporeality, then ascends before their eyes up to the heaven from which he came, from where he was expected to return during their lifetime—all this is dismissed as "mythology." It is tied up with belief in a three-story universe: a flat earth, the abode of men; the heavens above, the abode of God; and the bowels of earth, the abode of the "shades" of the dead and of evil spirits. There is easy traffic between these three abodes. Angels and evil spirits come and go, causing good and bad events. All this is no longer a possibility today when we know we live in a universe of which our planetary system is only the tiniest of specks.[5] We do not live in a world of angels and demons but of Salk vaccines and miracle drugs. Moreover, the whole notion of the coming of the heavenly being has been exploded because his expected return during the lifetime of his disciples did not materialize. Therefore, the whole "myth" must be reinterpreted to understand the meaning behind it. And this meaning is simply that God opens up a new future for those who have faith as Jesus had faith. The past is covered by forgiveness and so a new possibility arises out of the death of the old. This happens wherever the word of the cross as the complete self-giving of love is proclaimed. The crucifixion of Jesus of Nazareth is an actual event in history, but the stories of the resurrection and ascension are pious legend, not essential to Christian faith. This in very abbreviated form—and, therefore, a form which cannot do full justice to all that is involved— is the one alternative.

The only other alternative seems to be the literalistic one. Jesus, as the Christ, did come from another realm. He lived on the earth as a divine-human being. He actually died on the cross. Then he first showed himself to the spirits of the departed (not necessarily in a place in the bowels of the earth, but wherever they might be), and then on the third day he arose with the same body in which he had died, leaving the tomb empty. In this body he again walked the earth as he had once done. He convinced his disciples that he was not a "ghost"; he ate and drank with them; he presumably made himself available to all the senses of sight, touch, hearing, smell, taste. Of course, the body was not exactly like the body in which he had walked the earth before; it was a "glorified" body and, therefore, not subject to the same limitations as before—it came out of the tomb before the stone was rolled from the sepulchre, it passed through closed doors; it appeared and disappeared at will. Nevertheless, it was still earthbound and must go from place

180

to place; it was not everywhere present. The final change took place only at the ascension. Then he left the earth and never appeared on earth again so that he could be seen or touched. His presence now is of a different kind, a presence in the "Spirit" and therefore not just "physical." It is the "glorified" body which is present where two or three are gathered in his name, and which is present in the Lord's Supper in a peculiar way. This, again in a far too abbreviated form that cannot do justice to the view, is the other alternative.

Now the question is whether or not these two alternatives really exhaust the possibilities. There is, however, another possibility which regards the resurrection neither as a pious legend, nor as a way to the discernment of the true meaning of the cross, nor as a literal resuscitation of a corpse which is "proved" in various ways. The presupposition of this view is that the testimony of the New Testament is tied up with the world view of that day, and, therefore, does need to be interpreted. The simple notion of a preexistent heavenly being coming down from above, going up again, and someday returning is only one of the ways in which the New Testament speaks, and in so speaking it needs to be interpreted to reveal the meaning behind it. This we have tried to do by speaking of the action of God in condescension, self-emptying, entering fully into our human flesh and earthly condition.

This view sees that the *birth* of Jesus is witnessed to in various ways as a unique event. The witness, however, is clearly a testimony of faith. The night in which Jesus

181

was born as the Christ was, as far as anyone who just happened to be around was concerned, like any other night. The stars shone silently as ever, the heavens did not ring out, the angelic chorus did not appear for all to see. That God was acting in a unique way in fulfillment of prophecy was completely "hidden" as God's actions always are. We need not in any way sell short this testimony, as long as we keep in mind that whenever there is an attempt to make directly discernible what can be testified to only in "faith" we have to interpret what is meant without trying to force ourselves to believe what we can't believe. The world of today is not any different from the world of two thousand years ago. What does not happen now did not happen then. If angels do not literally appear as God's messengers now, they did not do it then. If devils do not cause disease now, they did not do it then. The God who ordered the world is faithful to his order. But this does not mean that God did not act in a unique way and that the meaning of this event cannot be testified to in a variety of ways.

When we come to the actual *life* of Jesus of Nazareth we discover that scholars have tried their best to get behind the New Testament witness of faith and arrive at the real historical Jesus, the man as he really was to his contemporaries, unencumbered by the later testimony. But this has been for the most part a vain quest.[6] On the one extreme we are left with only bare statements from extra-canonical sources that a man Jesus lived and was crucified. At the other extreme man's imagination runs riot to produce the greatest variety of characterizations from zealous revolutionary to impractical idealist. In between we have all kinds of attempts to bring the conflicting testimony into some kind of likely sequence. The New Testament writings are actually not biographies, but only, as someone has said, passion stories with long introductions. Without going into all the details of the fine-toothed criticism to which every line in the New Testament has been subjected by astute scholars over the years we may conclude that there is a sequence of events that roughly follows that of the three so-called Synoptic Gospels (Matthew, Mark, and Luke). On this, there is general agreement: The New Testament writings are the written precipitate, after a period of oral transmission, of the church's witness to Jesus as the Christ. What they witness to as God's action was not directly discernible by the actual contemporaries in time. The miracles which Jesus in all probability performed can all be explained in some other way than by the belief that he actually was the promised Christ. Many of his teachings could be those of the rabbis; those that could not were the very ones that gave offense. In any case, by the time he was brought to trial and found guilty on a charge of blasphemy by the Jewish court and on a charge of disloyalty to the emperor by the Roman governor, there was not a single one of his disciples, who, according to the witness, was not also offended in him.

Once he had died on the cross all hope in him as any kind of a deliverer was shattered. Then, however, something happened which changed all this. *It is the unequivocal witness of the New Testament that his fol-*

lowers were convinced that he was not dead but alive.
Without this certainty there would have been no New
Testament and certainly no church. As we have said,
tear the resurrection accounts out of the New Testament
and you have stark tragedy and not victory. So Peter
preached on the first Pentecost:

> Jesus of Nazareth, a man attested to you by God with
> mighty works and wonders and signs which God did
> through him in your midst, as you yourselves know—this
> Jesus, delivered up according to the definite plan and
> foreknowledge of God, you crucified and killed by the
> hands of lawless men. But God raised him up, having
> loosed the pangs of death, because it was not possible
> for him to be held by it (Acts 2:22 ff.).

So Paul wrote in the earliest recorded resurrection witness:

> For I delivered to you as of first importance what I also
> received, that Christ died for our sins in accordance with
> the scriptures, that he was buried, that he was raised on
> the third day in accordance with the scriptures, and that
> he appeared to Cephas, then to the twelve. Then he ap-
> peared to more than five hundred brethren at one time,
> most of whom are still alive, though some have fallen
> asleep. Then he appeared to James, then to all the apostles.
> Last of all, as to one untimely born, he appeared also to
> me. For I am the least of the apostles, unfit to be called
> an apostle, because I persecuted the church of God. But
> by the grace of God I am what I am, and his grace toward
> me was not in vain. On the contrary, I worked harder than
> any of them, though it was not I, but the grace of God
> which is with me. Whether then it was I or they, so we
> preach and so you believe (1 Cor. 15:3-11).

Paul's is the earliest of the resurrection accounts and

try as we may we cannot harmonize it with the others. The number and the sequence of appearances are quite different. There is no mention of an empty tomb nor of an ascension after forty days. Quite unabashedly Paul puts the appearance of Christ to him on a par with the appearances to the first disciples even though this appearance occurred years after the ascension. Paul's account may serve as a guide to our own understanding.

We note first how crucial the resurrection is for Paul. Without it all preaching is vain, those who testify to it misrepresent God, all men are still in their sins and there is no hope of anyone's ever rising from the dead. There is a curious reversal in Paul's witness (1 Cor. 15). Instead of basing the resurrection of others on the resurrection of Jesus, he says, first of all, "if there is no resurrection of the dead, then Christ has not been raised" (vs. 13). That is as much as to say that if there is no sovereign power which can bring life out of death, then neither is Jesus raised from the dead. Paul's concern is that there is a resurrection from the dead and of this resurrection Christ is only "the first fruits of those who have fallen asleep" (vs. 20). No matter that Paul thought this general resurrection would occur during his lifetime —that is not crucial to his argument. What is crucial is the certainty of the resurrection of which Christ was the first fruits of the harvest to come.

The second crucial point is that this resurrection is connected with Jesus' death on the cross. If Jesus had remained dead what possible significance could his death for sin have had? It is only because God raised Jesus from

185

the dead that there is assurance that sins are forgiven. It is the vindication of the sacrifice: to lose life unselfishly for others is to gain it.

The third crucial point for Paul is the manner of the resurrection. "With what kind of body do they come?" It would take volumes to review all the nonsense that has been written, both pro and con, concerning a bodily resurrection. To some this means a reanimating of the same chemical particles that composed the earthly body. But what if all the chemical particles have completely disintegrated after thousands of years without proper mumification or in the split second of an atomic explosion? Does resurrection really mean gathering these same chemical particles up again? They are the perishable components, but St. Paul says, "What is sown is perishable, what is raised is imperishable. It is sown in dishonor, it is raised in glory. It is sown in weakness, it is raised in power. It is sown a physical body, it is raised a spiritual body" (vss. 42-44).

Others have given up the notion of a bodily resurrection entirely. They have followed the Greek notion of the imperishable soul in an earthly prison house. The earthly house falls to pieces, but the soul goes on living. But this is, as we have already noted, an altogether unbiblical depreciation of the body and a denial of the oneness of man, who as a total creature stands over against his maker.

Therefore, St. Paul has an answer different from either of the above. He makes it all hinge on the creative power of God: he who gave man life in the first place will also again give man a body after the dissolution of the old. Paul makes a beautiful comparison between the seed sown into the ground which disintegrates, but out of which there grows a new body which cannot be compared to the seed. Think of any seed and compare it with the finished plant! You can stare at any acorn for a million years and if you had never seen an oak you could never imagine what the acorn could become. So it is with the resurrection body which God will provide.

> You foolish man! What you sow does not come to life unless it dies. And what you sow is not the body which is to be, but a bare kernel, perhaps of wheat or of some other grain. But God gives it a body as he has chosen, and to each kind of seed its own body. For not all flesh is alike, but there is one kind for men, another for animals, another for birds, and another for fish. There are celestial bodies and there are terrestrial bodies; but the glory of the celestial is one, and the glory of the terrestrial is another. There is one glory of the sun, and another glory of the moon, and another glory of the stars; for star differs from star in glory. *So it is with the resurrection of the dead* (vss. 36-41).

The point to be noted now is that it is precisely this kind of a body with which Paul sees Jesus endowed.

> "The first man Adam became a living being"; the last Adam became a life-giving spirit. But it is not the spiritual which is first but the physical, and then the spiritual. The first man was from the earth, a man of dust; the second man is from heaven. As was the man of dust, so are those who are of the dust. Just as we have borne the image of the man of dust, we shall also bear the image of the man of heaven. I tell you this, brethren: flesh and blood can-

not inherit the kingdom of God, nor does the perishable inherit the imperishable (vss. 45-50).

And then he goes on to exult how at the last trumpet's sound

the dead will be raised imperishable and we shall be changed. For this perishable nature must put on the imperishable, and this mortal nature must put on immortality. When the perishable puts on the imperishable, and the mortal puts on immortality, then shall come to pass the saying that is written: "Death is swallowed up in victory." "O death, where is thy victory? O death, where is thy sting?" The sting of death is sin, and the power of sin is the law. But thanks be to God, who gives us the victory through our Lord Jesus Christ (vss. 52-57).

This, then, is how Paul sees the resurrection of Jesus from the dead. This is everything but the resuscitation of a corpse. A resuscitation could take place in the coolness of a tomb after life had seemed to depart on the cross. Doctors have accomplished that through heart massage and there is the prospect that bodies put into a deep freeze may be thawed out again many years later. This always concerns what is still perishable and corruptible and of the earth. What Paul is talking about is a complete transformation from perishable to imperishable. What he sees in the resurrection is not just a temporary return to life, but a complete victory over death itself, for "the last enemy to be destroyed is death" (vs. 26). Paul knows nothing of a temporary resuscitation of the corpse of Jesus. He knows only the resurrected Lord who appears to the disciples, as well as to him, to assure them of the victory over sin and death.

Now we may draw some conclusions from this as far as the resurrection appearances recorded in the Gospels are concerned. Their vital concern is always to give assurance that the Jesus who was dead is actually alive. These appearances really occured. They were not hallucinations. It is quite clear that it was *not* because they expected to see him alive that the disciples then conjured him up in their imaginations. To see him alive again is the one thing they did not expect and according to all accounts the resurrected Lord appeared quite counter to all expectation. This also rules out any connivance on the disciples' part, as though because Jesus said he would rise again they made up the stories of his appearance. In this respect the conflicting, confused accounts of the resurrection, which are impossible to harmonize, are their best vindication. There was no attempt to clean up the accounts and bring them into harmony. They were simply allowed to stand in their stark incongruity, much the same as with any startling event when no two people, unless there has indeed been connivance, tell exactly the same story. Nor was it "faith" that produced the resurrected Lord. It wasn't because the disciples had "faith" in him as the Lord of life, that their "faith" then produced the appearances. This would be the kind of self-induced power that we have already rejected. It was rather the other way around. It was the risen Lord himself who convinced them that he was not dead but alive. So the resurrection appearances were real. They happened. If they happened at all, they happened in history, to men and women of flesh and blood.

Now, however, comes the crucial question. Can these resurrection appearances be put on an exact par with the crucifixion? Obviously not. Anyone who stood on Calvary's hill that day could witness the crucifixion. But who witnessed the resurrection? No one. That is conclusive: no one. And to whom did the resurrected Lord appear? He appeared to whom he chose: "They put him to death by hanging him on a tree; but God raised him on the third day and *made him manifest; not to all the people but to us who were chosen by God as witnesses, who ate and drank with him after he rose from the dead*" (Acts 10:39 ff.). Being a resident in Jerusalem did not, therefore, make one eligible to witness the resurrected Lord. It all depended on God's choice. All the seeming arbitrariness of God's action focuses here. As God chose the people of Israel to be the children of the covenant and to become bearers of his message to the world, so God chose certain ones to be the witnesses of the resurrected Lord and to carry the gospel of the victory over death to the ends of the earth. It was his first choices that started the chain of witnesses. Obviously the experiences these chosen witnesses had of the risen Lord were not shared, common experiences. They were peculiar to the witnesses, as the Christian experience of God always is. The awareness of God's presence is always an "inner awareness." To say this is not to make that presence "unreal." We fox around far too much with that word "real" in any case. Either the risen Christ appeared to the chosen witnesses so that they saw him, heard him, perhaps even touched him and became convinced against their wills that he was not dead but alive—or else he didn't. It is as simple as that, and Christianity stands or falls on this issue.

How, then, is this fact of the resurrection appearances established? Is it established simply as other facts are by piling up the evidence and striving for a high probability which does not necessarily involve you personally? This was the temptation to which the early Christians succumbed from the start. It is possible to trace how the story grew from the initially bare word of testimony to a supposedly guaranteed event. So, to cite only one example, in the apocryphal Gospel of Peter there is the assertion that as Jesus walked out of the tomb he handed the grave cloth that he had had over his face to the centurion keeping watch that he might keep it and show it as a memento and proof of the resurrection. The centurion is one who sees and shows something which obviously could be photographed. So the church became encumbered with all kinds of relics (for example Veronica's veil and the shroud of Turin) which would give a guarantee of the resurrection to the doubter. It is noteworthy that the canonical accounts contain no such *obvious* "objectification," but need we be disturbed if there are nevertheless evidences of a kind of "objectification" still present in the New Testament—like the appearance of angels who point to an empty tomb? This is not to say that the tomb was not empty. Perhaps it was. It is only to say that the empty tomb would prove neither the resurrection of the Lord nor the victory over death. It could always be explained in another way. Moreover, if we recall what St. Paul said about the resurrected body, then it is clear that we are not dealing with the perishable body that was laid into the tomb, although the disciples were convinced that he who appeared to them after the resurrection also ate and drank with them before the resurrection. The identity of the Lord must at all costs be preserved without getting hung up with the chemical particles again.

To recapitulate: the death of a man on the cross, we said, was directly discernible, but not the vicarious, atoning death for the sins of the world. This is not to be made highly probable. The resurrection of the Lord was witnessed by no one and the risen Lord was not seen except by those to whom he made himself visible. This we know only on the testimony of those who had the experience. That they testified to such appearances we can indeed establish with a high degree of probability, for it is the one-voiced witness of all the sources we possess, but whether or not their witness is true cannot be established. It cannot, in view of all the overwhelming counter evidence, be made highly probable, that one single man, out of all the millions who have died, not only came back temporarily and then only to die again, but was victorious over death forever and forever. At this point each man is finally thrown back upon himself as to whether he trusts that this Jesus, as the Christ, died for his sins and was raised for his justification (Rom. 4:25). There at least we are all on a par with those first disciples. We are no longer spectators trying calmly to establish a fact of the distant past. We are now ourselves addressed and involved by the biblical word of testimony. We are now challenged as to whether we really put our trust in the crucified and risen Lord. Did he die for my sins and was he raised for my justification? Do I trust him as my living Lord? We need not think that those first disciples had some kind of advantage because they were the privileged chosen witnesses. The time came for them, too, when the appearances ceased and when they had to live on trust alone. If anything, the temptation to doubt must have increased when the Lord was no longer seen. Why did he who had once appeared refuse to appear again? Why did he not keep his promise and come again? The New Testament closes with these words: "He who testifies to these things says, 'Surely, I am coming soon.' Amen. Come, Lord Jesus! The grace of the Lord Jesus be with all the saints" (Rev. 22:20 f.). This is the confidence in which we all must live and the prayer we must always repeat—that some day faith will turn to sight and we will know even as we are known.

CHAPTER VIII

THE SPIRIT AND
THE LIFE

The Holy Spirit's Work

God's sole purpose in creation was the establishment of the Christian pattern of life which we are calling *community of life together in love*. Sin spoiled this community, but in Christ a new beginning was made, a new state was prepared in which redeemed sinners might recognize and realize their brotherhood. It is essential now that we recognize that men enter into this fellowship only through the power of the Holy Spirit. In considering revelation we said that it is of the essence of revelation that God himself be present in that revelation. Hence the belief that Jesus, the Christ, is very God of very God. We also said that God himself must persuade us that it is he who confronts us, and he himself must cause us to recognize him; he himself must work "faith" in us. We cannot force ourselves to trust God, but such trust is creatively brought forth in us. This, too, therefore, is the work of God, the work of the Holy Spirit. It is the work of sanctification when we are transformed from sinners into saints.

The first Christian community was not established during Christ's lifetime. The Christian community was miraculously brought into being on the first Pentecost, when the ascended Lord, in accordance with his promise, sent the Holy Spirit upon a select group. Pentecost, therefore, is the third great festival of the Church Year, on a par with Christmas and Easter. Christmas and Easter would be meaningless and powerless but for the enlightenment of the Holy Spirit, and there would be no Christian community but for the activity of the Holy Spirit.

It is significant that Pentecost has never been adopted by the non-Christian world as have Christmas and Easter. Christmas can be turned into a sentimental celebration of good will; Easter is a natural for rejoicing in the reappearance of the roses after the death of winter; but what will the non-Christian world do with Pentecost, when its very purpose is to give an altogether different meaning to Christmas and Easter? When, therefore, Pentecost is not celebrated together with Christmas and Easter on an equal basis, it is a sad commentary on the state of Christendom. To the exact degree that Pentecost is minimized, to that degree are Christmas and Easter misunderstood, for they are understood only in the enlightenment of the Holy Spirit.

The Ascension of Our Lord

In the following account we must recall that the New Testament is testimony literature. It is to be taken literally but not literalistically. It is not to be allegorized according to our fancy, but it is to be understood as the writer addressing his situation intended it to be understood. The sequence of events which concerns us now is that given by Luke in the book of Acts. It is a highly stylized account in which numbers, like the forty days after Easter, play a significant role. The author's intent is to make it quite clear that the church did not come into being in the way any school of followers rallies to the master's memory after his death. It came into being only after the resurrected and ascended Lord sent the Counselor to lead men to the truth. The church is, therefore, a divine creation and not just a sociological phenomenon. This account in Acts, however, cannot be harmonized with the account in the Fourth Gospel. There the risen Lord himself gives his Holy Spirit to the apostles and there is no mention of an ascension (John 20:22 f.). Each writer has his own peculiar witness to bear and the exact sequence of events is hidden in the testimony. With this in mind let us look at Luke's testimony without getting bogged down in such silly questions as to whether the miracle of Pentecost was one of hearing or speaking. Let us keep in mind also what we said about Paul's testimony to the resurrection. Luke's account only reinforces what was said there. The resurrection appearances in themselves were not sufficient to give birth to the church, although they were an indispensable element. Not until the Holy Spirit made clear the significance of both crucifixion and resurrection was the church of transformed witnesses born.

According to Luke, forty days went by after the resurrection, during which time the risen Lord showed himself to his disciples on various occasions. Then came the day when these appearances ceased. The Lord ascended into heaven. This ascension stands at the end of Jesus' earthly manifestation, just as the virgin birth stands at the beginning. There it must stand *theologically* if the true significance of the virgin birth is to be recognized. Into the womb of the virgin the eternal preexistent Son of God descended to unite himself with human flesh. It was a divine-human Christ who lived on earth, died on the cross, and on the third day rose again. Then came the day when he returned to the glory from which he had come. He ascended into heaven to sit at the right hand of power. This does not designate a place but a function. Now he was to share again in the rule of the world. The state of humility was ended; the state of exaltation begun. He had performed his prophetic and priestly task on earth. He had made clear the nature and will of God, not just as the last of the prophets but as the one to whom all the prophets pointed. He had entered once and for all into the holy of holies and brought the all-sufficient sacrifice. Now, without ceasing to be prophet and priest, he was also to reign as king. From his throne on high he was to send his Holy Spirit; from there he was to watch over his church; from there he was some day to come again in the clouds of heaven to judge both the living and the dead. But this does not mean that he was to be far away from men. At his ascension he promised: "Lo, I am with you always, to the close of the age" (Matt. 28:20). Luther once said that while Christ was on the earth he was very far away, but now that he is ascended into heaven he is very near. He is present to all men everywhere, and he is among his own in word and sacraments as the gracious one.

The ascension is thus not to be understood as a space journey. It is nothing less than ridiculous to tie up its significance with first-century cosmology. Its profound theological significance is contained in the words, "sitteth at the right hand of God from whence he shall come to judge the quick and the dead." The God who is henceforth present everywhere is not the God who has remained aloof, but the one who has united himself with human flesh. To speak humanly, it is the God who bears the imprints of his sufferings in his hands and feet. It is the God into whose being is taken up the humanity he came to redeem. This is the God who now is everywhere present in his creation and not confined to any place. It is the one who gives himself to us as the God-for-us wherever the gospel is proclaimed and wherever the bread and wine are shared in remembrance of him. At the same time we must also remember that the work of redemption has been completed. It is the work of sanctification that is now going on and, therefore, the presence of God is now preeminently that of the Holy Spirit. We are not to think in spatial terms, of Christ present in heaven or on the earth, but rather in temporal terms: the work of reconciliation and redemption having been completed, the work of sanctification in the power of the Holy Spirit begins and continues until all the harvest is gathered in.

The First Pentecost

When Jesus ascended into heaven, according to Luke, he commanded his disciples to go to Jerusalem and wait there until they should receive power from on high to become his witnesses to the uttermost parts of the earth. We should note well the peculiar break here. Jesus had lived his life of love, he had died on the cross, he had risen again; yet there was no proclamation, there was no community charged with missionary fervor, there were only waiting, puzzlement, fear, misunderstanding. Luke is very clear about this. When the disciples are told to go to Jerusalem to wait for the promise of the Father to be fulfilled, they are still at their old tricks, still thinking in terms of earthly glory and power. They ask: "Lord, will you at this time restore the kingdom to Israel?" Jesus' answer does not deny such an eventual restoration. He says: "It is not for you to know times or seasons which the Father has fixed by his own authority. But you shall receive power when the Holy Spirit has come upon you; and you shall be my witnesses in Jerusalem and in all Judaea and Samaria and to the end of the earth" (Acts 1:7 f.).

Not until fifty days after Easter—ten days after the Ascension—did anything happen. But then it happened. It happened suddenly. It happened from above. It happened at God's initiative. It happened miraculously. It was another advent of God into the world. The Holy Spirit descended to enlighten men's minds, to empower them with zeal, to create the new community. This makes it clear that all this was God's doing, the creative work of the risen Lord.

Waiting, passive men were transformed, empowered, given new hearts and tongues. All this was not the result of slow, spiritual evolution, or the issuing forth of man's religious genius from within. It was sudden, from above. In order to show that men's wisdom did not produce this, they were unlearned, simple men. In order to show that men's fine moral qualities and their own efforts were not the cause, they were weak, timid, sinful men, but men who were at God's disposal.

See what happened on that day! First there was a sound as of a mighty rushing wind from heaven. Wind can be fearful in its destructive power. It sweeps away everything that is not solid and firm. It breaks dead branches from trees; it shatters flimsy houses; it sweeps the threshing floors and carries away the chaff. Just so is the Holy Spirit when he begins his clean-up in the human heart. But wind is also beneficent and creative. It ushers in life-giving rain; it drives away blistering heat; it turns windmills and turbines and generates power. So likewise is the Holy Spirit when he brings power to the human heart.

And the fire from heaven sat in little flame-like tongues upon each of the disciples' heads. This was no mass contagion or mob hysteria. Each individual received his own flame of enlightenment. Each individual was warmed within by the flame of love. Each individual was set on fire with enthusiasm.

Finally the disciples began to speak in other tongues, as the Spirit gave them the power to speak. Here was a new language for all to understand, each in his own tongue. This is what was meant at the beginning when we said that the Bible speaks a language of its own which is understood only by those who have had the Christian experience. Creation, sin, grace, love, repentance, faith, forgiveness—these are the words the Holy Spirit teaches. Christians understand them—they know the mysteries to which these words point for they have experienced them. This sounds as if we were here dealing with something that is not for everybody, but just the opposite is the case.

You can understand philosophers only if you have the necessary gifts of understanding, if you study faithfully for many years, and if you happen to belong to the right culture. Chinese and Hindu philosophy, for example, often stand as pretty much of a closed book to the western mind, while the typical Oriental may never succeed in grasping Plato's thought. But on that first Pentecost three thousand were converted in one day, and they belonged to all kinds of cultures. Not long years of study, not painstaking intellectual effort, but inner humility, openness, receptivity, the recognition of common human need were the conditions of understanding this new language which the Holy Spirit taught. Here is the one language that all men can learn, and that will bind them all together into one community. No longer will they be separated from each other by an abyss of misunderstanding when the Holy Spirit has taught them to speak in other tongues. Here is fulfilled the prophecy that the Bible would be translated into every language on the face of the globe, and in each language speak the language of the heart. Here is really the only hope for one united humanity. Russians, Americans, Hindus, Japanese, British may not understand one another. But Christians understand one another the world around.

It was on the first Pentecost then that a little group of Spirit-changed men and women formed the first Christian *community of life together in love*. It was in the power of the Holy Spirit that they recognized that they had crucified the Lord of glory, that this Christ was raised from the dead, that he is Lord, and that there is forgiveness and life in his name.

Entrance into the Community of Life Together in Love

It is quite clear from the preaching on that first Pentecost, and the response to it, how people entered into that first *community of life together in love*, and how that group grew. There is only one entrance into this love community. It is the narrow gate of repentance, which is nevertheless as wide as the measureless love of God. When the people asked Peter what they must do to be saved, he said simply: "Repent, and be baptized every one of you in the name of Jesus Christ for the forgiveness of your sins; and you shall receive the gift of the Holy Spirit" (Acts 2:38).

We are accustomed to associate repentance simply with sorrow over wrongdoing and the determination not to do it again. But repentance is here used in a much more inclusive and a yet more specific sense. Repentance means a complete change of heart and mind. It is the same as conversion. It means a change of direction, a complete turnabout. It is the sort of thing of which we have been speaking when we contrasted the first Adam and the second Adam. The first Adam has his life turned in upon himself, the second has it turned out toward God. The first tries to live out of himself and for himself, the second takes his life from God in trust and gives it back in obedience. Such a change is repentance; it is the straightening out of man.

Repentance: Contrition and Faith

We may say that there are two parts to repentance: contrition and faith. (The word "faith" is here used in a narrower sense than the one in which we have used it before as the comprehensive name for the right God-relation.) They are worked in man by the proclamation of the law and the gospel. The law is anything that proclaims God's holy will and his wrath against sin. The gospel is the good news of what God in Christ has done for man's redemption. The law is what God demands; the gospel is what God gives. Contrition is worked by both law and gospel; faith, however, is worked by the gospel alone.

Contrition

Contrition is heartfelt sorrow over sin and the turning away from it. If man is ever to be healed he must first realize that he is ill. If he is to be turned about he must realize that he is going in the wrong direction. If he is to learn to put his trust in God then his trust in himself and in the world must first be shattered. If he is to be humble before his God his pride must first be broken,

A beginning in this direction may be made by the proper preaching of the law. A man must realize what God demands of him. This means something other than that it is wrong to steal, to kill, to bear false witness, to lie, to be unfaithful to a trust. Men have realized from time immemorial that such things are wrong. Their consciences bore witness to this truth. But their realization was mostly that such things have bad consequences, that they make for unhappiness and the disintegration of human relations. Or they simply recognized that such things are not good, as some things are not beautiful, without being able to give any further reason. That such things are sins against God is a different knowledge.

It is something different that makes Adam cry out in fear after his disobedience. It is something different that causes Caine's anguished cry that his punishment is greater than he can bear. It is something different when David, after he had sinned with Bathsheba and cunningly contrived the death of Uriah, cries out, "Against thee, thee only, have I sinned, and done that which is evil in thy sight" (Ps. 51:4). As far as men might reckon, counting out the consequences, things had not turned out so badly. Uriah had died a hero's death in battle, ignorant of his wife's unfaithfulness. Bathsheba had become a queen and the mother of a king. David himself had possessed what he desired. Why, then, should he cry out? The reason was that David had become conscious of the fact that his sin was against God and not merely against a fellow man.

It is when a man sees not only single acts of wrongdoing, but his whole life as wrongly oriented, that he has a real consciousness of sin. That is not possible except where there is the proclamation of the gospel. Only when man's disobedience and mistrust are recognized as an offense against love can there be real contrition, genuine sorrow over sin, firm determination to abandon it, and resolute crushing of the evil purpose and intent.

The depths of contrition, however, are possible only where the fullness of love is revealed on the cross. Think of Peter going out and weeping bitterly at the look of his Lord after he had denied him. Surely it was love that called forth that sorrow, and because it was love that called forth the sorrow it brought with it the confidence of forgiveness.

Faith

There is a real difference between the remorse of Judas and the repentance of Peter. The one has faith, the other does not. There is a sorrow of the world that brings about death, and there is a godly sorrow that brings about repentance to salvation (2 Cor. 7:10). Judas regretted his deed because it had not turned out as he expected. It is hard to plumb to the depths of his heart, but whatever recognition of sin there may have been, it is clear that he no longer had any confidence that he could be forgiven. There was only despair. He went out and hanged himself.

It was different with Peter. He was drawn by love to recognize the shamefulness of his deed and to trust in that same love for forgiveness. This makes clear the nature of faith as we have previously described it. It is not a human achievement but the work of God in man; it is the achievement of love, as the contrite sinner is held by the love of the forgiving God. Faith is the hand which accepts the forgiving grace of God. It is the organ of reception and is itself created by God.

Justification

As trust and confidence are worked in man, he is at the same time forgiven. This is a man's justification. All the benefits of what Christ has done for him are bestowed upon him. There are many ways in which we can say this. We can simply say that he is forgiven, "for where there is forgiveness of sins there are also life and salvation." Or we can say that he is declared righteous when the righteousness of Christ is imputed or attributed to him. He stands before God, not in his own righteousness, but in that strange, foreign righteousness, which Christ has won for him. He has on the wedding garment the host himself has provided. Christ's obedience covers the sins of the world so that even the all-penetrating eye of God beholds them no longer. He who has repented, he who has been brought to contrition and faith, knows that his own sins are covered too.

This is said to be a synthetic judgment on God's part, not an analytic one. An analytic judgment is one which simply analyzes what has been done without adding anything new. In a chemical analysis the component elements of a given compound are determined. A synthetic product, however, is formed by adding new elements. An analytic judgment, declaring a prisoner innocent, would only be revealing that the prisoner who was thought to be guilty was not really guilty at all. The synthetic judgment, however, declares the guilty prisoner innocent. It adds the righteousness that was not there before. He is now a synthetic product, a sinner redeemed, a sinner declared righteous. This is the heart of the Christian confession: "We are justified by grace alone, for Christ's sake, through faith." We are the children of God only because God accepts us freely in his grace, forgives us for Jesus' sake, and works in us the trust and confidence that accept all this. But it is not the acceptance of this doctrine that saves. A person is saved by actual, personal trust in the Savior.

Actual Righteousness

We have said that it is the sinner who is declared righteous. He does not first become righteous and then have God recognize that fact. This must be maintained without the slightest toning down, if we are to maintain the truth and glory of the gospel. Yet there is more to be said, as we stressed when we talked of Christ setting us free from the power of sin as well as from its guilt. When a man comes to faith in Christ and is reborn he is not only declared righteous but he actually becomes righteous. It is not for this that he is accepted by God, but since he is accepted by God as a sinner he goes out and sins no more. He is henceforth the kind of man God wants him to be, fulfilling the commandment of love.

That the "righteousness of God" is this kind of saving,

forgiving, transforming righteousness is clearly stated by St. Paul in his letter to the Romans. "For I am not ashamed of the gospel: it is the power of God for salvation to every one who has faith, to the Jew first and also to the Greek. For in it the righteousness of God is revealed through faith for faith; as it is written, 'He who through faith is righteous shall live'" (Rom. 1:16 f.). The righteousness of God is thus a righteousness which comes down from heaven and makes man righteous by covering his sin and giving him a new heart and mind. "Therefore, if any one is in Christ, he is a new creation; the old has passed away, behold, the new has come" (2 Cor. 5:17).

This can also be put in other terms. We may, as Kierkegaard, put it entirely in terms of relations. The sinful self is improperly related to its own self, to God, and to the neighbor. We have talked of this self before as the one we name when we say "I," the center of responsibility within us. Such a self is not an independent self, but a dependent self. It depends for its being upon its relation to the God who brought it into being and preserves it in being. In addition this self is also related to other selves without whom it cannot be human—W. H. Auden says, "The ego was a dream within me, until my neighbor's need by name created it."[1] This dependent self can now either overestimate or underestimate itself. It can in defiance refuse to be the finite, dependent self that it is. It can presume to be self-sufficient in its finitude, defiantly determined to make the most of its limitations, without any falling back upon God. Or it can presume to be autonomous (a law unto itself), defiantly denying the limitations of its finitude and creaturehood. This also distorts the relation to the neighbor, without whose service and love the autonomous, self-sufficient self pretends to be able to get along. Such a misrelation is sin.

Or the dependent self that is related to God can underestimate itself. It can sink to the level of the animal even though it is not an animal. As Kierkegaard suggested, it can live in the basement of its three-story house never getting out where it can see the endless skies and the eternal stars, never recognizing that it is "spirit." Such is the way the masses of men live. Or it can simply succumb to its finitude in any number of a variety of different ways,[2] losing itself in all the trivialties of the finite, piling up money in vain efforts to achieve security, multiplying fornications in equally vain efforts to satisfy a hunger that is more than appetite, collecting *objets d'art* in the hope of finding an end to restlessness in a plethora of beautiful things.

All this is changed in "faith," when the promise of God is heard again and again. The self now wills to be the dependent self, neither overestimating nor underestimating itself. It is content to be the dependent, finite self, grounded in the creator God of love. At the same time there are opened up to it the infinite possibilities of God, so that there is no cause for despair. At the points of absolute *human impossibility* there is *the impossible possibility of God*. The unalterable past covered by God himself gives way to the new future. And when man is at his strength there is the grateful acknowledgment that all is from God. Man lives in the "already now" and the "not yet," that is, between the first advent as the beginning of the new aeon and the second advent which marks the end of time. He can enjoy the God-given world without losing his heart to it. He can possess as though not possessing. He is not stoically resigned to the inevitable, but like Abraham and all the heroes of faith he holds to God's promise. And because he has confidence in God, he will not use his neighbor in order to somehow secure himself.

The Heart of the Gospel

Thus "justification by grace alone, for Christ's sake, through faith, unto good works" must remain at the heart of the gospel message. Only when a man has been freed from working out his salvation has he also been freed from using his neighbor. This is what Luther found wrong with medieval piety and this is what still is wrong with the natural piety of every man who thinks that he is to earn his salvation by his good deeds. Then all the "good" he does to the neighbor, the alms he gives, the services he renders, however menial, is not really done for the sake of the neighbor. It is done ultimately to boost oneself one more notch up the ladder to the goal of holiness, perfection, and blessedness, even if this blessedness is described in no more glowing terms than the satisfaction one has in doing good. A man does not become good by doing good, but he must first *be* good before he can *do* good. The law then will serve a different purpose in his life than to goad him on to earn his salvation. It will always accuse him and remind him of his sin. At the same time it will still coerce him to do what he as a sinner is not inclined to do. But it will never be the means of his salvation. Good works will surely not then be absent but they will perform a different purpose. This is how Paul sums it all up, writing to the Ephesians, who had once been the slaves of sin:

> And you he made alive, when you were dead through the trespasses and sins in which you once walked, following the course of this world, following the prince of the power of the air, the spirit that is now at work in the sons of disobedience. Among these we all once lived in the passions of our flesh, following the desires of body and mind, and so we were by nature children of wrath, like the rest of mankind. But God, who is rich in mercy, out of the great love with which he loved us, even when we were dead through our trespasses, made us alive together with Christ (by grace you have been saved), and raised us up with him, and made us sit with him in the heavenly places in Christ Jesus, that in the coming ages he might show the immeasurable riches of his grace in the kindness toward us in Christ Jesus. *For by grace you have been saved through faith; and this is not your own doing, it is the gift of God—not because of works, lest any man should boast. For we are his workmanship, created in Christ Jesus for good works, which God prepared beforehand, that we should walk in them* (Eph. 2:1 ff.).

The Christian's Predicament

But this is not the whole story. The Christian's predicament is that he is at the same time always a just man and also a sinner. There are two men in him, the sinner who

211

is always in need of forgiveness, and the righteous man who has daily forgiveness and strives to do the will of God. The result is a constant struggle for holiness. People generally conceive of this in a quantitative way, using some kind of a chemical or medicinal analogy to indicate a gradual change and improvement. Man thus begins as thoroughly corrupt, like a body of water saturated with poison, or like a human body infected throughout with a foul disease. Then the cleansing process begins. Through God's grace the pollution in the waters is more and more cleaned out and the water becomes purer and purer. Some are willing to admit that the water never really gets to be one hundred per cent pure, but it gets so close that it takes God himself to detect the tiny bit of pollution that is left. Or people may mean that they are sick persons getting gradually better. The church is a sanatorium in which they are more and more restored to health, and where they will suffer relapses if they do not take their medicines regularly. The congregation, therefore, consists of people in various stages of health. Some are still very ill. Others have scarcely a trace of disease left and have developed almost total immunity so that they shed temptations like a duck's back sheds water. We ought to rid ourselves of these deeply ingrained ways of thinking.

Instead of thinking in chemical and medicinal terms, we must think in personal terms and in terms of dramatic struggle. There are two people in me, each one healthy and vigorous. Neither shows any traces of gradually being put to death, or becoming weaker. Both are vigorous, and remain so. What a fight that means! It means a daily fight—that daily fight signified by our baptism, when the old Adam in us must by daily sorrow and repentance be drowned and die, and the new man daily come forth and arise and live before God in righteousness and purity forever. The new man is healthy, vigorous, loving God, bound on serving him: "I will follow you wherever you go." The old man is just as healthy and vigorous, determined to live out of himself and for himself, unwilling to surrender, suspicious, proud of his achievements, taking all the credit. Unless a man wins a daily battle against this fellow there certainly is trouble ahead. This is the fellow who, when you do win a battle against him in the form of the grasping publican, suddenly turns up in the garb of the self-righteous Pharisee. He always turns up in a new form and never loses any of his wiles. The battle is life-long. There are always new temptations; each day is different and presents its own peculiar problems. The temptations of one situation are not those of another; marriage has its peculiar problems not presented to the unmarried; the temptations of old age are not the same as those of youth. The closer you get to the goal, the further it recedes. There is a new sensitivity and there are new possibilities.

This means that there is hope for progress in the Christian life. A man does grow in grace. That means that he grows up and matures in the grace offered him in Christ, in the new relation there opened to him. This is Peter's meaning: "But grow in the grace and knowledge of our Lord and Savior Jesus Christ" (2 Pet. 3:18). It is while

213

we are under the grace and in the knowledge of Christ that we are to grow. Victories become easier, for, after all, one does learn how to fight, and the Christian increasingly makes use of divine help. The Christian is not forever on a treadmill running like mad just to hold his own. One catches on to certain tricks of the enemy and learns the correct counter moves. It is not that the enemy has gradually lost his strength, nor is it that one is now more of a child of God. It is simply that long years of daily conflict have made one an expert fighter, more ardent in prayer, more open to God, more relaxed and maneuverable. This is the Christian's growth in grace and in sanctification.

The Mystical Union

The new birth to newness of life also includes the *mystical union* with Christ. This does not mean that man and Christ actually become one. This would be to forget that man stands over against Christ as he stands over against God, and this "over-againstness" will never cease. Yet there is a mystical union of the believer with Christ. How are we to picture this?

We realize how differently we act, all depending upon in whose presence we are. When we are with friends of our own age and sex we tend to drop our restraints and act more or less naturally. When we are with superiors whom we fear, we are immediately under restraint. When we are in the presence of those we respect, revere, love, we are again different. We try to put our best foot forward. We would be mortified if they could know all that we have done and the vagrant and evil thoughts that pass through our mind. The more intimate and close, the more genuinely loving the relationship is, the fewer the restraints, and the more open and natural and confiding we are. It is this sort of thing that indicates what is meant by the mystical union of the believer with Christ.

Peter feels that the Lord has seen into his doubting heart and cries out: "Depart from me, for I am a sinful man, O Lord." But the Lord does not depart. He stays with Peter and makes him a fisher of men. There comes a time when Peter is no longer ashamed to let the Lord search his heart: "Lord, you know everything; you know that I love you." That is the mystical union of the believer with Christ: the knowledge that the Lord does know all things, that all life lies before him like an open book, and that this does not cause him to draw his garments about him and disdainfully walk away. The Lord stays, and he forgives and encourages and helps. The believer, therefore, confides in him, tells him everything, hides nothing. Feelings of adoration and worship mingle with the most tender emotions of love for Him who has become one's equal even while he remains far above all that is sinful. The scriptures speak of the union of Christ, the Bridegroom, with his bride, the church, and the saints have slipped inevitably into the language of passionate love when speaking of their Lord. There is nothing in all the world to compare with what a man feels in that mystical union with his Lord.

The *life together in love* established by the Holy Spirit is the union of the individual believer with Christ. But this individual relationship does not exist apart from the wider community of which each Christian is a part. No Christian can be joined in the mystical union with his Lord without being joined through that Lord to all the members of the Christian community. This leads us to consider that wider community which is the Christian church, and the means whereby it is brought into being and is nurtured.

In discussing the individual's conversion prior to the discussion of the church we have simply made a fielder's choice. Just as there is no isolated individual except the individual in relation to his fellow man, so there is no Christian save the one who is in proper relation to both God and his fellow man. It is pointless to ask which was first, the church or the gospel message. God was first and he created witnesses and these witnesses were the church, created by a witness and bearers of the witness. It is to this church that we now turn.

CHAPTER IX

THE CHURCH AND THE MEANS OF GRACE

What Is the Church?

When we hear the word "church" we are most apt to think of some particular church: St. John's, or Holy Trinity, or the church in which we were baptized, or confirmed, or married. Perhaps we remember its altar, the crucifix and the candles. Perhaps we just think of people sitting together, work-worn hands folded, voices more used to shouting above the roar of machinery or the pounding of waves now raised in song. Perhaps we think of people kneeling together at the Communion, table after table, forming a chain, an endless chain that goes round and round the world. Here they come, one by one, each an individual, each one for himself alone, separate, with upturned face filled with peace and joy and rapture. Yet they all belong together; they are one family, one brotherhood, one body. They are the church.

Some people seem to think that it is very bad to have the word "church" suggest some particular church. They would prefer to have us think in world-wide terms, and so we must. But first we must go along with Mr. and Mrs. Brown, who think of the church as that little building on the corner where they meet their Lord and those who love him. This is exactly what the church is: a group of men and women gathered about the Means of Grace, and through those Means of Grace joined with their invisible Lord into one body. The church consists of such little groups. They are the cells that constitute a larger body. Each cell knows that it does not exist alone and that it is only a part of a larger whole. It is *fully the church* as long as the Lord is there in his word, but it is *not the whole Church.*

The Church, the Communion of Saints

In the Apostles' Creed we confess that we believe in "the holy Christian Church, the Communion of Saints." The words "Communion of Saints" stand in apposition to "holy Christian Church." It is the communion of saints who constitute the holy Christian, or catholic, that is, universal, church. The word "saint" is derived from the Latin word *sanctus,* meaning holy. The saints are all those who through their God-given faith are holy and spotless through the forgiveness of their sins, and also actually righteous through their rebirth to newness of life—always remembering, however, their predicament as life-long sinners.

This is the personal side of the church, making clear that it is a community of persons. But they are people with a mission in the world; they are under orders; they are witnesses. This is an absolutely essential characteristic. They are witnesses to the author of their new life. They must be witnesses in word and deed. They must proclaim love by the actual practice of it. A congregation that merely talks about love, but does not practice it, is no part of the church. It was through its witness *by word and deed* that the church was established in the first place.

We now have a further element essential to the church. The church is the body of believers brought into being by a witness, and itself bearing that witness. Christians, in other words, are torch-bearers, handing their lighted torches on from generation to generation. On Pentecost the fire descended from heaven and sat upon each of them, and now the flame is passed on and never allowed to go out. In some churches a light is kept constantly burning. It can be a fine symbol, but is worthless without that continuous line of living witnesses.

This should be sufficient warning against regarding the church as an isolated, esoteric, navel-staring group, separated from the world, intent only upon itself and its own growth. The New Testament insists that Christians should be *in* the world, but not *of* it (and world here means the old age of sin and death rather than the world of God's creation of which man is the crown). In fact, the only reason there is the gathered church, the assembly of God, is so that by what happens there the pilgrim people of God may be freed for their task in the world. Here they are freed from the idols that possess them for worship of the true God. They gather, as any family does, to be refreshed by their host, to rejoice in each other's company, to talk over their problems, to hear again from their commander the strategy of their task in God's world. They do not then go out into an alien world, but into God's world. They go out into the world as that part of the world in which God's purpose has been realized. They go out to be the salt of the earth and the light of the world (Matt. 5:13 ff.). They go out as God's agents of reconciliation.[1] Their influence is to spread far beyond the confines of their own little group; a little leaven is to permeate the whole loaf (Matt. 13:33).

This should also be warning enough against supposing that the church building is in itself some holy place. There are, in our evangelical view, no holy places to which you must go in order to meet God. That is a pagan notion which survives wherever it is believed that God can be permanently caught up in any material object and so confined to a place, as in a consecrated host, a tabernacle, a golden monstrance carried through the streets in a Corpus Christi procession. Such confinement localizes the living God in the wrong way; it puts him too much at man's disposal. It destroys the fact that God comes in an action, in a living personal encounter, and is not ever "thingified" in such a way that he can be carried about. Therefore, the church is the house of God and a holy place, not because Christ has taken up his abode there and dwells imprisoned in the tabernacle. The church is the house of God and a holy place because of *what happens there when the gospel is rightly proclaimed and the sacraments administered in accordance with the gospel.*

The history of the church gives witness enough to the fact that the external institution of the church, the priesthood that was in the right episcopal succession, the churches with properly consecrated hosts on the altar, did not in fact guarantee the gospel's right proclamation. If they had, no reformation would ever have been necessary. No place, no institution, is holy as such—but that place is holy, that place is "Bethel," ("How awesome is this place! This is none other than the house of God, and this is the gate of heaven" [Gen. 28:17]) where God's holy law and his gracious word of redemption are actually proclaimed. And this can happen anywhere where there is anyone whose life has been touched and transformed by that living word.

The Church as an Institution

Thus far we have emphasized the personal side of the church. But there is also an institutional side. The seventh article of the Augsburg Confession says: The church is "the assembly of all believers, among whom the Gospel is preached in its purity and the Sacraments administered according to the Gospel." This sets forth both the personal and the institutional elements, sides which belong inseparably together. There is always the danger of neglecting one at the expense of the other and failing to hold them in proper tension. So it becomes necessary at times to put renewed emphasis on one or the other. At the time of the Reformation it was the institution which had taken over while the personal side was neglected. The church was where the bishop was, meaning that in the *objective* ministrations of the institution and its properly ordained priests there was the guarantee of salvation and outside this institution there was no salvation. The personal character and life of the priest in no way affected the efficacy of his ministrations. This is Graham Greene's whiskey priest in *The Power and the Glory*.[2] He possesses the power and the glory by his ordination as a priest even though he is a weak and sinful man. He is the last of the priests in a godless land; he is the only one who can bring God down in the sacrifice of the mass and put him into the mouths of the people; if he goes, God goes.

There is truth, of course, in this emphasis upon the efficacy of the church's ministrations even though these be by sinful men. This is the issue that arose in the so-called Donatist heresy of the third and fourth centuries, when it was decided that those who had fallen away in times of persecution were still priests and their ministrations still valid and effective. This is true. The validity of God's promise, the power of his word, does not depend either upon the faith of him who proclaims it or upon his holiness of life, but its power rests only in the faithful God and his sure word of promise. If it depended upon man's "faith" or "sinlessness," then no one could proclaim the truth with efficacy, for "we have this treasure in earthen vessels" (2 Cor. 4:7): Everyone who proclaims the word of God always proclaims it first of all to himself as a "faithless" and "sinful" person; he knows that he, too, is always under both the judgment and the grace of God.

There is a vital difference, however, between those who restrict the effective ministration to the properly ordained priest and those who hold to the "priesthood of all believers," one of the most misunderstood concepts of the

Reformation. This does not mean that each individual person can just go to the Bible, interpret it for himself, and get into heaven by his own solitary route. Or even that each can find his own way, Bible or not. No! Outside the church, that is, the fellowship of believers among whom the gospel is rightly proclaimed and the sacraments administered in accordance with the gospel, there is no salvation. Every man needs the brother who must come running to him with the good news. Even when he is reading the Bible he is listening to the brother, for the written word without living proclamation is a dead letter. As Luther said, "the Church is a mouth house and not a pen house." And every man who has the good news is constrained to proclaim it to the brother.

This, then, is what is meant by "the priesthood of all believers." Every man *can be and is to be a priest to his neighbor* by ministering to him with the word of God. And such ministration always has full efficacy, whether it be the mother speaking to the child on her lap, or the father addressing his household, or a brother speaking to a brother in the most unlikely place. This is because all the power and efficacy lie in the word proclaimed. No episcopal ordination can add one iota of efficacy to such a "priestly" ministration. If, then, it would be a fearful and awesome thing to be ordained and as such to be the only one who can call God down from heaven and give him to the people, is it not equally fearful and awesome simply to be one of the "priesthood of all believers" and to know that you possess the good news and the powerful word of liberation upon which others depend? If you were the only one in a land who possessed this knowledge of the gracious God then you would indeed be the only one who could call that gracious God down from heaven and give him to the people. If you forsook your post, then the gracious God would go with you. If you were silent God would be silent. We lament today the lack of missionary personnel all over the world especially in lands where the church as an institution is not welcome. But in every land on the face of the globe, in all the far-flung business enterprises of the western nations, there are thousands upon thousands of those who are members of Christian churches, those who claim to be the "priesthood of believers." Yet their voices are silent and their deeds do not speak. What would happen if each were an active, vocal agent of reconciliation, one of the "priesthood of believers"?

We have now stressed the so-called objective efficacy of the Means of Grace, the word and the sacraments. We have said that in the medieval church this was one-sidedly centered in the institution and its priesthood. For this the reformation substituted the priesthood of all believers with objective efficacy in the word they proclaimed, not dependent upon the faith and life of the proclaimer. But can we so clearly divorce the message from the messenger? Does the efficacy of the proclaimed word depend in no way upon whether the one who proclaims it is really held by it and lives a life in accord with it? Can a word that promises a peace that passes all understanding be believable when proclaimed by one who himself has the holy jitters? Can a word of acceptance make a person really feel accepted when he who proclaims it does not himself accept? Did not the word become flesh, not just remaining on the lips, and must that word not always become again an enfleshed word? If the word proclaims a life together in love must there not actually be those who live together in such a life?

To ask these questions is to answer them. The tree is known by its fruits. Hence a necessary tension must be preserved. The seventh article of the Augsburg Confession is frequently criticized because it does not mention the life of the Christians among the so-called "marks" by which the church is recognized. This was done purposely because it was recognized that the church remains the church for sinners and is not only for those who meet certain man-made standards of goodness and respectability. It is precisely this wrong sort of housecleaning that has made the church into a club of the like-minded, the like-skinned and the like-heeled. Again and again men have set up their external standards of starched rectitude and excluded all who were not equally stiff. They have invariably toned down the demands of absolute trust and love to an attainable code morality, cut down to their own proper size: no smoking, no drinking, no open acts of adultery, etc. They have made clean the outside of the cup and the platter but inwardly they have been full of extortion and rapacity (cf. Matt. 23). And the issue is even broader, for men always fasten on what happens to be the urgent cause of the day as it strikes their own fancy in order to give the church a new "visibility" with it. For some, today, this is the fight against the Communists; for others it is the civil rights crusade. But the fear and the selfishness that may be behind such outward demonstrations of concern are never brought into the open. The necessary "hiddenness" of the true church is thus destroyed. If you are where the obvious action is you are in the church; if you are quietly and unostentatiously meeting the neighbor's need in the place where God has put you, you are not in the church.

So the church can never be restricted to those whom men consider clean enough and good enough and enthusiastic enough. It remains the "hidden" Church known to God alone. *Nevertheless,* the hidden life of love must be known by its fruits. This is the necessary tension. The only way to bring about these fruits, however, is not by scolding and insisting that they be there, but by faithful proclamation of the gospel which is their source and fountain. God's word will not return to him void but will accomplish that for which it is sent (Isa. 55:10 f.). The church was never reformed by making the rules stricter and shouting louder, but by recovery of the gospel. This, however, is not possible except on the basis of a clear understanding of the unyielding rigor of God's demands. Then the housecleaning will take care of itself. A church in which law and gospel are properly *distinguished and proclaimed* cannot be a popular refuge, the club to join if you want to be with the right people, a comfortable place where no one rocks the boat, the last place on God's earth where anything startling ever happens, the one safe group never in the vanguard of those who are concerned for the world's outcasts, the poor, the unjustly treated, the publicans and the harlots. It cannot ever be the staunch preserver of the status quo, afraid to venture out into the deep.

Because the organized, institutional church has failed in so many respects, there are many today who have simply dismissed it. The church is a fellowship and not an institution. The institutionalization of the church killed the fellowship.[3] The true church lives in spontaneous, unorganized groups that follow the action. Only in this way can there really be true followers of the Christ, the homeless wanderer, come to seek and save the lost (Matt. 8:20).

But is this realistic? Paul Tillich makes the point that one of the polarities of all human existence is "dynamics and form."[4] The dynamics is the free, burgeoning power of life which must take shape or form. A cancer is growth, but it is unstructured and therefore deadly. A sculptured Apollo by Phidias has form but he cannot blink an eyelash. One can kill the other. So it is with the church. It must have both dynamics and form. The question remains, then, as to which is the proper form. Here Christendom stands divided. There are those who insist upon the episcopal structure as the divinely ordained form, which if it is not essential to the church, belonging to its *esse* (Roman and Anglo-Catholics), is at least for its well-being, its *bene esse*. Others, however, say that although no particular form or church polity is divinely ordained, it is divinely ordained that there be a form, an institution, a polity which best fits the task for which the church exists. (Just as no particular form of the state is divinely ordained, while authority as such is.) It is, therefore, never a matter of indifference what form the church takes—even though there be no one fixed form. The form itself must be dynamic, flexible, free to meet the needs of the moment. This has been the Lutheran position, although Lutherans have been the last to capitalize on it. Whatever makes for edification out of the traditions of the past may be retained; if it no longer serves a purpose it must be junked. "Tradition," as Joseph Sittler has said, "gives our grandfathers a vote, although not a decisive one." Today, therefore, the church should be willing to capitalize on the rich heritage of the entire church as well as be open for all kinds of experimentation, so long as its central task is not thereby compromised but positively furthered.

The dynamics and freedom advocated, therefore, do need further qualification, other than saying there must be *a form,* an institution, a church polity. Church polity concerns the external arrangements, whether there shall be congregations organized with church councils, elders, deacons, Sunday schools, Ladies Aids, etc. Here the greatest flexibility should obviously commend itself. The church, however, does have a central task, and that is the proclamation of the gospel and the administration of the sacraments. Therefore in addition to the personal side there is an institutional side that is to remain constant. This institutional side is, however, not a group of persons, ranged in some kind of hierarchy. It is, rather, an office, a functional office to which certain definite tasks and responsibilities are entrusted. The church is a congregation (a gathering together, however organized), gathered about the Means of Grace, a group that is assembled to hear the word of God proclaimed in some way. And someone has to do the proclaiming. Members of the church were once baptized, and now they gather about the table of the Lord, and someone has to sit at the head of the table. This office of the public proclamation of the word and the public administration of the sacraments, is the necessary institutional side of the church and is inseparable from the personal side.

It works like this: Where there are believers, there the word will be proclaimed and the sacraments administered; and where the word is proclaimed and the sacraments administered there are bound to be believers. The church, the body of Christ, is not born whenever someone happens to be inspired by a sunset or by a baby nestled in its mother's arms. The Holy Spirit has bound himself to the Means of Grace. The church comes into being only where there is the proclamation of that event upon which the church is founded—the story of Jesus, his life, death, and resurrection. The church is nurtured and kept alive only where there is the continued proclamation of that event. In the word, which witnesses to that event, Christ continues to be present.

Many think that it would be easier for them to believe if they could see and hear Christ at first hand. Such people forget the "hiddenness" of God in his revelation. They forget that Christ is present in the church—in the same hiddenness—in the word and sacraments. There he speaks the same words of forgiveness and promise, the same words of condemnation and warning. It is there that he offers his very self, either as the rock of salvation or as the stone of offense.

As we have stressed when speaking of "the priesthood of all believers," anyone who possesses the gospel may as an individual proclaim it efficaciously to anyone. It is quite a different matter, however, whether he does so *to* the church and *in the name of* the church to others. This is where the functional office of the public proclamation of the word and administration of the sacraments comes in. No one can presume to this office unless he is asked to hold it. Hence the reformation churches have insisted upon a "call" from the church to the office of the ordained ministry.[5] The rite of ordination is considered the church's public ratification of the call of the church to someone to hold this office of the public proclamation of the word and administration of the sacraments. Only as long as a man continues to perform the functions of the office does he continue to be a minister. Ordination confers no indelible character upon him and confers no esoteric powers. The power lies in the word proclaimed. To hold the office of the word is therefore no mean thing because the word is no mean thing.

In stressing the necessary constancy of this functional office it goes without saying that the exact method of this functioning still remains flexible and open. There is nothing sacrosanct and permanently fixed about the typical eleven o'clock Sunday morning preaching service complete with somberly robed choir and cute little cherub to douse the light of God for another week. The day of the silver-tongued orator is just about gone in the pulpit as elsewhere, except for the good old silver-haired, baggy-eyed senior senator from Illinois, "over whose lips," as some reporter said, "the words roll like a string of over-ripe melons." Forms of proclamation certainly have changed in the past and must continue to change in these days of rapid change and mass communication.

The One Means of Grace

The Holy Spirit, we have said, does not come into people's lives in just any way. He has bound himself to Means of Grace, that is, to definite means through which at a definite time and place the grace of God, which is God himself in his gracious disposition, is imparted to individual men and women. The one Means of Grace, properly understood, is *the word*. This word then takes different forms. It may take the form of preaching, public proclamation, written witness, edifying writings, hymns, music, pictures, sculpture, or architecture, all of which may be transparent to the gospel when interpreted by the word. It may take the form of the word of absolution or forgiveness, spoken publicly or privately. This word of absolution is the heart and soul of the gospel. It may take the form of the sacraments, baptism and the Lord's Supper, which may then be called the visible word inasmuch as in addition to the spoken word there is also the "mask" of the earthly elements, the water, the bread, and the wine. Or it may take the form of ordinary Christian conversation, when Christian brothers console and encourage one another with the gospel.[6]

In all of these, however, it is the word, properly understood, which is essential. We are persons, not things, and God treats us as such. The only way that we can be called to a decision is through the word. Jesus Christ, therefore, is the Word become flesh and addressed to men, that they might respond to this Word. Jesus Christ is the Word that calls to decision. Luther sings in his great hymn:

> The Word they still shall let remain,
>   Nor any thanks have for it;
> He's by our side upon the plain,
>   With His good gifts and Spirit . . .

We note how naturally Luther speaks of the word, not as an "it" or a book, but as the living Christ who is actually with us in our battle. Yet we are accustomed to speak of the Bible as God's word, and rightly so. But this must be correctly understood, for the Bible must not be made into a "paper Pope." It was not that for Luther, and it dare not be that for us.

Strictly speaking Jesus is the Word of God, in whom God speaks and acts among men. The Old Testament is the record of the revelations which point forward to his coming. It is the record of how God confronted and dealt with men. These encounters are genuine revelations through which God makes himself known. Then comes the fullness of time, and the Word becomes flesh. The New Testament is the literary deposit of the first witness to this crowning event. This first witness was first of all the spoken word. There was a period of at least twenty-five years of such spoken witness when there was no written word of the New Testament. Then it took another three hundred years before there was any agreement about what books were to be included in the so-called canon of the Scriptures. There was a spoken witness, and there continued to be a spoken witness, and this, too, was truly the word of God.

It is perfectly conceivable that nothing might ever have been written down and that the oral witness should have continued through the years. This would only have been continuing that first twenty-five-year period indefinitely, but no one can deny that during those twenty-five years the word was being proclaimed, not only by the actual eyewitnesses of the crucifixion and resurrection but also by others who had received this witness at second hand. No one can deny that this was the period of the most rapid spread of Christianity. Men believed, not because they relied on the authority of a book, but because they experienced a living Lord. Yet there was a check upon willful proclamation. There was the witness of the Old Testament writings, of which the events being proclaimed were the fulfillment. Then there was the word of the eyewitnesses as long as they were still alive. Both of these are cited by St. Paul as the basis for his proclamation of the resurrection: "I delivered to you as of first importance what I also received, that Christ died for our sins in accordance with the scriptures, that he was buried, that he was raised on the third day in accordance with the scriptures, and that he appeared to [many]" (1 Cor. 15:3 ff.).

As time passed and the original eyewitnesses began to

die, it was natural that their witness should be recorded in writing and that it should remain as a constant check upon the oral proclamation. This is how the canon of the New Testament came to be accepted and to have authority. It was the literary deposit of the first in the long chain of witnesses that stretched through the years. This would necessarily make it authoritative and a constant check on possible aberrations as the witness got further and further away in time from the original events of revelation. Any subsequent proclamation which was not in harmony with that original proclamation could certainly not be the witness of the church.

The Bible, therefore, *with its center in the gospel,* became the norm of all preaching and teaching, and it still remains so today. If at any time a man has an experience or an interpretation of life which is out of harmony with that first witness and the witness through the years, then he may be sure he is on the wrong track. It was because Luther discovered that the proclamation of the church of his day was not in harmony with the original proclamation that he rejected it. He also discovered that his own experiences, as well as those of men throughout all the years, coincided with the original witness. He experienced the living Christ as his Savior from sin. He came to have a touchstone, therefore, for the word of God. Whatever proclaimed Christ was the word of God. The Bible, a thoroughly human book, written by fallible, sinful men who yet were used by God, was to him the cradle and the manger where Christ was laid. Therefore he treasured it and steeped himself in it, and with it defied the world and reformed the church. The Bible dare mean no more and no less to us today.

The Sacraments, the Word Become Visible

Although the word may also take the other forms we have mentioned above, we are accustomed to associate word and sacraments, because in the sacraments the whole gospel is contained and in them God's total redemptive activity takes place. Luther said, "The sacrament is the gospel."

The word is essential, we have said, because it treats us as persons, and so calls us to decision. We must at the same time, however, insist again upon the objective efficacy of the word. This means that the word has its own power to accomplish its purpose and it does not receive that power from the faith of the recipient. This faith is rather itself brought forth by the word. If we are careful not to forget that the word is never an impersonal thing we may compare it to a wire charged with electricity. What you happen to think about the wire cannot charge or uncharge it. If you touch it, the current will have its effects on you, regardless of what you think. So it is with the word of God. The power is there, and contact with it is bound to have an effect. It will cause you to either have "faith" or "be offended." It was so when Christ walked the earth. Those who came to him were either persuaded to have "faith" or else they were "offended." They could not come into contact with him and afterwards still be the same. (In this analogy as in every analogy, the one point of the comparison must be strictly observed. This is the fact that there is power resident in the word as in a charged wire, regardless of what you think. In other respects, of course, the word and the charged wire are quite different. You cannot give someone the holy jitters with a shot of the word the way you can make someone dance with a hot wire.)

What is true of the word is true also of the sacraments because they are nothing without the word. On the one hand we must insist on their objective efficacy. They are acts of God, no matter what we happen to think. They, too, are charged with power which is bound to have an effect. In baptism something always happens. In the Sacrament of the Altar the Lord is always present and imparts himself. Yet we must be careful not to reduce these acts to magic. We speak, therefore, of the sacraments as the word become visible, and insist that people must respond to them in the same way that they respond to a spoken word. Only those who have "faith" reap the blessings of the sacraments. To the others they become a curse.

Sacraments are acts of God by means of which God's grace is applied to the individual, that is, in which God graciously imparts himself. But they do not violate a man's personality. They remain in the area of personal encounter. This means that a man may reject the blessing which the sacrament has the power to work in him. He is free to make it impossible for the sacrament to work that trust and confidence in him which would make him a partaker of the blessing. Sacraments are added to the word because man needs the additional assurance which

236

comes through these sacred actions. But essentially the word and the sacraments are the same. God actually acts upon man, but never as though he were a thing. God's actions upon man are always personal dealings with him, to which he must respond.

Baptism

What then is the significance of baptism as a Means of Grace? To put it most simply: Baptism is that act of God by which I become his child. At the beginning of our life as Christians there stands this sovereign act of God's grace, whereby we are made the children of God and heirs of salvation and every heavenly blessing. Whether we are baptized as children or as adults, God's action always precedes our reaction; God is always beforehand with his grace. Baptism has therefore been called the sacrament of prevenient (coming before) grace.[7] Our whole Christian life is nothing but our response in God-wrought faith to what God has done. A Christian knows that he was not simply born into this state from his mother's womb. He knows that something else happened to him, causing him to be born again. By an act of God he was washed clean of all his sins and was admitted into communion with the triune God, Father, Son, and Holy Ghost. If ever he has doubts as to whether or not he is a child of God, all he has to do is to remind himself of that baptism. All his life he must now strive to remain what he has become through a gracious adoption.

Infant Baptism

Some people think that only adults should be baptized —after they have come to a conscious decision of faith. But this rests upon several misconceptions.

In a Christian home and community a child certainly ought to grow up in the conviction that he is a child of God. How is he to do that unless he is baptized in infancy? If baptism is omitted you face these alternatives: either you deny the doctrine of original sin, or you close the kingdom of heaven to the child. If you simply assume that all children born into the world are good and only need to unfold like flowers with the proper nurture, needing neither rebirth nor forgiveness nor reconciliation nor redemption, then you are making an assumption that is outside the Christian view as we have developed it. But if you hold to the doctrine of original sin, what are these children to think of themselves? What are they? By nature they are not the redeemed children of God. Are they to be denied the status of the redeemed until at some later age they come to a conscious decision? What are they then in the meantime? Are children who grow up in a Christian home constantly to be pressed to become converted, when they ought to be growing up as the redeemed children of God? If they are to grow up as children of God then they should be introduced into communion with their heavenly Father and the entire Christian community as soon as possible, much as the children born into Israel became members of the covenant people through the act of circumcision on the eighth day. But baptism is more than an externally discernible rite. It is an inner circumcision of the heart, and it requires the response of faith. Though the baptized child has, therefore, been adopted as child and heir, he may nevertheless through his own fault lose this precious heritage.

This naturally raises the question of whether an infant child can have faith. We could take an easy way out by insisting that it could in some way similar to the way it clings to its mother. But this certainly would not be the conscious response we ought to mean by faith. Or else we could say that it is only the seed of faith that is implanted, and that unless this seed is properly nurtured it will wither and die. But this strikes us again as a sorry substitute for the kind of active, living, busy thing which alone deserves to be called faith. There is one other way out. It consists in remembering that a thousand years are in God's sight as but yesterday.

We should take note of the different way in which "time" is conceived in the Bible from the way we most often think of it today. We are a time conscious people and our lives are regulated by the split second. We may call this "wristwatch time." It is the measurable time of seconds, minutes, hours, days, years. Time is a great mystery as it flows relentlessly on from the unknown future into the irrevocable past.[8] The present moment is nothing but the dividing line between a future not yet here and a past already gone. Yet we all live by our wristwatches, and our calendars, make our appointments, count off the hours, the days, the years.

But there is quite a different way of looking at time.

The little boy in the comic strip asks his mother, "What time is it?" and she answers quite naturally, "It is half past two." But the little boy answers: "I don't mean that kind of time. I mean, is it lunchtime or playtime or naptime or scolding-time or the time when daddy comes home?" This is a different way of looking at time, a way in which the flow of the seconds is not important. Time is the time for something; it is the time when something happens. In the Bible it is seedtime or harvest time; it is the time for work or for play; it is the time of opportunity, or it is the time when the opportunity is already past; it is the time in which God acts, in which he brings down his judgment or in which he visits and redeems his people. So there is the time or aeon of this world, the age before the Christ came into the world, and there is the new time, the new aeon, the new age in which the Christ has come. And this age, this decision-time, in which the two ages run concurrently, will be followed by the time of the final judgment and fulfillment. There is no point in asking how long is seedtime and how long is harvest time. It is the quality of time and what happens in it that matters. By way of contrast with "wristwatch time," we may call this notion of time "alarm clock time," the time when we are summoned to do something.

We may apply this now to our view of baptism. Baptism is the time of God's acceptance of us and our response to that acceptance. There is no point in asking, how long this time is. It is the time of God's gracious action and man's positive response and there may also come a time of "offense" and "rejection." What if, from

240

our point of view, there is an interval between a child's baptism and the first conscious moment when he responds as a child of God to that gracious act? God's love for us is from eternity. He has written our names into the Book of Life, not only at our baptism, but before the foundations of the world were laid. Therefore, God's approach to us in baptism and our conscious response is from God's point of view all one action. In the interval between the act of baptism and the first conscious response it is God who holds the child in faith. Since faith is not a "virtue," but a God-engendered new relation, is it not enough to say that God holds the child in this relation until he becomes consciously aware of what God has done? And then God intervenes to nurture that child by his word. There are deep subconscious roots into which we cannot penetrate. We must not be so sophisticated as to deny the power of the everlasting arms. As a child is secure in its mother's love without being consciously aware of it, so the baptized child is secure in the redemptive love of God. Baptism is and remains that act by which we become the children of God—a gracious water of life and a washing of regeneration through the Holy Ghost.

The Daily Significance of Baptism

Two things concerned Luther. The one was that men should have assurance of salvation, to put an end to their foolish fears and their frantic efforts at self-salvation. The other was that they should really live changed lives and conform to the will of God. In his view of baptism he found an answer to both concerns. Baptism stood like a bulwark at the beginning of the Christian's life and gave him the assurance of salvation. Whenever he was assailed by doubts Luther reminded himself, *"baptizatus sum,"* "I have been baptized." At the same time, this sacrament demanded of the Christian the constant struggle against the old Adam. Each day the old Adam was to be drowned and the new man born again. Only so could the Christian life be maintained.

The Sacrament of the Altar

Just as an act of God's grace stands at the beginning of our life as Christians, so God has provided that we shall also be strengthened along the way. The Sacrament of the Altar or the Lord's Supper may, therefore, be defined as that act by which God would strengthen us in our relation to him. By each Communion the bonds that bind us to our Lord, and through him to each other, are once more strengthened.

This Sacrament may be regarded as the fulfillment of the Old Testament Passover. The Passover was a family and community festival which united the people of the covenant. It had a backward reference to the time of their first deliverance from bondage in Egypt and their beginning as a separate people. It also had a forward reference to the coming of the Messiah and the perfection of the Kingdom.

It is exactly so with that Sacrament which is the seal of the new covenant. It unites God's people, the New Testament Israel, and it does so not on the basis of a symbolical lamb without blemish, but in virtue of the Lamb who actually takes away the sin of the world. Here full and real communion is restored and maintained.

A Memorial

The Lord's Supper therefore has a backward reference to Calvary. It is a *memorial*, a remembrance of what once happened at a time and place. "Do this in remembrance of me." Presumably the disciples would continue to break bread and share a cup of wine, but now instead of doing it in remembrance of God's act of deliverance from bondage in Egypt and of other acts of God's grace, they are to do it in remembrance of the Christ and all he has done. Without this anchorage in history the sacrament is nothing. The long line of memory must go back to that night in which he was betrayed.

A Sacramental-Sacrifice

There is thus a legitimate emphasis upon the sacrifice of Calvary in connection with the Lord's Supper, provided it is understood in a certain way and not made into some kind of an "unbloody" repetition of that sacrifice which was once and for all, all-sufficient and need not and cannot be repeated. Nor is this sacrament to be understood in any sense as a sacrifice made from man's side to God in propitiation for sin, an idea which would run counter to all we have said about Christ's vicarious sacrifice. This is altogether God's action; he provides the sacrifice; in fact *he is the sacrifice* that covers man's sin. Lutherans are used to regarding a sacrifice as that which is offered from man's side to God, while a sacrament is that which is given by God to man. Hence the pastor turns to the altar when speaking in behalf of the people to God (sacrifice) and he faces the people when he is speaking on behalf of God to the people (sacrament). If the words are so defined, then it would be a contradiction in terms to call the sacrament a sacrifice. If, however, we mean by a sacrifice "a giving up," "a suffering on behalf of others," then we could speak of the sacramental-sacrifice of Calvary. And then also we could speak of the Lord's Supper as a sacramental-sacrifice. The sacramental-sacrifice of Calvary is re-called, as we said; but it is not only re-called. In the Lord's Supper the sacramental-sacrifice of Calvary is brought forward in time and all who partake of the bread and the wine share in the benefits of that sacrifice. (It is the time of the once-and-for-all sufficient sacrifice, which is not measured by the clock.) All people of all generations become in this act contemporary with Calvary. We are there on Calvary's hill, as the spiritual puts it, while they are crucifying our Lord. Yet it is the risen, living Lord who is present in the Sacrament, making available to us all the benefits of his life of self-giving and his suffering and death. This sacrament is therefore also rightly called "the sacrament of suffering and victorious love."[9]

The Presence of Christ in the Sacrament

We must insist on the presence of the risen Christ in the Sacrament. Some regard the Sacrament as only a symbol which serves to remind us of our Lord. The bread and wine are like objects which belonged to an absent loved one, and which serve to recall him, while he himself is as far away as ever. But to us Christ is really present, as Luther says, *in, with,* and *under* the humble vehicles of bread and wine.

If we will recall Luther's notion of God's hidden presence in the so-called masks of creation by what John Baillie has called a "meditated immediacy" (See above, pp. 29 f.), this presence *in, with,* and *under* should not be so mystifying. The medium does not change but remains just what it is. Yet it is the vehicle of the divine presence. This presence is not *in* the bread and wine as eggs are in a basket so that it can be carried about. It is not *with* the bread and wine as a pencil and a tablet may be lying together in a drawer. It is not *under* the bread and wine as a biscuit is under a napkin.[10] Each of these prepositions (which Luther, incidentally, never used together), therefore, is used to deny the other and to say that the presence is really not like any of them. God is not far off but present in the sun, acting through it, giving light and warmth through it. There would then be nothing facetious about greeting the rising sun with a cheery, "Good morning, Lord," instead of the grumpy slugabed's, "Good Lord, morning!" So also Christ is not far off but gives himself graciously in the earthly medium. It is so when God acts in the waters of baptism. Without the word of God Luther considered such water nothing but a barber's bath, but *with the word of God* he held it to be a *gracious water of life and a washing of regeneration in the Holy Ghost* (The Small Catechism).

There is thus no need of a theory of *transubstantiation*, according to which the priest is given, by virtue of his ordination in the episcopal succession, the power to change the bread and wine into the body and blood of Christ, so that, though it still may have all the outward appearances of bread and wine in taste and smell and even chemical analysis, it actually has been changed into the body and blood of Christ. The presence of Christ would then be permanently localized and put at man's disposal. Such a view would justify the tabernacle on the altar, the holy place to which a deep genuflection is made. Then the host can be adored and carried to the sick and dying preceded by lighted tapers. It is quite different when the gracious self-giving is in the whole action of the sacrament, when bread and wine are actually given to a worshipper and received by him together with the words, "Given and shed for you for the remission of sins." The gracious presence and self-giving are then in the personal encounter, for which the bread and wine serve as vehicle. Throughout the celebration bread and wine remain what they are and when the celebration is over that is all they are. One need not therefore reserve the host or be unduly concerned about the disposal of the leftover wine. Since the first celebrations of the sacrament were in connection with regular meals it is quite certain that whatever was left over was either consumed at that meal, saved for the next one, or given to the poor. Bread and wine were holy in themselves as

THE CHURCH AND THE MEANS OF GRACE

precious gifts of God given for daily sustenance and therefore *always* to be treated with awe and proper reverence. Even when eaten at the table without the specific words "Given and shed for the remission of sins," they are masks of God whereby he gives earthly sustenance *graciously,* even though it is not "the body and blood of Christ given and shed for the remission of sins." Instead of worrying unduly about the elements left over after Communion we ought rather show more concern for the food we receive at our table and make of every meal a sacramental occasion at which God is present to bless us. Perhaps if we felt the pangs of hunger as millions in the world today constantly do, we would have more feeling for all this.

Such a view also rules out a so-called *consubstantiation,* which the Lutheran view is sometimes wrongly called. This word would imply that, after the words of institution are spoken and the Lord's Prayer recited over the elements as a formula of consecration, from that moment on until all the consecrated elements have been disposed of there are four substances involved: together with the bread there is the substance of the body of Christ, as though there were actual, inert particles of flesh; and together with the wine there is the substance of the blood of Christ, as though there were actual drops of blood. In this view also, you would be carrying Christ around in the bread and wine—a consecrated host could be actually reserved, carried to the sick, put at man's disposal, and you would be justified in the concern over a dropped host or a spilled drop of wine. But this would be in violation of the event character of Christ's coming. It would be a "thingification" of the personal encounter and would reduce the I-Thou relation to an I-It relation.[11]

Is it not altogether sufficient to say that Christ is present at his table and that he gives in sacred mystery the body that was broken and the blood that was shed on Calvary to all who partake of the bread and the wine? The sacrament was not given to be gazed at, but to be received as a gift. It is the life that is given in the broken body and the shed blood. Christians are not cannibals. Therefore, Lutherans particularly have spoken of the body and blood of the *glorified* Lord. They have made no separation between the human nature and the divine nature, which, according to the early creeds, were inseparably and indivisibly united. There is no point then in following those who confine the body to the right hand of God, and speak only of a "spiritual" presence in the sacrament. Such a separation between "material," which is spatial, tangible, solid and the "spiritual," which is non-spatial, intangible, invisible, non-solid, is altogether beside the point. The Bible knows of no such distinction. It is the total man with whom God deals. This means not only the seat of his emotions or the top of his head. It includes all his senses and every fibre of his being. Human beings who "know" each other in the embrace of love should not be "offended" if God too "knows" them in a tangible, physical way.

Finally it would be altogether out of keeping with the above orientation to suppose that the risen Christ remains at the right hand of the Father on heaven's throne, and that a man must fly to that throne on the wings of faith and there experience his presence. This would be to deny the whole sum and substance of our faith, namely, the Incarnation, when the Son of God left heaven's throne, came down to the earth, and sojourned among men. What he once did he can still do today. As once the Son of God imprisoned himself for love so does he imprison himself again and again and come to be with his own and impart himself to them so that they may feed on him as on meat and drink. Here the "mystical union" is realized, as the Lord accepts us just as we are, and we, laying bare our inmost souls, joyfully receive him, his body and his blood, under the forms of bread and wine, for the assurance of the forgiveness of sins and the strengthening of our faith.

All this is what Lutherans have designated as the "real" presence. This expression was born in a situation of doctrinal conflict and served its purpose in preventing a false "spiritualization" of the sacrament. It can, however, only serve to confuse today. To speak of a "real presence" is redundant. If Christ is present at all he can only be present in his totality. We have tried to spell out what this means without using the adjective "real." No doubt this will not satisfy some for whom the addition of the word "real" gives added assurance that this is not just an empty ceremony, a nice thing to do, a reminder that we belong together. For others, however, the word may be an unnecessary stumbling block, because they cannot disassociate from it notions of the ancient pagan mystery religions in which the worshipers thought that they were actually eating the flesh and drinking the blood of their god in order thereby to be filled with the strength and virtue of that god. So why try to explain the *how* of the presence in the sacrament? Is it not enough to assert the *that* and allow the mystery of it?

Unworthy Participation

A further concern in relation to the Lord's Supper is that of unworthy participation. This is based on Paul's words to the Corinthians, "Whoever, therefore, eats the bread or drinks the cup of the Lord in an unworthy manner will be guilty of profaning the body and blood of the Lord. Let a man examine himself, and so eat of the bread and drink of the cup. For any one who eats and drinks without discerning the body eats and drinks judgment upon himself" (1 Cor. 11:27 ff.). The context makes it clear that this certainly does not mean that whoever does not hold a certain view of the *how* of the "real" presence will be damned. "Discerning the body" has a twofold meaning. First, it refers back to what Paul has said earlier: "The cup of blessing which we bless, is it not a participation in the blood of Christ? The bread which we break, is it not a participation in the body of Christ?" (1 Cor. 10:16). A man must, therefore, be aware of this presence and act accordingly or that very presence will be a judgment upon him. It was in this respect the Corinthians had failed, for their behavior (see 1 Cor. 11:17 ff.) had been altogether unbecoming such a presence. Instead of meeting together as one body in Christ they were divided into factions. Apparently the rich who had leisure came first and glutted themselves and even became drunk, while the poor and the slaves, who had to work, came late and went hungry. This is then the second sense in which they did not "discern the body." The reference is to that body of Christ of which they themselves were members. So the concern that there be proper self-examination, lest there be unworthy participation, is justified, but it should not become a deterrent from participation in the sacrament. Some feel they must somehow make themselves worthy before they come and they often fear that they are not holding exactly the right belief. To them it must be said that the sacrament is for sinners "who hunger and thirst for righteousness." Here we have not a doctrine that is to be understood but a gracious Lord who is to be received.

A Eucharist

This leads to the further assertion that the Lord's Supper involves joyful expressions of thanksgiving. Some associate a mood of sorrow and sadness with reception of the sacrament. This is all too apparent when one observes the solemn faces of the communicants. In a way this is understandable, for sinners, at this time especially, feel the burden of their sin. But this mood of sadness should be left behind once the sins are confessed and the absolution has been received. The ancient communion hymns and liturgies are filled with joy and exaltation:

> Deck thyself with joy and gladness,
> Dwell no more, my soul, in sadness;
> Let the daylight shine upon thee,
> Put thy wedding garment on thee,

> For the Lord of life unending
> Unto thee his call is sending:
> Come, for now the King most holy
> Stoops to thee in likeness lowly.

The cry is "Lift up your hearts," and the answer is "We lift them up unto the Lord" and then there go up the joyful shouts of "Hosannah" as at the triumphal entry of Christ into Jerusalem. It is no wonder that the celebration of this sacrament was from very early times called the eucharist, which means "the thanksgiving." It is, however, not called that in the New Testament and there is good reason for not calling the *central act* of the sacrament "the thanksgiving." This would be to turn the sacrament upside down. The central act of the sacrament is not from man to God but from God to man, when man receives the body and blood of his Lord for the forgiveness of sins. *By this act of God he is then freed for the right kind of thanksgiving, for true joy, and for proper service to the neighbor.* It is much better therefore to reserve the word eucharist for "the entire gift-engendered response of the Christian life."

The Eschatological Reference

Finally, like the ancient Passover, the Sacrament also has a forward reference. This is a further reason for rejoicing. "As often as you eat this bread and drink the cup, you proclaim the Lord's death *until he comes*" (1 Cor. 11:26). The earthly table fellowship with the Lord in "faith" is only a foretaste of heavenly fellowship when faith has turned to sight. Each celebration is a joyful anticipation of the Lord's return in glory when the redeemed shall sit down in the new heaven and the new earth at the marriage supper of the Lamb.

Individuals in Communion

The Holy Communion preserves true individuality and true community. Here the Lord comes to each one individually and brings each one to full self-realization. It is only as each individual is joined in this way to his Lord that the Christian community is formed. Each person remains a true individual and receives the full measure of the Savior's love. Yet all are joined in true community. As the many grains of wheat are gathered from afar and crushed together into one life-giving loaf, so are the Christians gathered from the far corners of the earth, from every station and color, into this one community upon which the rest of the world may feed. Just as the many separate grapes are gathered from many different branches and pressed together into one cup of wine, so are the believers caused to flow together into one stream that energizes the world. In this way the Christian community avoids the evils of both a false individualism and a false collectivism and performs its function as the salt of the earth and the light of the world.

There is today a general revival of interest in the Sacrament and a desire for more frequent communions, and this can most certainly be for the good of the church. A word of caution, however, is in order, and this should not be interpreted as lack of appreciation of the Lord's Supper as a God-given means of grace. It is not just frequency of communion that matters. When the church was most in need of reformation there were hundreds of masses constantly being said not only on Sundays but on weekdays. The only thing that will revive and reform the church today, as in any day, is a clear proclamation of the gospel so that what goes on in the sacrament will be understood as really in harmony with that gospel. A liturgical revival is indeed a matter of first importance. This means first of all a reform of the liturgy itself and only then can it be a reform by means of the liturgy.[12]

Prayer as a Means of Grace

A Christian who does not pray is an impossibility. He would be like a child who does not speak to his parents. One of the five parts of Luther's catechism deals with prayer and the address of the Lord's Prayer, "Our Father, who art in heaven," is explained as follows: "God would hereby tenderly invite us to believe that he is truly our father and that we are truly his children, so that we may ask of him with all cheerfulness and confidence even as dear children ask of their dear father."

Expressions of praise, thanksgiving, and adoration thus come quite naturally to the Christian's lips. In fact, every confession of faith and this whole book on Christian doctrine is a kind of *doxology* (word of praise). He who feels that everything he is and has he owes to a gracious God will certainly be constrained to say so. He who is confident with St. Paul that "the sufferings of this present time are not worth comparing with the glory that is to be revealed to us" (Rom. 8:18), must break out in song.

How immeasurably impoverished our music would be without the music of praise to God!

Prayer, however, includes not only expressions of praise, thanksgiving, and adoration, but also prayers of petition. A child not only thanks his father, but he also asks. He asks for whatever he has on his heart. A Christian asks *with sincerity*, not to be seen of men, but to be heard of the heavenly Father (Matt. 6:5 f.). He asks *with confidence*, believing that his father will give him what is best for him. "What man of you, if his son asks him for a loaf, will give him a stone? Or if he asks for a fish, will give him a serpent? If you then, who are evil, know how to give good gifts to your children, how much more will your Father who is in heaven give good things to those who ask him?" (Matt. 7:9 ff.). Though he does not use vain repetitions, thinking that he will be heard for his great number of words (Matt. 6:7), he prays *without ceasing* and never gives up until he knows that his prayer has been answered (Luke 18:1 ff.; 11:5 ff.). There is nothing either too intimate or too trivial that he will not bring to his Father in prayer, from the forgiveness of sin to good weather for a picnic.

How glibly all this is said! Yet there is scarcely anything more contentious both to the insider and to the outsider than prayer—particularly the prayer of petition. To intercede for others, to bring to God our concern for the giant needs and agonies of the world, to ask for courage and strength in the face of difficulty, to plead for patience in tribulation, victory in temptation, increase of love and all the virtues, this is all natural enough—

but why clamor at heaven's gates for the things we want and will surely never get unless we work for them? Does it make any difference in what we get, whether or not we pray? Does prayer work? For everyone who cites the evidence for answered prayer there is at least one who is convinced that his cry was a cry into emptiness which no one heard. The Psalms are full of agonized cries against the God who keeps silent. For every confident "He brought me forth into a broad place; he delivered me, because he delighted in me," there is the anguished "My God, my God, why hast thou forsaken me?" Yet, what distinguishes the Psalms is the confidence that God is faithful, that he is both willing and able to help, and that eventually the righteous who depend upon him will be vindicated and will triumph. This is obviously the expression of a faith which runs counter to all the evidence.

There is no way of proving that prayer works. There is a story of the sceptic who was told that if he did not believe Neptune heard the cries of the mariners he should take a look at all the votive offerings heaped before his statue by grateful survivors. But the sceptic replied, "I want to hear first from those who drowned." On the other hand, it is equally impossible to prove that God does not answer prayer. So there is also the story of the small boy who prayed that he might get a pony for Christmas. When he didn't get it the other boys taunted him because God had not answered his prayer. But the boy answered, "Oh, yes, he did. He said no!" So the believer's prayers are always answered, like the cat thrown up into the air which always lands on its feet. There is no point in setting up a control situation and praying over some seeds and not over others, to see if it will make any difference.

Everything depends finally upon how one prays. If "faith" is the name for the right God-relation then every-thing depends upon "faith." The prayer of "faith" is always answered. Yet it is just this that causes the most difficulty. Whenever a prayer is not answered directly and one is not given that for which one asked, the peti-tioner tends to blame it on his lack of faith: "If only I had believed more firmly my prayer would have been answered." But does this not return us to our initial dis-cussion of "faith"? Is this not putting faith in your faith, rather than in God? If one trusts God, what other alterna-tive is there, but to take whatever comes and to affirm with St. Paul: "We know that in everything God works for good with those who love him" (Rom. 8:28)?

But then one may well ask: If prayer makes no dis-cernible difference, why ask for anything at all except that you should be enabled to take whatever happens without despairing? In *Honest to God* Bishop Robinson goes so far as to suggest that prayer *is* nothing other than this kind of submission to do God's will.[13] "He prayeth best, who loveth best, all things both great and small." It comes to that in the end. But does it really?

There are many moderns who frankly admit that they no longer pray. When we are ill we go to a physician. When we start out on a trip we make sure the car is in safe condition. When we drive along the highway we realize that all depends on the safety factors, above all on whether the drivers themselves stay alert and observe the rules of the road. A prayer for safety or a St. Christopher's medal seem equally superfluous. A prayer for good weather immediately after having heard the weather forecast of a deep low settling down for a week seems either funny or sad. There must, then, be some *other* way of praying if the "modern" man is to continue in it.

In coming to terms with this matter Bishop Aulén is unique—among Lutherans at least—in counting prayer among the Means of Grace, in addition to word and sacrament.[14] His justification for doing so is simply the fact that in prayer we do not only turn to God but God also turns and comes graciously to us. If that is what a Means of Grace is, a medium or vehicle in and through which God encounters us and graciously imparts himself to us without our merit or worthiness, and so strengthens us and enables us to become what we already are by virtue of our baptism, then prayer is most certainly a Means of Grace. Then God is not just another one of the means we employ in order to get what we want—something we *use* along with our own skill and knowledge, along with hoes and axes and telescopes and miracle drugs. In prayer we put ourselves at God's disposal so that he may work in us whatever *is* his will—to enlighten, comfort, strengthen, unsettle, prod, to break down and to build up. Prayer is then inclusive of all our thoughts about God and our whole inner relation to him and the recognition that God's gracious turning to us is always primary.

This seems again like a simple answer and yet, if we

are to be precise about what we mean by a Means of Grace can we let it go at that? Just calling "prayer," without any further qualifications, a Means of Grace will not do and it cannot have been the bishop's intention. The word "prayer" like the word "god" can refer to too many different things. If someone uses prayer as a gimmick to get what he wants, is it then a Means of Grace? Think of the Oriental prayer wheels, into which prayers are inserted and while one goes about one's work the wind does the turning. Is the thoughtless repetition of the "Our Father" any different? Or what about the boy who made a "novena" for a ticket to the World Series after it had been announced that for months all games had been sold out? Or suppose someone cuts an artery and, *instead of* putting on a tourniquet, prays? No—prayer as such is not a Means of Grace.

Or consider this: In prayer one is alone. The door has been shut, all voices, noises, distractions have been shut out. All is silent within. One is intent only to listen, to hear if possible a voice that might break the silence.

Now suppose that there is one who has never heard the gospel of the gracious God in Jesus, the Christ, who has never heard the news of the victory won and the new age begun. It is the proclamation of this gospel in word and deed that we have called the Means of Grace. A man who has never heard this gospel then goes into solitude and takes with him all the unanswered problems, the enigma of death, the accusing voices, the restlessness and longing. If then it were true that by retiring thus within himself he could find and hear an answer, then all that we have said about "revelation," about God's coming, about the church as the company of those to whom good news has come and has been entrusted, would fall to the ground. It would all be pointless and unnecessary. All men would need to do is to go into silence.

But, granting the boon of silence in a world so much distracted by noise, there is strictly speaking no "sacrament" of silence. A voice must break into the silence, as has indeed happened when the word became flesh and as happens again and again when that word is *rightly* proclaimed.

So it is only when a man has already heard the word spoken to him by his brother that he can hear it again when he goes into the silence. When Hanns Lilje was put into solitary confinement by the Nazis he rejoiced at how all the Bible passages he had once—perhaps reluctantly enough—committed to memory spoke to him in the silence. Out of the deep well of his subconscious they crowded up to address him once more as a Means of Grace, in which God himself addressed him. This was not because that "knowledge of God" was there deep within the well and now only needed the silence to enable it to surge forth—that would be to deny all we have said about man's basic alienation from the creator-ground of his being. It was possible only because once the good news had broken into the silence and God had spoken.

This then should provide the answer as to whether or not prayer as such is a Means of Grace in the precise sense in which we have defined it. The answer is no. It is not prayer as such which is God's gracious turning to and coming to man; that happens only in word and sacrament. If then in the prayer of faith, God does actually come graciously to man, it is because he comes in his word. Prayer is only the occasion for this gracious coming. This we *must* say, because we know only the God whose heart has been revealed to us in Jesus, the Christ. This we *can* say, without denying that God is God and that he may have his own gracious way of turning to the one who cries out in prayer without ever having heard the precious name.

Prayer then is part of the Christian's life. But this by no means solves the difficulties. It remains true that we do not ever really know how to pray. Prayer may come easily to the pagan who means to use his god. It never comes easily to the Christian who is to be put at God's disposal.

Listen to St. Paul's lament, in which he, at the same time, proclaims the answer to that lament: "Likewise the Spirit helps us in our weakness; for we do not know how to pray as we ought, but the Spirit himself intercedes for us with sighs too deep for words. And he who searches the hearts of men knows what is the mind of the Spirit, because the Spirit intercedes for the saints according to the will of God" (Rom. 8:26 f.). We do not know how to pray. This is all too evident from the fact that we make such a problem of prayer and write long tedious pages *about* it instead of just praying. Therefore, the Holy Spirit himself must teach us. He must pray in us. So then even our inarticulate groans, never formulated into words when our distress is deepest, will reach the Father's heart.

The restriction implied in the preceding paragraphs to *one* Means of Grace in many forms is not intended to result in a depreciation of the sacraments, nor is it intended to result in a depreciation of the many other ways in which God acts graciously although not redemptively. We must bear in mind all that has been said about the necessity of maintaining a proper distinction between creation, redemption, and sanctification. The specific Means of Grace of which we have been speaking is the means by which the gracious God himself encounters man to forgive him his sin and with such forgiveness to offer him life and salvation. This happens only in the specific word of judgment and of grace; and we are bound by that word even though God surely is not. We do not need, therefore, to rule out all the healing experiences people may have in encounter with the nature in which God graciously blesses them, or the gracious ministrations which two people may give to each other with their gifts. There is a "grace" in just being alive as a part of God's creation, related to the earth, to the stars, to the animals, and to fellow human beings. This we can and must say—without denying the uniqueness of our encounter with the gracious God in word and sacraments.

CHAPTER X

BEYOND TRAGEDY

The Ground of Hope

It would be strange indeed if men could dream of perfection and yet never attain it. It would be more strange yet, if they could experience love, particularly such love as men experience in Christ, and then have it all suddenly come to an end. It is not just youthful infatuation that causes people to vow undying love to one another, but it is in the very nature of love that it should brook no ending. Love that endures but for a season is not true love at all. Love is eternal, or it is not love.

The *community of life together in love* for which men were created will, therefore, be consummated, and will endure forever. The Christian who has been taken hold of by the love of Christ is secure in that love. Because he has *faith in the present*, he has *hope for the future*. He could not have faith without hope. His hope is not based on any argument for immortality but upon his faith in Christ and his promises. "Let not your hearts be troubled; believe in God, believe also in me. In my Father's house are many rooms; if it were not so, would I have told you that I go to prepare a place for you? And when I go and prepare a place for you, I will come again and will take you to myself, that where I am you may be also" (John 14:1 ff.). Christ is the ground of the Christian's hope as he is the author of his faith.

Two Common Mistakes

There are two common mistakes concerning man's destiny. The one is that man will finally escape this evil world for a world of eternal beauty and perfection. The present world order has no worth or significance; it is not quite real. The only real world is the world beyond, into which man enters through death, either immediately or after successive reincarnations.

The other mistake is the extreme of putting all emphasis on this world to the neglect of the world to come. It is supposed that an ideal state of peace and harmony can eventually be achieved on this earth. Such, for example, is the dream of the Communists, who believe that a classless society will inevitably come about by the disintegration of capitalist society and subsequent world revolution. Such also is the dream of many who believe that through the achievements of science man's control over nature will eventually give him complete security. Some think that this can be achieved solely by technical, scientific procedures learned in the laboratory. Others hold that it will come about only when men learn to follow the "Jesus way" and live in accordance with the principles of the Sermon on the Mount. According to this view all who do not happen to live at the right time are nothing but the manure that fertilizes the future.

No Immortality of the Soul

Nothing in the world of things is permanent. Everything changes, decays, and finally loses its identity in complete disintegration. This is what is meant by finitude. Even the diamond mountain will eventually be completely worn away by the brushing of the silk in the humming bird's mouth once every thousand years. Nothing which is composed of chemical particles can endure.

The scientist might add that the universe is running down. Energy itself is indestructible, but it passes constantly into unavailable forms. Our energy comes from the sun, but the sun is burning itself out. The same is true of other heavenly bodies from which we are learning to draw energy. They, too, are running down, and the prospect is for an eventual state of equilibrium in which nothing can happen unless, as some hold, there is a constant replacement of energy from somewhere in the vast reaches of space.

By way of contrast with this changing and disintegrating world of things, it is held by some people that there is within every man an unchanging and indestructible core, immortal in its own right. It is unaffected by time; it had no beginning, neither can it have an end. It has always been and always will be. It came into this world of changing things from the realm of eternity and will return to it. Views vary as to just how and when this will take place. Usually it is a long process of gradual liberation from the world of things, sometimes through successive reincarnations, sometimes through higher and higher realms of being, to eventual perfection. Sometimes the individual soul is said to lose its identity as it eventually merges with the great world soul.

Resurrection

As we have previously stated, the Christian view is by no means to be identified with any belief in the immortality of the soul. The Christian belief is in the immortality of the God-relationship, and in the resurrection. The Christian dualism is not that of soul and body, eternal mind and passing things, but the dualism of Creator and creature. Man is a person, a unified being, a center of responsibility, standing over against his Creator and Judge. He has no life or immortality within himself. He came into being through God's creative power. He spends as many years on this earth as in God's providence are allotted to him. He faces death as the wages of sin. Death is, as we said, the limit which God sets to man's proud pretensions that he has life within himself. But it would be a great mistake if man thought that death, therefore, ends all, and that he can escape God by dying. "It is appointed for men to die once, and after that comes judgment" (Heb. 9:27).

The prospect, therefore, is this: Through God's power all men will be resurrected, that is, brought back from death to life, to face the judgment. This resurrection and judgment is put at the end of time. It is connected with the return of Christ in glory. Christ comes again to judge both the *living* and the *dead*. The "quick," that is, those who are still living at the time of Christ's return, will appear before the judgment. At the same time the earth and sea will give up their dead and all will be arraigned before the throne: "We shall all stand before the judgment seat of God" (Rom. 14:10). "For we must all appear before the judgment seat of Christ, so that each one may receive good or evil, according to what he has done in the body" (2 Cor. 5:10). Christ himself tells of the final judgment when all men shall be arraigned before him and he shall separate them as the shepherd separates the sheep from the goats. Surely we can hold to such a return of Christ and a final judgment and fulfillment, even though we do not believe in a space journey Christ once made and will someday make again. When all this happens time and space as we know them are themselves sprung.

No State of Purgatory

All this is put at the end of time. It happens suddenly, abruptly, simultaneously for all men. In all the words and promises of Christ, and in all the New Testament witness, there is no single justification for asserting an intermediate state of partial fulfillment between death and the general resurrection which ushers in the reign of Christ in glory and the new heaven and the new earth. There is nothing about any purgatory in which the souls are gradually purged and made fit for heaven. This belief in purgatory is only the extension of a mistaken view of justification. The justification of the sinner is not a gradual process of transformation, but it is an "all at once" act of God, when the sinner is for Christ's sake declared to be completely righteous and a new man is born in him to live before God in righteousness and purity forever. This child of God is through God's grace able to stand in the judgment and, clad in the royal robes provided for him, may sit down *immediately* at the wedding feast. There is no need of any purgatory for those whom Christ has cleansed and caused to be born again. The old Adam, who in daily sorrow and repentance is drowned and put to death, is finally put off for good and aye, as the new man enters into life eternal in the Father's house of many mansions and is at home with his Lord. This is the significance of Luther's insistence: "Where there is forgiveness of sins, there is life and salvation."

It is when man is falsely split up into body and soul that speculations concerning an intermediate state arise. They arise also from a concern about the dead who have died in the Lord and who are assuredly at home with him and not just asleep in their graves, waiting for the last trumpet to sound. Because this thought was intolerable, men have speculated like this: At death the soul is separated from the body. It appears then before God in a preliminary judgment (mentioned nowhere in Scripture) and enters into a preliminary state either of blessedness or condemnation. Then, when the last trumpet sounds, the body is resurrected and rejoined with the soul, and complete once more, the reunited body and soul appear for the final, public judgment scene from there to enter either into final bliss or condemnation. It is no wonder that, with this view, men have had little use for a resurrection, and have finally dropped the notion altogether, satisfied with the redemption of only the soul.

The only way to cope with this is to take seriously both the fact that man is an inseparable unity of body and soul and the transition from time to eternity, that is, from the time of decision and faith to the time of fulfillment and sight. Since there is no clear statement in Scripture about an intermediate state and a preliminary judgment, every person should be held to pass through death immediately to the one and only resurrection and judgment. When a man dies, decision time is over for him and the time of judgment is come. All the people who have died along the line of decision-faith time, and will continue to die along it, pass at death into that other realm of eternity, that is, into the dimension of God. This realm is not just way off in the future somewhere. It crosses ours, like the vertical dimension crosses the horizontal one in ordinary space. To die means to pass to the resurrection and the judgment at the end of decision time. Even if someone says that all men sleep until the final trumpet sounds, what is the passage of time for those who are asleep? The transition from the moment of death to the resurrection is still instantaneous for them. It is no different from going to bed at night and being wakened in the morning. In sleep we are not aware of the passage of time. Rip Van Winkle knew that he had slept twenty years instead of the usual eight hours only because his beard had grown to a prodigious length and because when he returned home his children had grown up and his lonely wife had grown fond of the equally lonely boy next door. In the fairy tale, "Sleeping Beauty," there is no awareness of the passing of the hundred years when the whole castle lies asleep waiting for the deliverer prince to come along. Time just stands still for the princess as well as for the cook about to slap the scullery maid and for the eager yokel chasing the pig across the barnyard. When the moment of deliverance comes, life goes on exactly where it left off. The cook completes her slap and the yokel his chase without awareness of any interruption. Even so is the transition from the time of faith when we see as through a glass darkly to the time of fulfillment when we see face to face and know even as we are known (1 Cor. 13:12).

But this by no means is to say that we are to be troubled by the thought that the loved ones who have passed on before us are not at home with the Lord. Decision-faith time is over for them; they have arrived; they are no longer waiting. *It is we—still in the time of decision, still on trial, and still living by faith—who are doing the waiting.* The saints *are* at home with the Lord and we may have the full assurance of their blessedness.

We must be very humble at this point. We simply do not know enough about the realm of eternity to speak in any but ambiguous terms. The Bible itself does this. On the one hand, St. Paul speaks of the dead as asleep and waiting for the return of the Lord. He says this to the Thessalonians when they who were eagerly expecting the Lord's return in glory were worried about those who were dying before the dawn of that great day:

But we would not have you ignorant, brethren, *concerning those who are asleep,* that you may not grieve as others do who have no hope. For since we believe that Jesus died and rose again, even so, through Jesus, God *will bring with him those who have fallen asleep.* For this we declare to you by the word of the Lord, that we who are alive, who are left until the coming of the Lord, shall not precede *those who have fallen asleep.* For the Lord himself will descend from heaven with a cry of command, with the archangel's call, and with the sound of the trumpet of God. And *the dead in Christ* will rise first; then we who are alive, who are left, shall be caught up together with them in the clouds to meet the Lord in the air; and so we shall always be with the Lord. Therefore comfort one another with these words (1 Thess. 4:13 ff.).

On the other hand, Paul speaks of an immediate transition from the present vale of sorrows to the joys of heaven:

So we do not lose heart. Though our outer nature is wasting away, our inner nature is being renewed every day. For this slight momentary affliction is preparing for us an eternal weight of glory beyond all comparison, because we look not to the things that are seen but to the things that are unseen; for the things that are seen are transient, but the things that are unseen are eternal.

For we know that if the earthly tent we live in is destroyed, we have a building from God, a house not made with hands, eternal in the heavens. Here indeed we groan, and long to put on our heavenly dwelling, so that by putting it on we may not be found naked. For while we are still in this tent, we sigh with anxiety; not that we would be unclothed, but that we would be further clothed, so that what is mortal may be swallowed up by life. He who has prepared us for this very thing is God, who has given us the Spirit as a guarantee.

So we are always of good courage; we know that while we are at home in the body we are away from the Lord, for we walk by faith, not by sight. We are of good courage, and we would rather be away from the body and at home with the Lord. So whether we are at home or away, we make it our aim to please him (2 Cor. 4:16-5:9).

Luther also spoke in the same ambiguous way. On the one hand, he spoke of the resurrection morn when the Lord would stand over his grave and cry, "Martin, get up!" On the other hand, he spoke again and again of all the saints who were at home with the Lord and surrounding God's throne in everlasting joy.

Our funeral liturgy, too, has the same ambiguity, for, on the one hand, we speak of those "asleep in the Lord," while, on the other hand, we give full assurance that the dead are even now alive in the presence of God.

The all-important thing is that we do not put between death and the fulfillment a state of purgatory where men still need to be cleansed and made fit for heaven. They are made fit for heaven by the forgiveness of sins and are ready therefore for full face to face fellowship with God. We should not allow any false separation of body and soul either. It is the whole man who enters into bliss by means of God's resurrection power. Above all we should have the assurance that nothing can separate us from the love of God and that those who have died in the Lord are at home with the Lord. And finally we should remember that there is no individual blessedness. There are no private little heavens where individuals may bask all by themselves in the sunshine of God's presence. The Bible knows of no individual fulfillment apart from the fulfilled community and indeed of a fulfilled creation, a new heaven and a new earth. Hence we look not to an intermediate state but to the return of Christ in glory, the resurrection of the dead, and the descent of the new Jerusalem as a bride adorned for her husband (Rev. 21). It is because we look forward to a fulfilled creation, therefore, that we must take quite a different attitude toward the world, the earth, the sea, and the sky around us. This is not just scaffolding that can be thrown away once the building is complete. All this is material for the finished building.

The Final Judgment

All men shall be resurrected and shall appear for the judgment. How shall they fare? We may reckon with three possibilities: The first is that some shall be saved and enter into everlasting bliss while some are lost and enter into everlasting torment. The second is that all shall be saved and none lost. The third is that only those who are saved shall continue to exist; the others shall simply cease to be.

Let us grant, to begin with, that the thought of everlasting torment is intolerable to man. We, sinful and vindictive as we are, would not want even our worst enemy to be tortured gruesomely forever and ever. Can God be less loving than we are? Did not Christ die for his enemies and is his death not the atonement for the sins of the whole world? Is not God's love precisely for those who do not deserve it? Whose would be the victory, if billions spent eternity in torment, while only a lucky handful enjoyed eternal bliss? If the relationship to Christ is all decisive, then what of all those who have died never having heard of him?

An answer to the last question is found in our Lord's descent into hell, or better, Hades, the place of the shades. After our Lord had died victoriously on the cross he showed himself in triumph to all God's enemies. We are told that he also preached to the spirits in prison. We need not get hung up at this point with the geography and the time schedule, a descent into a place in the bowels of the earth, etc. What is meant is that God has ways and means beyond the portals of death to reach with his saving love those who were passed by in this life by an accident of time. This does not mean a second chance, but it does mean that the way in which a man meets his responsibility in this life will decide his destiny when in eternity he is confronted by the Lord who died for him. We need not concern ourselves about God not being fair to all. God, we know, is more than fair; he is loving. What we need to concern ourselves about is that we will be faithful in fulfilling our Lord's command to bring the gospel of his love to all peoples upon the face of the earth.

This is the clue to our puzzlements about everlasting punishment. We have no right to assert without qualification that anyone shall be lost. We are not the all-knowing judge. Neither have we the right to assert categorically that all shall be saved, or that those who are not saved shall be annihilated. We dare speak only in a hypothetical manner. All we can say is this: *If* any man *will not believe,* he shall be damned. Jesus himself said, "He who does not believe is condemned (John 3:18). We must take seriously that God "desires all men to be saved and to come to the knowledge of the truth" (1 Tim. 2:4). We must take seriously the fact that Jesus died for all and that his death atones for the sins of the world. But we must also take seriously God's respect for man's freedom, and must not take the heart out of responsibility and the crucialness of decision—if we do that, we cease to be human. In the final analysis it is a personal matter. Grant to all others that they shall respond to God's love and live, if you will, but be concerned about yourself. Remember that if you spurn God's love, if you insist on being your own god, if you who can have life only in God nevertheless insist on getting it out of yourself, if you will to continue in your rebellion, then God himself cannot save you.

But the Christian has no fear. In faith he is even now beyond the judgment. "If God is for us, who is against us? He who did not spare his own Son but gave him up for us all, will he not also give us all things with him? . . . [Nothing] will be able to separate us from the love of God in Christ Jesus our Lord" (Rom. 8:31, 39). And this which we hope for ourselves we certainly will desire also for all men.

The Coming Kingdom of God

We have considered the destiny of the individual. Now what of the course of the history of the whole world? One reason for rejecting the notion of an intermediate state is that it allows individuals to enter a state of blessedness apart from the perfected community. This is out of harmony with the biblical view. Men live on this earth in the Christian fellowship of the church. This is the church militant. Then they enter through the resurrection into

275

the church triumphant. This is the perfected community, the perfected kingdom of God, the new heaven and the new earth. This is the goal toward which the whole creation moves. There is no blessedness for the individual apart from it.

End of History Beyond History

We must be clear about the nature of historical existence. Things and animals have no history. Only human beings have a history, because they are responsible beings. They live, as we have said, in a time of decision in which they are called to trust and obedience. It is a time of struggle against all kinds of obstacles. It is an intense drama of conflict. The players are sinful, finite creatures, who must live by faith and not by sight. It is a time of pilgrimage, with the goal of the promised land always beyond us. Now and then from a mountain top there are granted glimpses of its glory, but the land itself is not attained (Deut. 3:23 ff.). To be engaged in this struggle and pilgrimage is what it means to be a human being.

Conceivably this kind of thing could go on forever, in endless cycles of repetition, one civilization following the other in a succession of birth, growth, flowering, maturity, and final decay. So the philosopher Nietzsche promulgated his doctrine of "eternal recurrence" as a sorry substitute for the Christian hope. Everything, including all the stupid things each one of us has ever thought or done, not only has happened an endless number of times before, but will happen again an endless number of times. What a ghastly prospect!

According to our hope, however, history shall itself one day end. Time itself shall be over for all men. Historical life as we know it shall be no more. What happens after that is no longer history, trial, decision, but fulfillment. It cannot be described at all in terms of history, as we know it.

We know life only as struggle, and we advance toward a goal. What life shall be like after we have attained the goal we do not know, but we must not make the mistake either of prematurely putting the time of arrival on this earth, or of carrying the struggle itself over into eternity. It is impossible to have any notion of a perfected kingdom of God upon this earth. However close we may get, we shall always still be on the way. We shall always be strangers and pilgrims upon this earth, who have here no continuing city but seek one to come. This is what is meant by saying that the end of history lies beyond history.

The Second Advent

Christians confidently expect the return of Christ in glory. Some make the mistake of placing this event *in time* and so envision a sort of "sputnik" descent conveniently located to wherever they happen to live. But this is absolutely impossible. Under conditions of space and time a direct vision of Christ's glory is impossible. We must live by faith and not by sight. Only when decision-time itself is over can we see God's glory in any other way than by faith. This is what men of all times fail to understand when they expect a Messiah in anything other than the form of a servant. As long as time endures we shall have to worship the Christ of the manger and the cross and see his glory only with the eyes of faith. But when time is over then "he will come in the clouds of heaven," and we shall see him as he is. C. S. Lewis says somewhere that when the author comes out on the stage the play is over. Exactly so. When the Lord returns in glory it is too late to still play a part. This is the judgment, the punishment or the reward. This is the entrance into or exclusion from the perfected *community of life together in love.*

The New Heaven and the New Earth

The seer of the Apocalypse (Rev. 21) sees a city foursquare, coming from heaven down to earth. Its streets are paved with gold and studded with jewels. In it the tabernacle of God is with men. There is no more sea. There is no need of the sun for God himself is men's sun. Sorrow and weeping have flown away and God has wiped away all tears from men's eyes. In such pictures human language is trying vainly to describe the indescribable, but the import is clear. God's whole creation is redeemed, recreated, perfected. The tabernacle of God is with men. No longer is he hidden behind the veil. All see him face to face. The sea, the symbol of insecurity, with its restless, billowing waves and its limitless horizon, is no more. And men do not have to depend upon any intermediary being such as the sun for their sustenance. They draw their life directly from God.

We cannot really imagine what this is like. The best we can do is to have God on a time schedule, paying us an occasional visit. We do not know what it is like to have all men continually basking in his presence. We know only that we shall see him as he is, be like him, and know him even as we are known. But that should suffice, for that will be perfection of joy. An attempt to describe the joys of heaven in detail requires the use of poetic pictures which are little more than the products of the imagination.

Sameness and Difference

We can give no real description of the hereafter. We are caught in a peculiar dilemma. If we say that we shall have arrived at perfection we destroy life, because we know life only as struggle and as the march toward perfection. Once we have arrived, there is nothing to do but vegetate. On the other hand, if we assert that we shall go on living, then we destroy perfection and deny that we have arrived. We can, therefore, only assert both sameness and difference. The life of the hereafter is a genuine continuation of this life, and yet it is different, altogether different. "In the resurrection they neither marry nor are given in marriage, but are like angels in heaven" (Matt. 22:30). In heaven it will be the same you and the same I; we shall preserve our identity. The same Christ we love here will welcome us. Yet everything will be different. "No eye has seen, nor ear heard, nor the heart of man conceived, what God has prepared for those who love him" (1 Cor. 2:9).[1]

A History of the End

We have asserted the end of history. Can we also give a history of the end? Jesus did speak of the signs of the times and counseled men to read them. However, honest criticism of the New Testament makes it impossible always to distinguish the actual words of Jesus from those of the interpreting, witnessing church. If we examine the signs recorded we shall discover that they give us no blueprint of the future and do not tell us when the end will come. All that these signs of the times can do is make us *so live at all times that we will be prepared and never found sleeping.* The record speaks of false Messiahs and false prophets, of wars and rumors of war, of physical disturbances of various kinds—earthquakes, famines, pestilences, unusual portents in the heavens—persecutions of the faithful, and widespread falling away from the faith. Finally it speaks also of the manifestations of the antichrist, in whose person all the pretensions of evil come to a final focus. A little thought will reveal that we find these manifestations in all times, and that every age has its antichrist. And so it shall always be until the end of time. What are we to conclude, then, but that the end is always equally near? The night is far spent, the day is at hand. We must not be found sleeping, but waking and working. At any moment the end may come for us when we must pass to the judgment. Yes, and at any moment history and time may be over for good. But in the meantime there is always work to be done. It would be misreading those very signs of the times if we made any definite predictions from them.

The record makes it clear that no man—not even the angels in heaven or Christ himself—but only the Father in heaven knows the day and the hour of his return. "Watch and pray." And above all this: We are told that Christ will not return until the gospel has been preached to the ends of the earth. But this also is no clue to the time of his return, for we can never know when this command has been fulfilled. It is an endless task and a constant obligation as each new generation is born into the world and needs to be confronted with the gospel.

We must preach the gospel to the ends of the earth. Only so can we hasten the coming of that great day. We will have no illusions about an earthly kingdom of God as a sorry substitute for that new heaven and new earth which loom beyond, but we shall know where our only hope lies. It lies in the gospel of Christ spread to the ends of the earth. We shall have that degree of peace and harmony upon the earth which is compatible with living by faith and not by sight, in the measure and to the degree that men and women surrender to and are taken possession of by the love of God in Jesus Christ.

This twentieth century has witnessed the most gruesome destruction of all history. Now the world is tragically divided and the threat of nuclear destruction is always imminent. How shall it end? This is the world in which we must live. It is not our business to play God in it, and by fair means or foul try to change it nearer our heart's desire. We have only one obligation—each one of us in our station, whether we be father, mother, son, daughter, master, mistress, servant, ruler, subject, teacher, preacher, factory worker, soldier, business executive, private secretary, labor leader, politician, grocery clerk, grease monkey—to see ourselves constantly under the judgment and under the mercy of God, and so try to practice that love wherewith we were loved. This is true Christian stewardship. Let us do what our hands find to do, at one with that great community of God which in every age has looked back to the cross and resurrection and forward to the coming of Christ in glory. Life without hope is tragic. But there is a "beyond tragedy." "If in this life we who are in Christ have only hope, we are of all men most to be pitied" (1 Cor. 15:19). "Blessed be the God and Father of our Lord Jesus Christ! By his great mercy we have been born anew to a living hope through the resurrection of Jesus Christ from the dead, and to an inheritance which is imperishable, undefiled, and unfading, kept in heaven for you, who by God's power are guarded through faith for a salvation ready to be revealed in the last time" (1 Pet. 1:3 ff.). So absolutely fantastic is God's promise that for this reason alone it must be true.

"He who testifies to these things says, 'Surely I am coming soon.' Amen. Come, Lord Jesus!" (Rev. 22:20).

NOTES

SUGGESTED READINGS

INDEX

NOTES

Preface

1. Søren Kierkegaard, *Concluding Unscientific Postscript,* trans. D. F. Swenson and W. Lowrie (Princeton: Princeton University Press, 1941), p. 325.

Chapter I: The Character of Faith

1. It is interesting to note that "hocus pocus" is a contraction of the Latin words, *hoc est corpus (Christi),* "this is the body of Christ"—as though these words in themselves had the magical power to produce what they say.

2. *Philosophical Investigations I,* trans. G. E. M. Anscombe (Oxford: Basil Blackwell, 1958), No. 43, p. 20e.

3. E.g., J. C. Archer and C. E. Purinton, *Faiths Men Live By* (New York: Ronald Press, 1958).

4. *The Faith of the Christian Church,* trans. Eric H. Wahlstrom (Philadelphia: Fortress, 1960), p. 19. Italics mine.

5. David Hume's *An Enquiry Concerning Human Understanding* (1758) ought to provide the necessary corrective to any man's pretensions to certainty.

6. See Kierkegaard, *op. cit.,* p. 208.

7. See Kierkegaard's eulogy to Abraham in *Fear and Trembling* (with *The Sickness Unto Death*), trans W. Lowrie (New York: Doubleday Anchor Books, 1954), pp. 30-37.

8. See Martin Luther's explanation to the First Article of the Creed in The Small Catechism.

9. See Luther's explanation to the Second Article of the Creed in *ibid.*

10. See my treatment of "the absolute paradox" in *The Moment Before God* (Philadelphia: Fortress, 1956), pp. 21 ff.

Chapter II: The Living God

1. Kierkegaard, *Concluding Unscientific Postscript*, p. 219.

2. See J. A. T. Robinson, *Honest to God* (Philadelphia: Westminster, 1963).

3. See Rudolf Bultmann, *Jesus Christ and Mythology* (New York: Scribner's, 1958).

4. Aulén, *op. cit.*, pp. 102 ff.

5. See Rudolf Otto, *The Idea of the Holy,* trans. J. W. Harvey (New York: Oxford University Press, 1950).

6. See Anders Nygren, *Agape and Eros,* trans. P. S. Watson (Philadelphia: Westminster, 1953); and Paul Tillich, *Systematic Theology,* Vol. I (Chicago: University of Chicago Press, 1951), pp. 280-82.

7. Karl Barth, *The Doctrine of the Word of God* (Edinburgh: T. & T. Clark, 1936), pp. 339 ff.

8. See Claude Welch, *In This Name* (New York: Scribner's, 1952).

9. Only a reading of Isaiah 40 *in toto* will do justice to this paean of praise to "the Holy One of Israel."

10. Augustine, *Confessions,* Book 11, Chapter 4, in *Augustine: Confessions and Enchiridion,* trans. and ed. A. C. Outler ("Library of Christian Classics," VII [Philadelphia: Westminster, 1955]), p. 248.

Chapter III: The Image of God

1. Fyodor Dostoyevsky, *The Brothers Karamazov* ("The Guild Classics" [The Literary Guild of America, n.d.]), p. 252.

2. As was done, e.g., by H. E. Jacobs in *A Summary of the Christian Faith* (Philadelphia: United Lutheran Publication House, 1905), pp. 88 ff.

3. Gerhard von Rad, *Genesis: A Commentary,* trans. J. H. Marks (Philadelphia: Westminster, 1961), pp. 56 ff.

4. *Ibid.,* p. 58. See also Edmond Jacob, *Theology of the Old Testament,* trans. A. W. Heathcote and P. J. Allcock (New York: Harpers, 1958), pp. 167 ff.

5. *Systematic Theology,* Vol. II (Chicago: University of Chicago Press, 1957), pp. 62 ff. *et passim.*

6. See especially Kierkegaard's *The Present Age,* trans. A. Dru and W. Lowrie (New York: Oxford University Press, 1940); also, Libuse Lukas Miller, *In Search of the Self* (Philadelphia: Fortress, 1962).

7. It needs to be acknowledged that, strictly speaking, the above are not all theological affirmations based on revelation. They rely, in part, on what man has discovered about himself with his God-given brains (which does not make them invalid). They make no claim to be the inspired word of God. They can perhaps be challenged on purely rational grounds or from the point of view of revelation and the Christian witness. Possibly these affirmations leave the impression that only one with all his powers fully developed is a child of God and in his image. This would exclude vast numbers from the sphere of humanity. We need the balance, therefore, of what was once intended by the assertion of the "infinite value" of every human soul. We need to affirm that every human being born of human parents is equally the object of God's boundless love and concern and, therefore, must be so for us also. It is the potential of human development that puts upon mankind the tremendous burden of human nurture, upbringing, and education. No one is expendable.

And it could be asserted that all the powers and prerogatives we have mentioned indicate only a quantitative degree of difference from the animal and, therefore, are not theological affirmations but the product of human science or philosophy. Theologically, it is enough to affirm that man was created in, for, and by love in order to reflect that love —and this alone is what it means to be in the image of God (a point made so well in the work of Emil Brunner and Karl Barth). But, in spite of the possibility of misunderstanding, something needs to be said about what theologians have in the past called the "formal image" of God in man, that is, the structural image which then needs to be filled with a certain content or a "material image." It is the "formal image," of which we have been speaking, which makes man the kind of creature who is potentially fitted for fellowship with God and life together with God and who is capable of coming under both God's judgment and grace.

Chapter IV: The Rebel

1. Søren Kierkegaard, *The Concept of Dread,* trans. W. Lowrie (Princeton: Princeton University Press, 1944), pp. 27 ff., esp. p. 31.

2. Reinhold Niebuhr, *The Nature and Destiny of Man* (New York: Scribner's, 1941), I, 242.

3. See Denis de Rougemont, *The Devil's Share* (New York, Meridian Books, 1956); C. S. Lewis, *The Screwtape Letters* (New York: Macmillan, 1943); Edwin Lewis, *The Creator and the Adversary* (Nashville: Abingdon-Cokesbury, 1948).

4. Compare 2 Sam. 24:1 with 1 Chron. 21:1.

5. See also Kierkegaard, *The Concept of Dread;* Niebuhr, *op. cit.;* Tillich, *Systematic Theology,* Vol. II; and Heinecken, *The Moment Before God.*

6. E.g. by W. H. Auden, *The Age of Anxiety* (New York: Random House, 1947).

7. *The Concept of Dread,* pp. 32 ff.

8. The Augsburg Confession, Art. II in *The Book of Concord,* ed. T. G. Tappert (Philadelphia: Fortress, 1959), p. 29.

9. *The Concept of Dread.* pp. 14 ff.

Chapter V: God Revealed

1. J. B. Phillips, *The New Testament in Modern English* (New York: Macmillan, 1959).

2. See Kierkegaard's analogy of the king who loved a humble maiden in *Philosophical Fragments,* trans. D. Swensen (Princeton: Princeton University Press, 1936), pp. 20 ff.

3. See Kierkegaard's lengthy Holy Communion address, *Purity of Heart Is To Will One Thing*, trans. D. V. Steere (New York: Harper Torchbook, 1956).

4. E.g., Franz Pieper, *Christian Dogmatics*, trans. T. Engelder and W. W. E. Albrecht (4 vols.; St. Louis: Concordia, 1950-57), *passim*.

5. It is significant that Luther connects the virgin birth of Christ with his true humanity.

6. According to the studies of Wolfhart Pannenberg there are dozens of "Christologies" in the New Testament; see his *Grundzüge der Christologie* (Gütersloh, 1964). See also Oscar Cullmann, *Christology of the New Testament*, trans. F. V. Filson (rev. ed.; Philadelphia: Westminster, 1964); and Donald Baillie, *God Was in Christ* (New York: Scribner's, 1948).

7. This discussion has been sharply precipitated by the "demythologization" program of Rudolf Bultmann. See John A. T. Robinson, *Honest to God*.

8. From *The Green Pastures*. Copyright 1929, 1930, © 1957, 1958 by Marc Connelly. Holt, Rinehart and Winston, Inc. edition of 1929, 1930, © 1957, 1958, pp. 155-56. Reprinted by permission of Holt, Rinehart and Winston, Inc.

9. *Ibid.*, pp. 171-73. Reprinted by permission.

Chapter VI: The True Man

1. See Paul Tillich, *Systematic Theology*, Vol. II, pp. 127 ff.

2. Rudolf Bultmann, *Jesus and the Word*, trans. Louise Pettibon Smith and Erminie Huntress Lantero (New York: Scribner's, 1958).

Chapter VII: The Reconciler

1. See my *The Meaning of the Cross* (Philadelphia: Fortress, 1962), pp. 15 ff.

2. Carl F. Burke, *God Is For Real, Man* (New York: Association Press, 1966).

3. Gustaf Aulén, *Christus Victor*, trans. A. G. Hebert (New York: Macmillan, 1951).

4. (New York: New American Library, 1964).

5. See my description, based on Sir James Jeans' *The*

Universe Around Us (4th ed.; Cambridge: Cambridge University Press, 1944), of the immensity of the universe in *God in the Space Age* (New York: Holt, Rinehart and Winston, 1959), p. 90.

6. Albert Schweitzer, *The Quest of the Historical Jesus* (3rd English ed.; New York: Macmillan, 1954).

Chapter VIII: The Spirit and the Life

1. *The Age of Anxiety* (New York: Random House, 1947), p. 8.

2. Kierkegaard, *The Sickness Unto Death* (with *Fear and Trembling*), trans. W. Lowrie (New York: Doubleday Anchor Books, 1954), pp. 176 ff.

Chapter IX: The Church and the Means of Grace

1. Arnold B. Come, *Agents of Reconciliation* (Philadelphia: Westminster, 1964).

2. (New York: Viking, 1946).

3. Emil Brunner, *The Misunderstanding of the Church,* trans. Harold Knight (Philadelphia: Westminster, 1953); and *Dogmatics,* Vol. III, trans. David Cairns and T. H. L. Parker (Philadelphia: Westminster, 1962). Cf. Colin Williams, *Where in the World?* (New York: National Council of Churches, 1963) and *What in the World?* (New York: National Council of Churches, 1964).

4. *Systematic Theology,* Vol. I, pp. 178-82; Vol. II, pp. 64-65.

5. Augsburg Confession, Art. V, "In order that we may obtain this faith, the ministry of teaching the Gospel and administering the sacraments was instituted." *Book of Concord,* p. 31; see also Art. XIV, p. 36.

6. See The Smalcald Articles, Part III, Art. IV. *Book of Concord,* p. 310.

7. Aulén, *The Faith of the Christian Church,* p. 338.

8. For a delightful essay on the mystery of time see O. K. Bouwsma, *Philosophical Essays* (Lincoln, Neb.: University of Nebraska Press, 1965), pp. 99 ff.

9. Aulén, *The Faith of the Christian Church,* p. 353.

10. One should notice the difference, which Martin Heidegger points out, between the way *things* are in a place and together with each other and the way in which *people* are in a place and with each other. A person is in a room in a different way than a match is in a box. Two people are with each other quite differently from the way in which two matches lie side by side.

11. For a Roman Catholic statement see, Edward Schillebeeckx, *Christ: The Sacrament of the Encounter with God,* trans. Paul Barrett (New York: Sheed and Ward, 1963).

12. For a fuller treatment of these problems see: "The Sacrament of the Altar and Its Implications," a statement of the United Lutheran Church in America, 1960; *The Meaning and Practice of the Lord's Supper,* ed. H. T. Lehmann (Philadelphia: Fortress, 1961); Gustaf Aulén, *Eucharist and Sacrifice,* trans. E. H. Wahlstrom (Philadelphia: Fortress, 1958); Donald M. Baillie, *Theology of the Sacraments* (New York: Scribner's, 1957).

13. *Honest to God,* pp. 91-104, esp. 99 ff.

14. *The Faith of the Christian Church,* pp. 355 ff.

Chapter X: Beyond Tragedy

1. See above, pp. 266-67, concerning the resurrection.

SUGGESTED READINGS

GENERAL

Aulén, Gustav. *The Faith of the Christian Church.* Trans. Eric H. Wahlstrom. Philadelphia: Fortress, 1960. A complete statement of the Christian faith for the more advanced.

Forell, George. *The Protestant Faith.* Englewood Cliffs: Prentice Hall, 1960. A widely used college textbook presenting what Protestants hold in common.

Hordern, William. *The Case for a New Reformation Theology.* Philadelphia: Westminster, 1959. A reinterpretation for today of the theology of the Reformation in clear, simple language.

————. *A Layman's Guide to Protestant Theology.* New York: Macmillan, 1957. A good introduction to the history of Christian doctrinal developments from the beginning of the Christian Church to the present.

Watson, Philip. *Let God Be God.* Philadelphia: Fortress, 1948. An excellent presentation of Luther's theology for more advanced readers.

Whale, J. S. *Christian Doctrine.* New York: Macmillan, 1941. A British Congregationalist writes clearly and persuasively about the Christian faith.

CHAPTER I:

Brunner, Emil. *Truth as Encounter.* Philadelphia: Westminster, 1964. For the more advanced. Deals with revelation as the personal self-disclosing of God.

Hordern, William. *Speaking of God.* New York: Macmillan, 1964. This is a clear presentation, distinguishing the language of Faith from the different uses of language. For the serious student.

Lewis, C. S. *Mere Christianity.* New York: Macmillan, 1953. The well-known English don comes to the defense of the Christian faith.

Wolf, William J. *Man's Knowledge of God.* Garden City: Doubleday, 1955. An introduction to the distinctive nature of revelation and faith.

CHAPTER II:

Barth, Karl. *Dogmatics in Outline.* Trans. G. T. Thompson. New York: Harper Torchbooks, 1959. Chapters 1-5 are particularly relevant to this chapter.

Gilkey, Langdon. *Maker of Heaven and Earth.* Garden City: Doubleday, 1959.

Hendry, George S. *God the Creator.* Nashville: Abingdon, 1938. A lively, clear presentation of the Reformation view.

Welch, Claude S. *In This Name: The Doctrine of the Trinity in Contemporary Theology.* New York: Scribners, 1952. A good presentation of the doctrine of the Trinity in its historical context and its permanent significance.

Heim, Karl. *The World: Its Creation and Consummation.* Trans. Robert Smith. Philadelphia: Fortress, 1963. For the advanced. By a Lutheran theologian who was recognized also as expert in the scientific developments of his day.

CHAPTER III:

Brunner, Emil. *Man in Revolt, A Christian Anthropology.* Trans. Olive Wyon. Philadelphia: Westminster, 1947. A theological classic. Definitely for the advanced reader.

Lazareth, William. *Man in Whose Image.* Philadelphia: Fortress, 1961.

Miller, Alexander. *The Man in the Mirror*. Garden City: Doubleday, 1958. A brilliant presentation of the Christian understanding of self-hood.

Owen, D. R. G. *Body and Soul*. Philadelphia: Westminster, 1956. This will dispel the false notions of a separation of body and soul which have destroyed the biblical view of man as a unity.

De Rougemont, Denis. *The Devils Share*. New York: Meridian Books, 1956. For those troubled by traditional views of the devil. See also C. S. Lewis, *The Screwtape Letters*. New York: Macmillan, 1962.

CHAPTER IV:

Bonhoeffer, Dietrich. *Creation and Fall*. Trans. J. C. Fletcher. New York: Macmillan, 1959. This puts into proper perspective the biblical view of man's fall into sin.

Cherbonnier, Edmond L. *Hardness of Heart*. Garden City: Doubleday, 1955. Presents the biblical view of man as sinner in contemporary terms.

Kierkegaard, Søren. *The Sickness Unto Death*. Trans. W. Lowne. New York: Doubleday Anchor Books, 1954. For the more advanced. Shows that man is a sinner and does not just now and then commit sins.

CHAPTER V:

St. Athanasius. *The Incarnation of the Word of God*. New York: Macmillan, 1943. A beautiful apology for the incarnation that has not lost its relevance.

Brunner, Emil. *Revelation and Reason*. Trans. Olive Wyon. Philadelphia: Westminster, 1946. For the more advanced.

Bring, Ragnar. *How God Speaks To Us: The Dynamics of the Living Word*. Philadelphia: Fortress, 1962. Highly recommended to dispel false notions of the Word of God.

CHAPTERS VI AND VII:

(The subject matter of these two chapters is closely related.)

Aulén, Gustaf. *Christus Victor*. Trans. A. G. Hebert. New York: Macmillan, 1951. A most influential view of the history of the various views of the atonement.

Baillie, Donald. *God Was in Christ*. New York: Scribners, 1948. A clear presentation of the different views of the person and work of Christ.

Dillistone, F. W. *Jesus Christ and His Cross: Studies in the Saving Work of Christ*. Philadelphia: Westminster, 1953.

Whale, J. S. *Victor and Victim*. New York: Cambridge University Press, 1960. A popular presentation of Christ's work of atonement.

Heim, Karl. *Jesus the Lord*. Trans. D. H. van Daalen. Philadelphia: Fortress, 1963. For the more advanced. A more comprehensive study of the person and work of Christ.

CHAPTER VIII:

Bergendoff, Conrad. *One Holy, Catholic, Apostolic Church*. Rock Island, Ill.: Augustana, 1954.

Dillistone, F. W. *The Holy Spirit in the Life of Today*. Philadelphia: Westminster, 1947.

Jenkins, Daniel. *The Strangeness of the Church*. Garden City: Doubleday, 1955. An excellent modern interpretation of the church, reflecting an ecumenical spirit.

Nelson, J. Robert. *The Realm of Redemption*. New York: Seabury, 1953. An excellent review of the development and present articulation of different views of the church.

On the sacraments in particular:

Marty, Martin. *Baptism*. Philadelphia: Fortress, 1962.

Lehmann, Helmut (ed.), *The Meaning and Practice of the Lord's Supper*. Philadelphia: Fortress, 1961. A helpful symposium on the New Testament basis, the history, and the contemporary interpretation of the Lord's Supper.

CHAPTER IX:

Crabtree, Arthur. *The Restored Relationship: A Study in*

Justification and Reconciliation. Valley Forge: Judson, 1963. A stimulating presentation.

Miller, Alexander. *The Renewal of Man: A Twentieth Century Essay on Justification by Faith.* Garden City: Doubleday, 1956.

Routley, Erik. *The Gift of Conversion.* Philadelphia: Muhlenberg, 1955. Lutherans particularly need to ponder this emphasis on the necessity of being converted.

Wingren, Gustav. *Gospel and Church.* Philadelphia: Fortress, 1964. Makes clear the specific function of the church. For the more advanced.

On prayer:

Lewis, C. S. *Letters to Malcolm: Chiefly on Prayer.* New York: Harcourt Brace & World, 1964.

Buttrick, Georg A. *So We Believe, So We Pray.* Nashville: Abingdon-Cokesbury, 1951.

CHAPTER X:

Baillie, John. *And the Life Everlasting.* New York: Scribners, 1933. The biblical view as opposed to belief in immortality.

Brunner, Emil. *Eternal Hope.* Trans. H. Knight. Philadelphia: Westminster, 1954. The crown of this great theologian's belief.

Heinecken, Martin J. *The Beginning and the End of the World.* Philadelphia: Fortress, 1960.

Kantonen, T. A. *The Christian Hope.* Philadelphia: Fortress, 1954.

INDEX